My Journey
THROUGH A
CHANGING
SOUTH

My Journey
THROUGH A
CHANGING
SOUTH

Charlie Grainger

MY JOURNEY THROUGH A CHANGING SOUTH

iUniverse books may be ordered through booksellers or by contacting:

iUniverse
1663 Liberty Drive
Bloomington, IN 47403
www.iuniverse.com
1-800-Authors (1-800-288-4677)

Photo Credits: The author is shown on the top front of this book walking down Dexter Avenue at the conclusion of a legislative session in 1973. Photo by Tommy Giles, Montgomery, AL.

ISBN: 978-1-5320-8537-6 (sc)
ISBN: 978-1-5320-9485-9 (hc)
ISBN: 978-1-5320-8538-3 (e)

Library of Congress Control Number: 2019918054

Print information available on the last page.

iUniverse rev. date: 03/20/2020

To Mary S. Grainger, who served as the last minute editor
of this book and has been my loving wife for 52 years.

PREFACE

Chronicler, witness and participant in some of the Twentieth Century's and early Twenty First Century's most interesting history.

I grew up half-country, have-small city—ten years on a small farm and ten years in a city that would falter and decline due to union domination that forced job-providing production plants to leave the region and force most of my 1955 high school class of 106 to go elsewhere to pursue careers. The history of how things happened is why I wrote this book: To capture the essence of a booming region in the eight decades from the thirties through the first two decades of the 21st Century. It began in 1937 in my grandparents' home along an unpaved road in Lawrence County, with the whimper of a newly-born child. And it ends with a satisfied old man who made a deal with God, his long-lost but not forgotten savior, for him to live another 10 years. The reader should read the full litany of this man's life up to that point by reading all eight chapters. A good bit of the history he was directly involved with. Like when the Freedom Riders rode into Montgomery to be greeted by an angry mob determined to do harm to the young black riders and others supporting their cause. There is politics, as when he took his oath as a legislator in 1968, to having spent more than half a century lobbying Congress. There is sports writing, like a trip to Detroit to observe Ted Williams hit a thunderous grand-slam homerun to win the game. "Ted Williams was never more magnificent," the headlines of the *Detroit Free Press* read. There is space. It is the culmination of space pioneer Werner von Braun's dreams that began in Germany and came to fruition in Huntsville, Alabama.

Will Trump be "Convicted" by the Voters?

Then, while writing this book, the question became "Will the people 'convict' President Donald Trump in the election of 2020 as did the House?" The indictment by the House occurred shortly before Christmas in 2019. Early in the new year, the author was convinced, the Senate would acquit the President of the allegation, which was regarded by the partisan House as a dereliction enough to remove him from the job to which he had been elected in 2016. I see a campaign poster: Speaker of the House and Trump glaring at end other, nose to nose. Stenciled across the page are those words: "THE RECKONING!"

Will he win? Over the slate of Democrats now in the race for the White House, I would have to say the answer to that is "Yes." Unless he sticks his big fat mouth into it between now and election day.

Two years ago, I was one of his victims. During a typical Trump speech, after 49 minutes, I grew weary, and had a brief "stroke warning" following the event. Seven days later, the real thing hit me, and I have spent the past 29 months trying to learn to walk again.

CONTENTS

CHAPTER 1

The Terrible Thirties

"This generation of Americans has a rendezvous with destiny." ~Franklin Delano Roosevelt

Once upon a time, in the Depression era of the 1930s, a doctor hitched his buggy and drove out to the C.C. Smith Community on the western side of Lawrence. That's where I came in. I was a "blue baby" born to Olen and Lorene Grainger.

After the largest stock market crash in American history in 1929, most of the following decade was consumed by a terrible economic downfall called the Great Depression. Some people starved, many others lost their farms and homes. A recovery began in late 1935, but in 1937 a new depression occurred.

A Child of the Great Depression and Aftermath

I was born in 1937, in a dark part of the Great Depression. I also am a proud child of the Tennessee Valley Region. Franklin D. Roosevelt created the Tennessee Valley Authority which brought electricity to the region.

My father, Olen Emanuel Grainger was born in 1910 in Lawrence County, Alabama. His middle name was Emmanuel, taken from Matthew:1:23: *"Behold, a virgin shall be with child, and shall bring forth a son, and they shall call his name Emmanuel, which being interpreted is, God with us."* Of course, our father was not a saint, but the life he lived was as close to sainthood as anyone I ever knew.

Olen Grainger became attracted to Lorene Marsh when she was a teenager riding a gray mule to school at C.C. Smith in rural Lawrence County. She and her cousin rode their mules to school on a route that crossed the back side of T.L. Grainger's farm. Olen, nine years older, was smitten by the pretty young girl on the gray mule. He waited along the wooded route every day, playing a clown role by foolishly trying to attract her attention. As he laughed and mimicked her, she would say to her cousin, *"There's that ol' Olen Grainger again."* After they were formally introduced at a party, they began dating. Like other rural people who tended to marry early, they soon married. She was 16 he was 25.

On May 22, 1937, the Graingers were deeply enmeshed in what was regarded as the second phase of the Great Depression. Dr. Price Ervin hitched up his one-horse buggy for the 15-mile ride from Moulton to the C. C. Smith community on the western edge of rural Lawrence County. He was responding to a message he needed to come, Mrs. Grainger was preparing to deliver a baby.

Several hours after Dr. Ervin had headed down the gravel road back to Moulton, my mother's mother noticed that I was not breathing normally. She grabbed me up and bounced me vigorously, forcing infant breathing. Those first few hours were touch and go. I was diagnosed as being a blue baby, a life-threatening malformation that robs the blood of oxygen, causing a bluish cast to the skin. The first successful blue baby surgery was seven years later when a John Hopkins surgeon joined an artery from the heart to the lungs of a small, frail child---giving the blood a second chance at oxygenation. The rest of us simply outgrew ours. I grew quickly, weighing 22 pounds at five months, compared with a birth weight of six pounds, eight ounces.

To this day, the government bureaucracy has had a problem with the origin of my birth. On the form for a top-secret clearance background check, it asks for the city of your birth. I was not born in a city or town. I was born far back in the country in my grandfather's house, where my mother and dad made their first home in one of its six rooms. It was three hundred yards to the closest neighbor, a quarter mile to C. C. Smith School, three miles from Flat Rock, 15 miles from Moulton, the Lawrence County seat, and two miles from the Franklin County line. Our address was Route 4, Russellville, AL, the county seat of Franklin County located 20 miles away. Some security forms show my birthplace as Moulton. It was so far out in the country it was difficult to designate. To further complicate matters, Dr. Ervin misspelled our last name on my birth certificate. Before I got around to correcting it with the state Department of Vital Statistics in the early 1960s my birth certificate listed my last name as "Granger" when most, but not all, of our family for generations had been "Grainger." The limited literacy of early generations led to inconsistent spelling. The Graingers and Grangers were mostly one and the same, all in some manner related to English *keepers of the grange*. It is for a name given to a farm bailiff who was responsible for the collection of the rents due and other accounting for the Lord of the Manor.

Almost all expectant mothers experience cravings during pregnancy. Mother's was mayonnaise. She ate an entire jar the day before I was born. I have a total aversion to mayonnaise all my life. "Waitress, one hamburger without mayonnaise please." Mother insisted she was responsible for me being "the Mayo Kid."

Women married young at the time and babies came soon thereafter. My mother was barely 17 when she and Daddy married. She was 18 ½ years old when I was born. My birthplace was in the crowded home of the Rev. Thomas L. Grainger, my father's father. It was their home the first two years of their marriage. The Rev. Grainger farmed while serving as a Cumberland Presbyterian minister and part-time deputy sheriff. My father deeply respected his father, inheriting his devout spiritualism, and was particularly close to his mother, Etta Cole Grainger. She died a year before I was born.

When I was one year old, near-disaster struck again. I was infected by colitis, which was making the rounds among infants at the time, often fatally. Dehydrated from constant diarrhea, nothing would stay on my stomach. As I continued to weaken, my Grandmother Marsh came up with a home remedy.

"Olen, get somebody to get some brandy in a hurry!" she said. Daddy was then and for the full 92 years of his life, a non-drinking "tee-totaler" in the strictest sense. There was no alcohol in our home, or anywhere close by. He had no idea where to find brandy in a county so legally dry no one knew about anything other than corn whisky. But Uncle Underwood Berryman, already dreaming of moving on to a better life in a northern factory town, knew about a liquor store at Sheffield, 28 miles away. He returned with a bottle of apple brandy, which they mixed with egg whites. Recovery came quickly and miraculously. Now that I have reached four score years of age, perhaps that alcohol sample can be attributed to my continued great health---or at least my happiness many late afternoons of adulthood.

One of my first words was to call Grandmother Nancy Marsh "Mawmaw" in "baby talk." As is normally the case with the first grandchild, that became the name her grandchildren used for Nancy Marsh throughout the rest of her life. And then I named Grandfather Ernest Marsh, "Pawpaw." Living three miles away on a small sandy road on Mount Hope Route 2, they became second parents and more. They were our pals, always entertaining, as we grew in those early years in the cotton fields and on the banks of tiny, serpentine Town Creek.

The names I gave my parents were simply, "Mother" and "Daddy." They became "Mimi" and "Pops" when our children came along. Grandpa Grainger was stern, rarely smiling, whose manner intimidated my young nervous mother. We three were stuffed together in a tiny room in the large house. As the room closed in on Mother, she experienced claustrophobic horror. They escaped in early 1938 after Daddy bought 82 acres of land from his father for $750 and built a two-room, unpainted house with a stone fireplace on the rear of the farm that they called "the James Place." That little house became heaven on earth for Mother and Daddy and their young child. Those three years living at the James Place, they always said, were the happiest years of their lives. Our farm stretched northward from the cotton and corn fields of the James Place through a hardwood forest, to five more acres of cultivated land with a cattle pond called the Landers Place, that Daddy bought from a neighbor.

Before the beginning of World War II, we moved into a beautiful four-room, house that our father had built on the Flat Rock-C.C. Smith road. Our little fairytale house was painted bright white, with a green tin roof. It fronted the county road, 250 yards west of the Grainger family home. It featured a barn, a peach orchard, and an outdoor storm cellar. Half-covered by a mound of dirt, the storm cellar was both our refuge from tornadoes and the repository of canned vegetables. Younger sister Joyce was born in 1939 and Linda in 1943.

Thomas L. Grainger, the grandfather that we called "Grandpa," sold his farm a few years later and moved to Phil Campbell in nearby Franklin County. I was around him infrequently as I grew up. But while working at the *Birmingham News in* the early 1960s, I sometimes stopped by to visit on the way to Sheffield on weekends.

Grandpa Grainger was older and kinder then, and I enjoyed his company. When Grandfather Grainger died a few years later, two older cousins had first claim on items left for division among his grandchildren. They chose his pistol and rifle. Picking third, I wound up with what to me was the greatest of his inheritance: his family Bible and Book of Sermons. The sermons were typed on thin paper on an old Underwood typewriter. Poor grammar and spelling reflected the limited formal education of a man who gave up school for farming by the time he had reached high school. His Book of Sermons was filled with common sense sermons and a deep understanding of the Bible. His Bible contained the "family record" that had been passed down from the previous generation. His grandparents lived in Carroll County, Georgia in the 1800s. His parents moved to East Alabama where Thomas L. Grainger was born in 1876 in Cleburne County.

The Grainger family bible traced his relationship to his grandmother, Mary R. Crockett of Tennessee, a first cousin of the frontier hero, Davy Crockett. Grandpa Grainger wrote in the family bible:

"David Crockett,

American pioneer and politician, were born in Tenn.1786. He was noted chiefly for his adventuresome habits. He was a member of Congress from 1827 to 1833 and from 1833 to 1835. He joined the Texans in their revolt against Mexico; was taken prisoner at Fort Alamo in 1836; and, with the five other survivors of the battle, was massacred by order of Santa Anna…

My grandmother Mary R. Crockett, Grainger, was a Ft. Cousin to David Crocket, borned and reared in Ga.Apr.17-1826.

So, he and I were 3rd Cousin's.

T. L. Grainger

CHAPTER **2**

The Fantastic Forties

America had not recovered from the Depression when the Japanese attacked Pearl Harbor and Hitler's armies advanced relentlessly across Europe. Historians were astounded by the level of Americans' unity

The massive war effort provided jobs that caused the Great Depression to disappear in a sea of patriotism. "V" for Victory" posters sprouted up everywhere. Our parents' generation became justifiably known as America's Greatest Generation."

My Earliest Contribution to Patriotism

Too young to completely comprehend its meaning, I sensed the patriotic zeal and found my own way to join in the spirit of the times. On the north side of our county, the United States Army Air Force built four 5,000-foot runways in eight months in 1942. Courtland Army Air Field became a center for training of pilots and aircrews of fighters and bombers. Planes constantly buzzed over our farm 15 miles to the southwest. Across our front yard there was a clean dirt path at a 45-degree angle from the mailbox to the front porch. I took a garden hoe and dug a second angled path to the road to create my own "V for Victory." The pilots noticed my homemade signal of patriotism and, often tipped their wings to the kid in the front yard.

The remarkable unity of World War II was bolstered by radio, newspapers, and flag-waving propaganda movies. We drove to Moulton for my first movie, at the Ritz Theater. It was *God is My Co-Pilot,* featuring the heroics of an American pilot in the Pacific who prevailed against the Japanese because God was on his side.

Our closest identity to the war effort was the Courtland Air Base. It was there that I experienced my scariest early childhood moment. On a hot summer day, our family joined a crowd at a military parade that was so large it frightened this five-year-old. As we picked along the crowded sidewalk, I stopped to stare at military hardware passing by. I was frozen with wonder for minutes. When I looked around for a parent's finger to hold, they were gone! It seemed like a lifetime before they retraced their route and found me standing on the corner desperately trying to decide what to do.

Our primary link to the fighting on both sides of the globe was a battery-powered Philco radio. Every night, a booming radio voice reverberated throughout our little house, updating battles won and lost around the world. The announcer sounded like what I imagined the "voice of God" would sound when He was unhappy. The voice came from Gabriel Heatter of Mutual Network, one of the era's leading radio commentators. During a particularly bleak period, Heatter constantly opened his nightly commentary with the exclamation: "Good evening, America---there is bad news tonight!" We sat silent and fearful. As the war wore on and the Allies' victories mounted, Heatter's opening became "there is good news tonight." In 1945, we celebrated as Heatter announced that the war was finally over. Those old enough to understand its horror would be shocked to learn after the war that Hitler had directed a horrible Holocaust, where six million Jews were murdered by German Nazis.

Midway through the four-year war, my dad learned of his draft notice in a strange way. The family had moved to Birmingham where Daddy had been selected by Southern Railway for a mail clerk job. They were living in a small furnished rental house in East Lake while I spent the summer with Mawmaw and Pawpaw Marsh. When my grandparents picked up the mail from our big mail box at C.C. Smith they found a draft notice to Olen Grainger. Without a telephone and miles away from a telegraph office, Mawmaw communicated the news of the draft notification at the bottom of a post card I wrote. In large first-grade handwriting, I took up the allotted space describing my concerns about a sick chicken. In tiny letters at the bottom my grandmother penciled in: "Olen, you have a notice to report to the Selective Service Board in Moulton." The sentence went unnoticed for days. When it was finally noticed, they rushed home, fearing that he would be drafted immediately and forced to leave behind a sickly wife and three children. But ours was a small county and the Lawrence County Selective Service Board was made up of neighbors who knew most everyone personally. The board had established a practice that permitted middle-aged farmers with small children to stay home and raise peanuts to help meet the nation's war emergency. Daddy was exempted from the draft on that basis, as were Pride Saint and Julius Anderton of our community.

Peanut Farming to Aid the War Effort

"Those who labor in the earth are the chosen people of God." ~Thomas Jefferson

We spent the last half of the war digging peanuts from ground where cotton and corn normally grew. At age six, I crawled around and helped separate the green peanuts from the soggy, sticky ground. My parents' original understanding was that the oil from peanuts was to be used to make the jelly-like substance for producing heavy bombs for the war effort. Later they learned that growing peanuts had become a vital part of the "Food for Freedom" program to feed a famished world. The federal government encouraged farmers to switch from other crops to peanuts and bought up all available peanuts to ship them to war-famished countries.

Beyond providing peanuts and foodstuffs for the war effort, Americans cut back their consumption of food and materials. The Food Rationing Program deeply affected the way of life for most of us. Commodities such as meat, sugar, butter, coffee, gasoline, tires, shoes, and clothing were rationed. Each family received a specified number of ration coupons. Most automobile drivers received coupons for three gallons a week, aimed as much at conserving rubber as gasoline. Families and neighbors sold or traded coupons. In our case, we bought gasoline, tires, and sugar coupons from a tenant farmer whose family lived in a tiny house my father had built 100 yards west of ours. They had no car and used very little sugar.

There are many happy memories of our life on our parents' 87 1/2-acre farm. Joyce, two years younger, was my regular playmate. She played the role of cowgirl Dale Evans while I pretended to be the heroic Roy Rogers, galloping to her rescue on a broomstick "horse" in the peach orchard out back. That peach orchard also was where we were sent to cut a peach tree limb when our mother disciplined us. When we misbehaved, she would demand, "Go get me a switch." We carried out her orders as slowly as possible, dreading the "switching" the she applied to our naked legs. That nettlesome corporal punishment was more instructive than abusive.

Our little white house with the green roof was on the north end of the farm on a gravel road. The outdoor toilet and the pump that brought water from a well a few feet below the surface and a big black wash pot were just outside the back door. Our heat in Winter came from a Warm Morning stove. It was my job to bring the coal in and take the ashes out. The barn provided stalls for two mules and four cows; calves, hogs, and chickens found their own shelter. On Saturday nights our screechy, battery-powered radio brought the entertainment highlight of the week: the country music show from Nashville, Tennessee called the Grand Ole Opry.

Light for working on our homework at night was limited to the faint yellow-tinted light of a kerosene lamp until the mid-Forties when Daddy bought an Aladdin lamp with a mesh wick and tall globe that filled the entire room with a refreshing white light. Much of our food came from canned vegetables, which Mother stacked in rows in our cool storm cellar. Somewhere in our part of the South, tornadoes came through two or three times each year. As the skies blackened, we quietly crowded into the cellar, protected by a large mound of dirt.

Surviving the Depression and the Aftermath

The Great Depression and its aftermath had taught our parents frugality and self-sufficiency. Fortunately for us, our father was able to pay cash for both parcels of our land and, unlike many small farmers, we were not under the threat of losing a mortgaged farm due to inability to make interest payments. We didn't have much money to spend, but we didn't need much. Like almost everyone else in our remote part of the planet, ours was a close-knit community which took years to completely recover from "hard times." Neighbors cared for neighbors, particularly poverty-stricken sharecroppers and tenant farmers. Our mothers mended socks and sewed patches over holes. Younger children inherited hand-me-downs from older siblings or cousins or friends. My hand-me-downs came from a cousin whose father had migrated to Pontiac, Michigan, where he found a job in an automotive factory. Other kids in our little country school ridiculed my "Yankee clothes." I remember a pair of woolen knicker pants that ended just below the knees. I quit wearing them because of my friends' ridicule.

Fried chicken was the main course for Sunday lunches after church. About once a month it would take a heavy hit when the preacher and his wife came for lunch following his Sunday sermon. They were served first and given their choice of the best pieces. While my mouth watered, the preacher always chose my favorite part of the chicken, the meat around the "y"-shaped bone from the breast that we called the "pulley bone." After the adults had filled their plates, the children were stuck with the "left-overs," mainly bony necks and feet.

We went barefoot all summer except on Sundays. Our feet would grow tough as we walked on gravel roads and through briar patches without hesitation, somehow without being snake-bitten. How is still a great mystery to me. As much as we walked through knee-high weeds and stepped over logs along the creek my only conclusion was that they heard us coming and hid.

Most threatening to us were the aggressive cottonmouth water moccasins. Once, fishing at the "pasture hole" under a willow bush on the short stretch of creek that flowed through my grandfather's farm, focused on fast-biting bream, I suddenly sensed a slight peripheral movement just overhead. I looked up, and moving toward the branch was a cottonmouth moccasin hanging from a limb directly overhead. I scrambled away and gave him plenty of time to clear the area before pulling my string of bluegill from the creek. Another time, less than 100 yards west, just below the shallow ford that connected Pawpaw's fields, I had another scary moment. My bare feet were a couple of feet away from a full string of fish hanging in the creek when I noticed a heavy ripple in the water. Instinctively I jerked my feet back. There was another snake, this one interested in eating fish off the stringer. In my haste to get away I did not get enough of a view to determine if it was a cottonmouth. Under those conditions, a snake is a snake. I had nightmares about those snakes for the decades to follow when, at almost 80 years old, research suggested the odds of fatal snakebites were so low we should not fear any snakes except the coral snakes not found this far from the Gulf of Mexico. I have not had a nightmare about snakes since.

My First Bike Earned the Hard Way: Picking Cotton by the Pound

Half of our 87 1/2-acre farm was in heavy woodlands of hickory, pine, and oak trees. The other half was in cotton, corn, and pasture land. It was lowland with logging roads filled in Winter with foot-deep puddles of freezing water. Our dad paid us at the same per-pound rate that he paid the cotton pickers he recruited each morning and brought back to the farm from Russellville. At age ten, I could pick almost 100 pounds a day. Adult pickers could pick 300 or more pounds a day. As was the case with most other farmers in that new age of agricultural mechanization, Daddy could farm more acreage than he owned by plowing fields by tractor light long into the night. So, he leased land for expanded operations from other farm owners.

In late 1946, we were finishing picking the cotton on Julius Anderton's land along Franklin-Lawrence county-line road. That cold, wet December lint cotton remained in the fields. Lint cotton is the stringy strands left over after the field has been picked twice and the truck-loads of cotton pickers have finished their work for the year. Picking it is a slow, tedious task, but we needed the money to pay for our Christmas presents. The three of us---mother, eight-year-old Joyce, and ten-year-old me---slowly crawled along picking the scant remains of that cotton crop. Too young to help was four-year-old sister Linda, who hitched rides on Mother's pick-sack. It was Christmas Eve morning before we finished. From what

I earned, I bought my first bike, a Schwinn, with classy fenders, a chrome-plated headlight, and a push-button bell---the "Cadillac" of cruiser bikes of the day.

'Big Jim' Folsom Pulls Us Out of the Mud

Walking the half mile from our house to C. C. Smith school the first through fourth grades seemed like a million miles in winter. There was no way to avoid stepping ankle-deep in the cold, watery pot holes. I wore "hand-me-down" galoshes that had been passed along after being outgrown by our cousin in Michigan. One was at least two sizes too large and was lost somewhere along the way. I started my school day waiting in line to warm my wet feet by the big coal-fired Warm Morning heater.

Miraculously, the following summer, the man who was promising to black-topped country roads, James E. Folsom, brought his campaign to the Summer picnic at nearby Hatton. A handsome, six-foot-eight giant, James E. (Big Jim) Folsom, was running for Governor in 1946, making "stump speeches" far out into isolated communities. We were in what was called "the branch heads and brush arbors and forks of the creeks." He was like a big teddy bear with a natural smile. He stooped over, patted my sandy head, grinned and asked in a baritone drawl, "Who is this young man?" Then he kissed my young mother on the forehead, and inquired, "And who is his purty momma?" Folsom chose crossroads communities like this one because these were the people he felt closest to and knew other candidates would bypass. Hatton was typical of the places he visited: a cotton gin, a post-office, and three stores. They came from miles around to hear this new folk hero, and excitedly carried his words to the folks they associated with in Moulton when they went there on Saturdays. The word spread from there. He was our neighbor from Cullman, the county to the southeast, who would help the people in the section of the state never known to South

Alabama politicians. Rural North Alabama would have a friend who would at long last pave our roads.

Since rural Lawrence County was one of the counties that turned out the most Folsom votes, state crews paved our little gravel road early in his first four-year term in office. The miserable potholes that I had waded through walking to school and back on so many cold, wet days were filled with asphalt. President Franklin D. Roosevelt had created the Tennessee Valley Authority to control floods and help stimulate the economy during the Depression. Our lights at C.C. Smith came on in the mid-Forties, just before we moved to town. My parents said it this way: "FDR turned on the lights and Big Jim Folsom got us out of the mud."

With little statewide name recognition, Folsom had surprised the political establishment by entering the 1942 Alabama Gubernatorial Primary against five opponents, including two former Governors. One newspaper referred to him as a "funster" candidate, one of those who frequently ran for Governor "for the fun of it," with no realistic chance to win. Folsom ran a surprising second, positioning himself for a serious run in 1946. After the war, the big city newspapers and special interests discounted Folsom as a candidate who would be unable to raise money, but he turned the fact that he was not part of the elite political class into an image of independence, obligated only to the little people. A student of Southern politics, Folsom had noted that in other states some candidates used string bands to attract and excite campaign crowds. Big Jim pulled together a band of amateur "hillbilly" musicians which he named the Strawberry Pickers. He spoke in parables and used colorful gimmicks to make his points. He produced a corn-shuck mop to "clean out the capitol" and passed around a collection bucket bearing the words "Suds for Scrubbing." He needed the "suds to do the job," so the crowds dropped nickels and dimes into the suds bucket to pay the expenses for the cash-strapped campaign to move on to the next town.

Folsom was elected governor, his first public office, at the age of 38. His populist agenda represented a critical threat to the establishment forces that had dominated Alabama government and politics for a half-century, known as the "Big Mule-Black Belt" coalition. Alabama politicians preparing to fight to retain segregation anticipated a battle at the 1948 Democratic National Convention. Slates of rabid segregationist Dixiecrats opposed a slate of Folsom candidates and another slate of national party loyalists. When a civil rights resolution was introduced, the Dixiecrat members joined the Mississippi delegation in walking out of the convention. After underdog Truman won the election, Folsom tried legal action to force the Dixiecrat electors to vote for Truman but they voted for U.S. Senator Strom Thurmond of South Carolina. What I remember from that election was my grandfather Marsh's complaint that "They wouldn't even let me vote for the President of the United States."

My Grandparents, My Closest Pals

Our childhood was blessed with an extra set of loving "parents." From the time I was a tot through my college years, my constant companions, my closest pals, were my mother's parents. I fished with my grandmother and hunted with my grandfather. I, as their first grandchild, bestowed on them in "baby language" the names all their grandchildren would call them in the future. Two of the first words I uttered were "Mawmaw," the closest a two-year-old could get to pronouncing "grandma," and "Pawpaw," for "grandpa."

Both my maternal grandparents were small: my grandfather at 5'5", 130 pounds, and my grandmother shorter than five feet tall, weighing less than 100 pounds. But both were strong and overflowing with energy. Mawmaw was remarkably kind, understanding, and patient. She was slightly stooped with a hump in her back and a dip of snuff in her lower jaw. She and I fished

Spring through Fall for orange-bellied bream and yellow catfish in the rocks along Town Creek. She led the way into branches that were chest-high in depth, seining for crawfish bait with a seine made from burlap sacks with a cut-off log chain at the bottom to keep crawfish from escaping underneath. Brownish-purple earth worms worked as bait. But not nearly as well as the tails of crawfish, which with their striking white colors attracted bream from a wide radius.

Determined and fearless, Mawmaw never worried about the cotton-mouth moccasin snakes that lived along Town Creek and its tiny tributaries. The impatient Pawpaw would join us to fish for yellow catfish, particularly after heavy rains flooded the creek and on a frantic rampage for food. It was with my mother's parents that I celebrated the happiest days of my youth. Fishing, hunting, working in the fields and as a teenager sitting on the front porch watching for approaching rain while reading Pawpaw's paperback novels.

Our favorite fishing story was the time Mawmaw and I caught the big turtle. I was fishing in a pile of tree limbs above a tiny rock divide when an enormously heavy turtle latched on to the bait at the end of my thick black line. Both of us fought the monster for an hour. Finally, as I held firm, Mawmaw laid my dull hunting knife across its neck and pounded the knife blade with a heavy rock until it stopped snapping. When we returned home, a neighbor helped cook the turtle into turtle stew. Ugh, after a couple of bites I decided I preferred fresh-caught fried bream.

Pawpaw and I mostly worked together until crops were gathered and hunting season arrived. They awakened early in the morning and Pawpaw found ways to sneak a nap after lunch, before charging back into heavy farm work. When he and I hunted, I carried a light-weight, single-shot .22 rifle for hunting squirrels and he carried an old single-barrel shotgun. Once I shot a possum hiding in the hollow crack of a tree, which we tried to cook into something edible but tasted no better than turtle meat. With only one shot available before reloading I learned to make the first shot count. Pawpaw found the ultimate test for my sharpshooting when he spotted a cone-shaped hornets' nest hanging from a quarter-inch tree limb overhanging the creek. He dared me to see if I could shoot the twig in two. It was not over 10 or 12 feet away but I have still never understood how I hit that little limb. Yet "plop" was the sound as the nest fell into the creek. My dad even let me shoot hogs at hog-killing time in early winter. A tiny twenty-two bullet took but a single shot if it was shot directly between their eyes.

My grandparents' house was near the deadend on a dirt road so tiny it was too small to qualify under Governor Folsom's farm-to-market paving program. The tiny dirt road, loosely sprinkled with gravel, branched off from the Flat Rock to Mount Hope asphalt-covered road a quarter mile north of Town Creek. On the right was a large, unpainted shotgun house with a yard full of old cars. The man of the house was the community mechanic. The women mostly sat on the front porch shyly waving at the eight or ten cars that passed by each day. There were three houses down that road. In the center was our grandparents' white, green-roofed house on a slight rise above twenty acres of pastureland and cotton fields between the house, barn and Town Creek.

In the early spring the creek always flooded, bringing rich fertilized soil from upstream and depositing it in Pawpaw's sandy cotton fields. The farm was divided almost equally by the creek. A large tree served as a foot bridge, connecting pedestrians to the twenty acres of plowed fields on the south side of the creek. That was the same footbridge my dad used when he walked two miles through the backwoods to the Marsh farm to court our teenage mother. It was alongside shallow crossing where mules pulled wagons across the creek, at the point they called the "ford." From there, the mules pulled their load up a sharp incline to the "new ground," a new cotton field acquired on 20 acres. Pawpaw farmed two fields. A couple of miles south on prairie land riddled with limestone rocks and cedar trees, a small branch, about ten feet wide and four or five feet deep, flowed through the property. When I was eight or nine, Pawpaw waded across the branch and coaxed me to dog-paddle to him. I did that enough times that he announced that I had "learned how to swim," although I could barely swim. A few years later when I almost drowned in a Tennessee River lake, I regretted not having the opportunity to practice more.

On my frequent visits to my grandparents' home I slept in a small uninsulated, unheated/uncooled room, under heavy layers of quilts and feather beds during Winter. My grandparents rose every morning before daylight and always had the fireplace going before I climbed out of bed. Mawmaw was a great cook on her wood-burning stove, specializing in fried chicken, country ham, corn, butter beans, peas, fried pies, and tasteful teacakes.

I was attacked by a large rooster in their sandy back yard when I was four or five years old. Pawpaw angrily killed the rooster with a hoe. We celebrated by eating the big rooster for lunch but it tasted like tough old rooster instead of the tender taste of a young chicken. The big rooster left me with a permanent scar below my nose. Little sister Linda remembers Pawpaw later killing a big black snake that frightened her. He hung it on a barbed wire fence as a warning to other snakes and, as some neighbors superstitiously maintained, to attract rain in the dry summertime. The house had a beautiful green, regularly-mowed front yard but clumps of grass made the sandy back yard somewhat of an eyesore. When I was seven or eight years old, I was scraping away at those clumps of grass with a sharp hoe used for chopping cotton to create the appearance of a flat, sugar-colored beach common in most rural yards at the time. My aunt Mary, ten years my senior, demanded that I "stop doing that." I kept at it. She snatched the hoe out of my hands, which caused it to accidentally cut my ankle. I screamed and Pawpaw came running. He whipped his teenage daughter with a wide leather strap used for sharpening razor blades, known colloquially as a "razor strop."

A terrible crash occurred in those days on two-lane Highway 24 between Moulton and Russellville when a pickup truck abruptly turned left without signaling, just as a car was attempting to pass. After the collision, the old man climbed out of his pickup truck and said to the shaken driver of the car, "Didn't you know I always turn here?" That could have been my grandfather, who was 90% blind but navigated the back roads of Lawrence County without incident, his neighbors got out of the way when they saw him coming.

Tranquility: Riding on a Cotton Wagon to the Gin

Pawpaw was known for miles around for the mammoth size of his mule team. Products of a strain of mules so large and strong that they could only be bought at auction 100 miles to the north at "the mule capital of the South," Columbia, Tennessee. Pawpaw's mule team featured "Ol' Hattie" on the left and "Ol' Ider" on the right. His command of "Gee" meant turn left, "Hah," right. They both topped 1,000 pounds, stronger than a horse of similar size with the endurance and stubborn disposition of the mule breed.

I was just growing into my early teens when I found myself hanging on to a "turning plow" behind those giant mules in a stump-infested patch of new ground on the south bank of the creek. It was the first year that land previously wooded was to be cultivated for row crops. Rather than guiding the plow, I was racing and doing my best to hold on behind the fast-walking giant mules as the plow bounced among the roots of tree stumps. By afternoon, I had a severe stomach ache from dehydration, and the acrid taste of sulfur-flavored water only worsened the dizziness. But I was too proud to admit the discomfort to my grandfather.

One of the saddest events of my childhood was the time my grandfather's favorite mule, "Ol' Hattie," injured her leg when she stepped through a hole caused by a missing plank in a wooden bridge over the creek on the Mount Hope road. The accident permanently damaged a hoof tendon and broke Pawpaw's heart. Ol' Hattie was a sad sight limping around the barn for years afterward, unable ever again to pull her share of a wagon or a plow. After that, her face seemed to me to have developed a pitiful frown.

My favorite time of year was when I rode on frosty mornings burrowed in deep holes dug in the cotton on the way to cotton gins at Mount Hope or Flat Rock. In the remaining decades of my life, when obstacles were high and disappointments deep, I could briefly make the world go away by pretending that I could burrow into the soft cotton once again, lie in a thick feather bed, listening to the patter of steady rain on the tin roof, or recline on my back in a springtime meadow, staring upward into a blue sky.

On the Front Porch Watching for Clouds

By my college years, when I still spent most of the Summer visiting them, I often lay in my swing reading paper backs by Mickey Spillane, with graphic details about a tough detective and his flings with women, and Erskine Caldwell, whose description of poor Georgia white trash were so vivid I had no desire to visit the Georgia backwoods.

After Pawpaw read from his paperback novels for a while, he tended to become restless, announcing he needed to "go to the store." He was in paradise at every country store within a five-mile radius. We sat on nail kegs around iron stoves visiting with neighbors, drinking Nehi grape colas with a pack of peanuts poured inside. The men told old jokes, talked politics, and caught up on the latest local news. One of the happiest moments on his seven decades on earth was years later when I was campaigning in my first political venture shortly before he died of cancer in 1970. Lawrence was one of seven counties in the district from which members of the State Democratic Executive Committee were elected. Pawpaw proudly led me into each store smiling proudly, exclaiming, "This is my grandson, and I want you to vote for him." He was overjoyed when I won, mainly because of the margin provided by Lawrence County, my native county, and Colbert County where I grew up from elementary school through college and later published a newspaper.

While Pawpaw was a heavy roll-your-own smoker, he avoided alcohol most of his life. When doctors prescribed medicine to combat prostrate problems in his later life, he refused to take it. Our parents always took us to our Mawmaw and Pawpaw Marsh's house on Christmas Eve, a tradition we followed with our own children. The traditional highlight of our Christmas was seeing a beaming Pawpaw enjoying the chocolate-covered coconut and Coca-Cola drinks as much as any of the young grandchildren.

Summer Revivals at the New Zion Baptist

"If we had more hell in the pulpit, we would have less hell in the pew."
~ *Evangelist Billy Graham*

Our church was New Zion Baptist Church at Flat Rock. I loved that little white church, especially Vacation Bible School each June. Pawpaw Marsh, and my dad were both deacons. When babies became hungry during services, mothers flopped out breasts and nursed them openly. No one thought anything about it. It was a special time in America, when we lived in blissful naïveté, which in so many ways was far superior to enlightened times. Summer brought week-long church services each evening known as revivals. Usually held between "laying by and gathering" time for crops, the purpose was to revive the spiritual commitments of all and especially to gain new converts.

Evangelists concluded their sermons at emotional peaks, then stepped down in front of the pulpit, arms stretched wide, appealing for sinners to come forward and accept Christ. The rest of us, those too young or those already "saved," would sadly sing the invitational hymn, *"Just as I Am, without one plea, but that thy blood was shed for me, and that thou bidst me come to thee, O Lamb of God, I come, I come..."* Members sneaked glances at the targeted sinners. If their response was too slow, an aggressive deacon would move to sit by the sinner and with arms over their shoulders, appeal to them in low voices. That usually pried one or two to leave their seats for the slow walk down the aisle to the alter to confess his sins and accept Christ.

Other evangelists came to our county to preach at brush arbor revivals. Brush arbors were a throwback to America's pioneering days. In our community, they were generally looked upon as entertainment. Young people brought their dates to observe from a safe distance in the woods as "holy rollers" rolled in the aisles and spoke in unknown tongues. Wild drunken gatherings further back in the woods invariably led to fights, sometimes even stabbings.

My kind, trusting father showed real anger for the first time in my young life, when he discovered our hogs had been poisoned by the farmer next door. The pigs had worked their way out of their pen, looking for food in the wooded area of the farm next door. They died from the poisoned food that had been left for them. The first time I ever heard my dad curse, he angrily said, "I ought to take a gun to the SOB." The impact of having someone poison our basic year-long food supply when times were still tough was beyond comprehension. But I knew my dad's temptation to respond violently was too uncharacteristic to represent a real threat. So, he prayed about it, and kept his distance from the evil neighbor afterwards.

To my saint-like father, harm to his family was even more provocative than killing his hogs. He dealt directly with the tenant farmer, whose sons tore down my tree swing that gave me so much pleasure and then laughed at me when I cried. Even though he was a lazy worker, the tenant farmer had served a useful purpose during the war by selling his sugar and gas rationing coupons to us. But after he failed to apologize or discipline his rowdy sons, Daddy insisted that the family move away from our farm in short order.

Moving for Greater Opportunities

After the great war ended my father began looking beyond our small farm for a better career. An excellent carpenter, he had built our little white country house with the green roof during the war. After the war, he began commuting the 20 miles to Sheffield where he built custom homes with Julius Anderton, the farm owner whose cotton land we were renting when the war ended. By 1948, Daddy had built a brick house, complete with a basement and attic. It was at 601 12th Street, directly in front of Sheffield High School. We moved in that Summer, in time for me to enter the fifth grade and Joyce the third grade.

When we moved to town, we brought along our milk cow, Bossy, and staked her out in a rocky hollow between our house and the Tennessee River. I was responsible for feeding and milking her. She had a nasty habit of putting her manure-encrusted foot in the milk bucket, polluting that day's supply. An even greater challenge occurred when neighborhood kids threw rocks in our direction to panic Bossy. While I was hanging to the rope for dear life, Bossy bolted, dragging me at full speed across the rocky ground.

Work was a basic part of my world from the time I helped dig raw peanuts during the War to two years of hoeing and picking cotton before we moved to town. In Sheffield, as I grew up, I always had at least one job. That practice was to become financially rewarding in my college days when I wrote for two newspapers, served as news director as a student, and promoted horse shows, rodeos, and rock 'n' roll music concerts.

Lessons Learned as a Newspaper Carrier

In addition to milking Bossy, I found a job as a newspaper carrier for the *Birmingham News* while waiting for a route to become available with the local paper, the *Tri-Cities Daily*. The *News,* published over 100 miles away, was a thick, heavy paper and my 50 or so customers were scattered over nearly three miles. J.D. Savage was the local *News* circulation manager and my childhood hero, who became an all-time favorite boss. Mr. Savage treated young, impressionable boys with respect and fairness. The challenge for a eleven-year-old carrier was to keep the bicycle balanced with papers bulging from a wire basket attached to the handlebars. I would lean the bike on its kick-stand, with the front wheel snug against the curb. But when hit by a sudden gust of wind, the bike toppled and papers spilled into the watery gutter.

We newspaper carriers did not realize it at the time but we were learning about business in the real world, with real customers, at an impressionable age. Most of our customers responded kindly by answering our knocks on the door and paying their bills promptly. Then there was the occasional cynical adult who enjoyed bedeviling young newspaper carriers. One character, who had moved from the

North to work for TVA, was obstreperous, a pain to deal with, but he tipped well. While I was bent over one day writing his payment into my route book, he spotted the name I had given him: "The Mean Tipper." He roared with laughter, and tipped more than ever afterwards.

After several months, the coveted *Tri-Cities Daily's* Nashville Avenue route opened and I was next on the waiting list. Instead of carrying the much heavier *Birmingham News* to the few of its subscribers on three streets in far-away Sheffield, I now had a route with a customer at nearly every house in the half-mile up Nashville Avenue from downtown to the bluff above the Tennessee River. For the next four years, I delivered the local daily newspaper seven days a week to over 100 customers along the eight blocks from downtown to the river bluff on the north edge of town.

Easy to fold into thin eight-inch squares, we flipped the papers back-handed, frizbee-style. A good throw made the front porch; a miss went into the shrubs. It took about 30 minutes to fold our papers on benches in a carrier room below the *Standard and Times* offices on the alley behind Montgomery Avenue, the town's main street. We folded the papers into flat rectangular discs and arranged them in rows in cloth bags to place in the bicycle baskets. Some of the older boys even had motor scooters and larger routes. It was a congenial young group that came together to fold newspapers for delivery. We looked forward to those gatherings as social events. Jack Gravett, an older carrier, entertained us by singing Ernest Tubb's "*Walking the Floor Over You"* in a gravelly voice.

Our subscribers wanted the news while it was hot. I would rush along Nashville Avenue, sailing the *Tri-Cities Daily* Frisbee-style in the general vicinity of the front porches of my customers. The wind sometimes interfered and a customer's paper wound up in the shrubs. If the customer was old or handicapped, I climbed off the bicycle, fished it out from under the bush, and dropped it on the front porch. Otherwise, I kept pumping the pedals and flipping the newspapers.

Our playground at Atlanta Avenue Junior High School was covered in small river stones, called pea-gravel, mixed with sharp stones, which had been dug from the river. Most, but not all, of it was washed smooth by the current. We played tackle football every recess.

In sixth grade I ran into my first problem in class, learning that studying the subject of health should have required at least some homework preparation. A "D" grade one six-weeks period led to a note to the parents---and direct parental involvement. My mother jerked my ear to emphasize that she would not tolerate her children slacking off. In seventh grade, Miss Pollard taught us how to multiply, divide, add, and subtract. It stuck to the point that when I became a manager, I looked back with appreciation at being taught to calculate numbers in my head long before I ever discovered a calculator.

The Mighty Tennessee, Our Region's Greatest Asset

I was fortunate to have grown up, and lived almost all my life, in the great Tennessee Valley region of the Southeast. Fed in its upper reaches by the thousands of streams from the forested coves and misty ridges of the Appalachian Mountains, the 652-mile-long Tennessee River was our region's greatest asset and represented the path to great economic progress in the decades to follow. Increasingly visible in the 1940s were the benefits of FDR's Tennessee Valley Authority (TVA). In my early childhood, we lived a few miles south of the river near Wheeler Dam.

Living in Sheffield we were in easy view of Wilson Dam, built a year after the United States entered World War I. The federal government built dams for the making of explosives and Wilson Dam was constructed to supply the electricity needed to power the plants. TVA acquired Wilson Dam in 1933.

We were directly impacted by programs brought about by the TVA, which was responsible for at least one memorable improvement in the quality of our lives. Our old one-seat outdoor toilet, on the worn path between the house and the barn, was replaced by TVA shortly after World War II with a handsome new two-seater, elevated to increase air circulation, and sporting a lightning rod on top.

CHAPTER **3**

The Fabulous Fifties

By the decade of the Fifties, America had recovered from World War II and a Cold War had developed into a hot competition between the United States and the Soviet Union. The parents of the Fifties were properly called America's "Greatest Generation" because of their sacrifices in the Depression and World War II.

I was a child of the Fifties, labeled the "Luckiest Generation." I visited the White House as a 13-year-old newspaper carrier who luckily won the trip largely at the behest of a cantankerous customer.

Then they invented a new kind of music which was popularized by Elvis Presley of Memphis as rock 'n' roll. I was a young reporter when a new friend and Florence native, Sam Phillips of Memphis, took a liking to me and began inviting me to Memphis. He would become known as "The Father of Rock 'n' Roll." One night, I spoke with Elvis on the phone when my date, a former girlfriend of Elvis called him so I could speak personally with him.

I rode a bus to Detroit to cover the pennant race when I was invited by my hero, batting star Ted Williams to a one-on-one interview. That was before the game that sunny Saturday when the headline read: "Ted Williams was never more magnificent," the next day following a bases-loaded grand slam homer in the ninth.

Miracles Come from the Strangest Places

As a 13-year-old newspaper carrier, I found myself lagging in a major competition selling U.S. Savings Bonds. I needed a miracle to pull ahead of the other *Tri-Cities Daily* carriers to win a trip to Washington, D.C. hosted by President Harry S. Truman.

President Harry S. Truman, left, and Treasury
Secretary Snyder promote saving bonds, 1952

I was pushing hard, soliciting subscribers up and down my paper route on Sheffield's Nashville Avenue. But, try as they might, these were middle income people, and few could afford to spend heavily on savings bonds. I was knocking on doors on the 700 block when I reluctantly entered an old two-story rooming house. Mr. Backus was a gruff old man, the most dreaded customer on the entire route. I quietly slid the brochure under his door and moved on to the next house.

The next day Mr. Backus was waiting for me at his front door, holding the Savings Bond brochure in his hand. "Why did you skip me?" he demanded. "I saw you knocking on everyone else's door!"

I mumbled that I hadn't wanted to bother him. "Well, come on in here, young man. I want you to understand that I am a strong believer in Savings Bonds. I believe I can help you win your contest." Whereupon he signed a pledge for an incredible amount. It put me over the top.

And off to Washington, D.C., I headed early that Summer. Riding on two-lane highways through the Blue Ridge Mountains, we stopped in Pulaski, Virginia, for lunch. Well-cooked Virginia country ham was the specialty of the little restaurant. A melancholy feeling consumed me as we drove across the awesome Shenandoah Valley, speckled with rail fences remindful of the area's importance in the Civil War. I silently hummed a popular waltz song, *"In the Shenandoah Valley of Virginia, lives a girl who is waiting just for me…"*

Our week in Washington as guests of the Treasury Department and President Truman was highlighted by the gathering in the White House Rose Garden. Wearing a light suit with a carnation, President Harry Truman addressed the small group of "paper boys," and stressed the importance of citizens investing their savings in the bonds that had helped finance America's war effort.

A few years later, while I was in college, I learned that Mr. Backus had died. I went to the rooming house to pay my respects. There were only a handful of friends sitting by the casket. I sat there with them all night, regretting that more people had not discovered this grand old man. To the few who were there I said, "I don't know most of you. But, based on the few of us that are here, he didn't have many friends here on earth. But I am praying that he makes it through the Pearly Gates because if he was half the friend to God that he was to me, I know what his final destination will be." He was the biggest benefactor my young life had seen.

A Life-Threatening Experience

I experienced a life-threatening trauma in the summer following the seventh grade. At a Pickwick Lake picnic area near Savannah, Tennessee, I was dog-paddling from the pier to a floating life boat just 10 or 15 feet away. It was only about six feet deep, but over my head. I had barely learned to swim on my grandfather's farm. About half-way to the life boat it began drifting away. I tired and my head dropped underwater. A tall classmate, JoBelle McWilliams, standing on an underwater rock with her head above the water, reached out and plucked me from beneath the water. My mother was on shore saying, "Thank God! Thank God!"

We Got in the First Lick, Then Fled Before Reinforcements Came

Teenage fighting started out badly for me. The first was with a neighborhood bully named W. J. Thurmond, who beat me up with his fists, when I was in the eighth grade. It happened on the high school campus. I went home crying to our Mother. The first time she kept her cool. It was simply a disagreement which anyone could have. The second time set her blood to boiling. She raced toward the high school, then saw the bully walking down the street and confronted him. My mother was a fiery little woman, and you were not safe if you beat a child of hers. I just knew that it was safe for me to play in the neighborhood from that day forward.

The next time was when I was a senior in high school. I was working for the *Florence Times-Tri-Cities Daily* as a stringer, meaning I got paid so much a month times the cumulative length per column inch of the stories turned in for the month. It was a game at Greenhill with T.M. Rogers as the host team. I was joined by Buck Locke, the center on Sheffield's football team. We sat in a section with several attractive high school girls. We flirted throughout the game. The girls were from there, in rural Lauderdale County, and some of the local boys became angry over the flirtations. As the game ended and we came near my car in the parking lot one of the boys challenged me to a fight. I had always heard that if the first one to swing in a fist fight hit the other hard enough there would be no need to fight further. Instead of wasting time talking I hit him before the question had left his lips. That ended that! One of his buddies stepped forward and my football player friend knocked him across the hood of my car. We jumped in the car and raced away. We won the fight by leaving before reinforcements could follow up. He and a group of his pals looked for my buddy and me on the drive-in circuit for several weeks without any success. I thought later how lucky we had been that they didn't recognize the byline on the game story the next day.

Sheffield's Colorful Coaches

Our football and baseball coach, Walton Wright, was a legend in high school circles for inspiring a team always smaller than its opponents. Never weighing as much as 140 pounds while starring as a high school and college tailback, his highly-disciplined teams were formed in his image---small, quick, and hard-hitting.

A characteristic of his was that his players must focus only on football and avoid distractions such as dating. One Spring day, Coach Wright spotted our third baseman, Don Armstrong, chatting intimately with a girl at her locker. At baseball practice that afternoon he positioned Armstrong halfway between third and home. He hit blue-darter grounders with the fungo bat until Armstrong had knots covering his shins. In 28 years at Sheffield, Coach Wright won nearly twice as many as he lost in football and eight times as many as he lost in 11 years of coaching baseball.

Walton Wright always showed his appreciation for my coverage of their games. I sat by him in the dugout and kept the scorebook.

I had a somewhat different experience with his assistant football coach, who also coached track. The problem developed when I wrote a Sunday feature article about the burgeoning prospects of an underclassman who was showing great potential as a versatile star. He excelled at throwing the discus, shot-putting, broad jumping, high jumping, and running on relay teams. I portrayed him as a high school version of Jim Thorpe. The next day, as the coach presided over our study hall, he peeked over his thick glasses and signaled for me to come up to his desk. He administered the tongue-lashing of my young life for heaping such misplaced praise on the athlete. Maturity was not the hallmark of the young track star. He was an undisciplined thrill seeker who died a short time after high school from a late night high speed collision.

Carl Boley, an Educator on a Fast Track

As a high school senior one of my assignments was working as a clerk in the office of the principal in the middle of the day. Our principal was Carl Boley, an outgoing young man on a career fast track. A football star at Florence State Teachers College while majoring in English, he had assisted Ms. Daves as a practice teacher my sophomore year. Ms. Daves, who passed her enthusiasm for writing to me, shared with Carl Boley her pride when I began writing for the local daily newspaper. We became friends.

My junior year, Mr. Boley taught English at SHS. By my senior year he had ascended to the position of Principal.

While enjoying my other classes, I hated chemistry! It was taught by a volatile teacher, so scatterbrained she had failed to notice that I had been skipping laboratory classes all year. I would sometimes sneak off to the nearby river to fish for Crappie lying on my stomach on a flat rock from a bluff above the water. It was almost at the end of the school year that our flaky chemistry teacher finally noticed that I was missing. I was in the cafeteria eating an early lunch when a classmate burst in to warn me that the chemistry teacher had begun shouting, "Where is Charles Grainger?" I rushed to Carl Boley's office to give my friend a heads up that we had an angry chemistry teacher. "I'll take care of it," he assured me. Somehow, he calmed her.

Nearly two decades later my friend came through again. I was serving in the State Legislature and he had become Superintendent of Sheffield Schools as well as Chairman of the State Mental Health Commission. I was looking for funds to offset a $300,000 inflation-caused construction overrun on the new Mental Health Facility in Huntsville. The Deputy State Budget Officer searched until he found enough funds left over in a forgotten account from a bond issue. There still was the problem of the lack of a precedent for the state to provide local funding for mental health facilities. We made the case to the State Board that these were special, unique circumstances. Carl Boley convinced his colleagues to support our request.

Impersonated by a Peeping Tom

I learned about another form of strange behavior in a most unbelievable way.

The phone rang late one night. Mother answered. It was the police department.

"Do you know where your son Charles is?"

"Yes," she answered, "he's in his bed asleep."

"Ma'am would you mind double-checking?"

MY JOURNEY THROUGH A CHANGING SOUTH

She checked my bedroom, then confirmed to the policeman that I was indeed in bed sound asleep.

"OK, that's good," said the officer. "We caught a "Peeping Tom" outside a lady's bedroom in Village One and he's saying his name is Charles Grainger. We'll get his real name now."

Word of the incident got around quickly as well as the identity of the voyeur who had maligned me. When I confronted him, he turned red, then said, "Yours was the first name that popped into my head." Years later, I could still see his face. The only thing I will say is that he has long been dead.

"Oh, to be like Grantland Rice"

The 1955 Sheffield High annual, *The Demitasse,* pictured me with a flattop haircut above the words, *"Oh, to be like Grantland Rice."* In spite of the editor's catchy phrase, I knew I could never produce eloquent prose with the flair of the legendary sports writer Grantland Rice. The most famous Rice account was of the 1924 Notre Dame-Army game. He led it with the Biblical reference to the *Four Horsemen of the Apocalypse*:

"Outlined against a blue-gray October sky the Four Horsemen rode again. In dramatic lore they are known as famine, pestilence, destruction and death. These are only aliases. Their real names are: Stuhldreher, Miller, Crowley and Layden. They formed the crest of the South Bend cyclone before which another fighting Army team was swept over the precipice at the Polo Grounds this afternoon as 55,000 spectators peered down upon the bewildering panorama spread out upon the green plain below."

The Demitasse summarized my student involvement as *Hi-Lites* Sports Editor, Key Club, Student Council, baseball, basketball, football,

Senior Play cast, Quill and Scroll, and Boys State. I was proudest of my selection to attend Boys State, a week-long conference at the State Capitol consisting of students chosen statewide. A student Legislature was elected and we went through the process of enacting laws. I was elected to the State Senate, serving with Sonny Hornsby as Lieutenant Governor. He later became Chief Justice of the Alabama Supreme Court. With classmate Jean Quinn as my speech-writer, I finished second in the Colbert County Oratorical Contest. The winner was Jimmy Gullett of Tuscumbia, a big guy with a booming voice who was preparing for a career as a Baptist preacher. We would become close friends in college.

Mid-Fifties in Small Town, America

Some other quick recollections of those days:

- Playing basketball at our backyard goal with my sister Joyce, who was an excellent athlete, head majorette, and salutatorian of her graduating class. She would help coach me through College Algebra when we took the same class one summer at Florence State. I loved to work the numbers in math but I learned algebra took some time studying.

- The Standpipe, a tall, round water reservoir on the bluff overlooking Pickwick Lake at the north terminus of Montgomery Avenue, Sheffield's main street. Playing among those high bluffs, we once were chased into the arms of the police by two fishermen upset that we stupidly threw rocks into the river close to their boats.

- Close friend Charles Beck, who watched television at our house at the beginning of the Fifties. The reception from the Birmingham and Nashville stations was so bad we looked away from the screen into a mirrored reflection to reduce the amount of "snow" caused by poor reception.

- Mother's business enterprise, The Candy Store, in downtown Sheffield. She never made a profit but the three Grainger children loved her merchandise.

- A woman known as "Shug" and her husband with their push carts roving the back alleys of downtown Sheffield picking up junk. That was before any of us had ever heard the word "homeless."

- The old mustachioed Mexican who sold tasty tamales, hot in the shuck, from his push cart. Jo Jo attracted attention by yelling, "Cold today, hot tamale."

- The strawberry sodas at The Smoke Shop Drug Store.

- Using onion-soaked dough-balls for bait to catch carp where the sewer drained into the river across from the Naval Reserve Station. We never ate those sewage-eating fish, but the crappie from that lake were delicious. In the Fifties, the Naval Reserve Station was the site for our teenage dances and "sock hops." In 1979, Sheffield grad, guitarist and Muscle Shoals Sound producer Jimmy Johnson and his partners bought the building and created some great records in the unusual studio environment.

- Our high school play, *"Ten Little Indians, (And Then There Were None)."* The production was based on Agatha Christie's tale of 10 people invited to an isolated place where an unknown person killed them one by one. My character, an aging professor with white eyebrows, was among the last to die. The *Demitasse* snapshots section featured a photo of me thrusting my hands in the air in theatrical surprise, exclaiming "Dead??!!??" when learning that another of the ten had been killed.

The Legend of Hawk Pride Mountain

My senior year I was victimized by a "farmer's daughter" prank. The guys who talked me into going to Hawk Pride Mountain were Peewee Nelson, Gene Harris, Don Armstrong and Johnny Williams. The girl was Nancy Snyder. They were all in on the joke, of which I was the butt.

I had shared the urgings of a maturing young man with some of my buddies and one Spring night, they drove me to an old country house on Hawk Pride Mountain. There, I had been promised, sat a young lady who was eagerly waiting. When we shouted from outside to the girl inside, Nancy's voice came back almost as a whisper. The weak "yes" was a sign something was amiss. So, I decided to run away when I heard the shotgun blast! Harris, the fleet shortstop on our baseball team, fell. Then he shouted to me to get help! He said he had been shot! I ran and ran until I found a light on about a half-mile away. The neighbors called the law. They finally arrived, lights flashing---an ambulance plus deputies' cars.

When we rode down the mountain to the Sheriff's Office, the law enforcement officers lectured us about the gravity of pranks like that. I took the ribbing from classmates the next day. But I was to remain short in the birds and bees department. But not for long.

The Summer of Fifty-Five

The Summer of 1955 was filled with magic. I branched out into a broad range of news writing and public relations activities. I wrote radio spots for WLAY in Sheffield, promoted a Tennessee Walking Horse Show, a rodeo, and publicized rock and roll and country music shows. The horse show was the most lucrative. I learned that those who support horse shows tend to be financially capable of easily filling a program with ads. As part of the build-up for

MY JOURNEY THROUGH A CHANGING SOUTH

the rodeo event, I picked a "rodeo queen," who was pictured on the front page of the *Times-Daily* atop a wooden fence sporting a cowgirl hat and a beautiful smile. I dated her only once before her Church of Christ parents learned I was a Baptist and ordered her to restrict her social life to fellow church members.

I had a Fall job lined up with the *Birmingham News* covering Tennessee Valley high school sports. I was continuing as a twice-a-week sports columnist for the *Times-Daily*. My column was headed by a two-column box titled, *"Sports Chatter With Grainger."* Sports Editor Hap Halbrooks, a cynical sort, gave it the name, probably because as a young eager beaver I chattered excitedly while hanging out in the newsroom. The atmosphere in that newsroom, the smell of hot lead and printers ink, the excitement of unfolding news events was intoxicating. I was a "stringer," a newspaper writer paid by the column inch. They literally measured monthly clippings with yardsticks and multiplied the small amount per inch to arrive at the monthly payment.

Halbrooks and City Editor Ben Knight, who was to become one of my closest friends the next few years, also steered me toward a college job. I planned to commute to Florence State Teachers College, living with my parents and sisters on Sheffield's Cliff Haven, on the bluff overlooking the Tennessee River bridge. On the recommendation of Halbrooks and Knight I was hired by the FSTC Sports Information Director to be his assistant to maintain statistics and cover daily football practices.

Ben Knight, My Mentor During my Early Maturity

Ben Knight, the *Times-Daily* News Editor, was a talented, clever writer who maintained the best sources in sports, politics, and entertainment. Newsmakers called Ben first when something important happened and maintained close personal relations with him. His friends included Sam Phillips of Sun Records fame, and actor George "Goober" Lindsey. In sports, he was a personal advisor to two of the legendary high school coaches in small school football, C. T. Manley at Leighton and Bud Mills at Cherokee. Ben also was close to Line Coach George Weeks at Florence State, State Senator Barry Lynchmore Cantrell of Tuscumbia, Colbert County Circuit Solicitor Bryce Graham of Tuscumbia, and Colbert County Circuit Judge Clifford Delony. His apartment was their refuge from the public for having a drink since our county was "dry" at the time.

He was my mentor, sharing contacts and writing tips. He flavored his writing with the regal thrusts of his sports columnist hero, Walter Steward of the Memphis *Commercial Appeal*. Beyond writing and editing local news stories, Ben wrote a comical column about entertainment. He was the recipient of several Associated Press news-writing awards. He received national attention when a network television series entitled *"The Big Story"* featured his successful investigation of a man erroneously convicted of murder who was released as a result of Ben's investigative reporting. He was presented the Pell Mell" award for investigative journalism.

Knight's dry wit was uplifting. When he answered the phone, if a friend said, "Knight?" he would respond with a gravelly, tired voice, "Knight-MARE." Ben Knight had an outstanding career, the promise of an even more spectacular climb cut short by an early death. He died as a result of alcohol at the age of 53 in 1984, living just a year longer than his idol, Walter Stewart, who had died at 52 in 1958.

Introduction to Rock 'n' Roll

Beyond my sports column, I wrote articles about entertainment, which led to promoting rock 'n' roll and country shows. The most significant events of the Summer of 1955 for this 18-year-old were:

- The return of young Elvis Presley to Sheffield.

- Becoming a close friend of Presley's discoverer, Sam Phillips of Sun Records and being a part of early performances of several of his miraculous rock 'n' roll discoveries.

- Getting an up-close look at the 1955 American League pennant race, highlighted by a one-on-one interview with the greatest hitter of all time. The same day Ted Williams made a point of giving a kid columnist an exclusive interview about how he had always wanted to be a pitcher, he hit one of the most memorable home runs in an extraordinary career.

Sam Phillips, the Father of Rock 'n' Roll

"Well Nashville had country music but Memphis had the soul
"The white boy had the rhythm and that started rock 'n' roll
"And I was here when it happened don't you all think I ought to know
"I was here when it happened,
"I watched Memphis give birth to rock 'n' roll." ~ "Birth of Rock and Roll," written and sung by Carl Perkins.

The Fabulous Fifties, America's happy days, spun off the greatest cultural force of the Twentieth Century: the coming together of black and white music into rock 'n' roll. I was fortunate enough to be in the center of those events.

Sam Phillips was the visionary who created the dominant strain of rock 'n' roll during the last half-decade of the late Fifties that transformed the landscape of music and American culture for generations to come. He was its father, the man who invented rock 'n' roll. All that happened in short span of six years. It began with the magical discovery of Presley in 1954.

During the next eighteen months Sam Phillips worked tirelessly promoting Elvis. Sam *was* Sun Records. He produced, engineered, and marketed the Sun label. Sam loaded his Cadillac full of the little yellow label "45s" and drove from city to city, sixteen hours a day, marketing Elvis records one record distributor at a time. In 1955, Elvis Presley rocked his way across the South on the way to becoming the most influential cultural figure of the Twentieth Century. His discoverer, Sam Phillips, became universally accepted as the "Father of Rock 'n' Roll." Associated Press, July 30, 2003, AL.com.

A year after he discovered Elvis Presley, other talented entertainers beat on his door. Johnny Cash, Carl Perkins, Jerry Lee Lewis, and Roy Orbison formed a constellation of stars that dominated the music of the last half of the decade of the Fifties. They all came from near-poverty backgrounds. Elvis, a truck driver and aspiring gospel singer, was living in a low-rent Memphis housing project when he went to Sun to record. The others were fresh from the country. After Presley came Carl Perkins and Johnny Cash from the Arkansas and Tennessee cotton fields growing up directly across the Mississippi River from each other. Perkins brought a rocking style developed in small town honky-tonks that sounded somewhat like Presley's sound.

Cash revolutionized country music with a unique new sound enthusiastically accepted by both urban and rural America. Jerry Lee Lewis, a Louisiana rocker who played a piano like a wild man, showed up at Sun in late 1956. Then came Roy Orbison a nondescript young Texan, whose career began with Sun rockabilly songs and exploded in the Sixties, when with another label, he recorded the greatest ballads of the century.

Sam Phillips used the friendly audiences of the Sheffield Community Center across the river from his home town of Florence as early launch sites for his developing stars. In January of 1955, Elvis drove to Sheffield from a performance the previous night in Corinth, MS. When he went on stage young girls jumped up and down and screamed wildly. The *Florence Times-Tri-Cities Daily* wrote that "many who had not previously heard the just-turned-twenty 'fastest rising country music star in the nation' left the show as full-fledged fans." Afterwards, excited young girls, known as bobby-soxers, clustered in a large pack near the stage waiting for autographs. Many hoped to be selected for a date to ride in his pink Cadillac. That night Elvis picked Carol Cahoon, a 17-year-old Sheffield High junior. "Carol Cahoon went out with Elvis Presley!" echoed along the corridor at Sheffield High. Girls were jealous and boys were puzzled why they hadn't noticed her before. Carol was slim, with attractive eyes and an interesting face. She was in the eleventh grade. I was a twelfth-grade senior.

Elvis was among the lower-billed entertainers on two All-Star "hillbilly" shows on August 2. The name at the top of the ads in the *Times-Daily* was Webb Pearce, the recognized "Mr. Country Music" of the mid-Fifties. My article that day was headlined, "Big Hillbilly Show Tonight in Sheffield."

The morning of the event I received a call from Sam Phillips saying the tour producer was adding to the shows a young singer with a record that was stirring the Memphis radio audience. I had already written the article, leading with, "Tonight is the night that the country, folk, western, and bop fans of the Tri-Cities have been waiting for..."

I added a quick paragraph: "A late addition to the show is a fast-rising young star who is not well known locally. He's Jimmy *(sic)* Cash, who is rising rapidly with a new hit called *Cry, Cry, Cry.* All reports indicate that he'll be well liked by Tri-Citians." Oops, I noticed later, in my first article about Johnny Cash we had gotten his name wrong. In the interest of time, I had called to dictate the update to City Editor Ben Knight. In his haste, Knight typed the wrong first name.

The Sheffield Community Center was unique for a small town, the largest entertainment venue in the region. With a large balcony, it packed some 2,000 spectators, all seated relatively close to the stage. Bouncing around back stage was a hyper Elvis Presley, with long dark hair in greasy ducktails, eyes highlighted by mascara, striking in black and pink. Strumming on his guitar, he flirted with pretty 17-year-old singer Wanda Jackson. He sang Johnny Cash's trademark song, "Cry, Cry, Cry." Johnny Cash was not a happy observer.

In his deep baritone, rural Arkansas voice, Cash glared at Elvis and said, "Elvis, ah'd 'preciate it if you wouldn't be sanging my song."

Elvis ignored him, flashing his dark eyes directly at the young female singer. She smiled back.

With more feeling, Cash repeated, "Elvis, I said, ah'd 'preciate it if you wouldn't be sanging my song."

The backstage episode ended without violence when Elvis finally got the message. (Postscript: The last time I checked, Wanda Jackson, then age 75, was back on tour singing the rock 'n' roll songs Elvis encouraged her to sing when she began dating him on that early tour. "Now girls, don't get ahead of me here," Ms. Jackson would say in her concerts. "That was way back in 1955.

45

My daddy traveled with me and kept my reputation intact." Her publicists called her "the Queen of Rockabilly and America's first female Rock and Roll singer.") Sullivan, James. "Wanda Jackson Remembers Elvis," Rollingstone. December 9, 2005.

My coverage of the August 2 event in the *Tri-Cities Daily* exclaimed that upstart Elvis had stolen the show from the hillbilly king, Webb Pearce. I also wrote, "Johnny Cash...was simply great," describing him as "a coming star with tunes that sounded like the best of Presley's bops, with a "voice that was different...deeper." Two years later, in a long visit at Sun Studio, Cash remembered that as among the first times he had seen his name in a newspaper. By November 15, when Elvis returned to Sheffield, it was his name at the top of the marquee.

Sam Phillips' Personal Story is Filled with Fun

"If you're not doing something different, you're not doing anything."

~ *Sam Phillips*

Florence, Alabama, prides itself in having given birth to two American music icons: W.C. Handy, the father of the blues, and Sam Phillips, the father of rock and roll. Both settled in Memphis as young men because of the musical attraction of Beale Street, the home of the Mississippi Delta blues.

Of great significance to me, the Summer of 1955 was the beginning of a close, two-year personal relationship with Sam Phillips. Our relationship was enhanced by my mentor and our mutual friend, Ben Knight, *Tri-Cities Daily* News Editor. Sam and Ben were already close friends at the time and would remain close drinking buddies in the Seventies when Sam began developing radio stations in the Shoals area. Sam always enjoyed being with people from his home town, particularly those of us who reported his Memphis successes to the home folk. He clearly had a special yearning to be a recognized "prophet in his hometown."

In spite of his tendencies to control conversations, Sam Phillips was an extremely likeable man. Time spent with him was never dull and always pleasurable. When I began visiting him, I was 18 and Sam was 32. He was comfortable with my age group: When they began their careers with Sun, Elvis Presley was 18, Jerry Lee Lewis and Roy Orbison were 21, and Johnny Cash and Carl Perkins were 22 years old. Following the two August 2 shows in Sheffield, Sam invited me to come to Memphis as his house guest and to hang around the studio while he recorded. The magnetism of the studio was remindful of the excitement of the news room where I hung out on Saturdays in my high school days. Only the smell of printer's ink was lacking.

After his work in the control room was finished after midnight, we would sit in his den listening to recorded music until daylight. Our favorite was *C. C. Rider* by black rhythm and blues artist Chuck Willis. Sam had no business interest in the singer. We just liked his music. We played it over and over and over.

Another artist whose records we enjoyed in those early morning hours was Charlie Rich, a Sun studio musician, whose country-soul ballads reminded me of the old Southern expression, "as smooth as syrup poured over pancakes." "He's an arrogant so and so, but he can flat sing a song," Sam said more than once. As we listened to the Rich renditions, I could almost see Sam's mind spinning, looking for the path to a hit record. However, few Rich songs were released by Sun Records. It was the late Sixties, after both Sam and Charlie had left Sun, that *"Behind Closed Doors"* and several other million-seller ballad hits were released by another record label.

As he conducted recordings from his seat behind the glass, Sam Phillips reminded me of a football coach. He was a sound engineer looking for whatever technique it took to unlock a person's unique quality. He explained that he was looking for a *feel*, not technical perfection. Sam said Elvis always began his recording session anxious and overly energized. Carl Perkins loosened his nerves with Early Times bourbon. There was no red light on the wall to hurry his singers. When he got what he was looking for Sam would burst out of control room laughing and clapping his hands, announcing that they had a hit record.

The success of the Sun sound was due to both the talents of his budding stars and Sam's creativity in the studio. His signature sound was the product of a one-room storeroom studio with the barest of basic recording equipment. The artificial echo effect he called "slap-back" came from manipulating sound through the heads of his reel-to-reel tape recorder, combining the same notes played in the studio with those delayed by a fraction of a second. He used wooden crates as baffles and wads of paper to deflect sound reverberation. A haunting sound emanated from the tiny studio. It was the beat that America came to love.

Always energetic when story-telling, Sam relived the magical date in 1953 when a timid 18-year-old Elvis Presley walked in the studio door to record a record for his mother as a surprise birthday gift. With greasy hair, eyes highlighted with eye shadow, in flamboyant clothes, Presley looked and sounded like no one else. He sang ballads with such a yearning quality in his voice that Sam was hearing the pure emotion of gospel music. He made a note of Presley's name and phone number.

Elvis often dropped by the studio over the next several months hoping to be noticed by the busy Phillips. Each time Sam's assistant asked if she could help him, the young man responded by asking if anyone knew of a band that could use a singer.

She asked what he sang. He replied, "most anything."

"Who do you sound like?" she asked.

"I don't sound like nobody," he stammered.

Ten months later, Sam was searching for a prospect to record a sad ballad. The singer who came to mind was the weird looking shy kid who had stopped by the previous summer to cut a record for his mother and had been hanging around since. When he got the call, Elvis Presley grabbed his little guitar and ran to the studio. Guralnick, Peter. "Last Train to Memphis: The Rise of Elvis Presley", Little Brown & Company, September 1, 1995, pp. 62-64.

Sam scheduled an audition on June 7, 1954. Presley sang ballad after ballad but Sam was looking for something else. After trying every song they could remember, Presley and his two-man band took a break while Phillips stepped away from the control booth. Elvis relaxed and began fooling around with an old blues tune he had heard a black singer sing when he was a young kid in Tupelo. His band picked up on Presley's bouncing rhythm and joined in with a heavy beat. "What's that?" Sam said as he walked back into the control room. None of them knew. "Well, back up and start over," Sam said. "Do it again." Presley sang, "That's all right Mama, that's all right for sure. That's all right Mama, just any-thing you do." Sam knew he had something special when he recorded this sound that was so unlike anything he had heard before.

The next session became an urgent search for a second side for the record. They again stumbled on the right song. The bass player began slapping out an old slow bluegrass song, *Blue Moon of Kentucky*. As the band played it faster and faster, Phillips shouted, "That's it. That's a pop song!" The record was released as Sun #209 on July 19, 1954.

Presley's record exploded across Memphis, played repeatedly by almost every disc jockey in town. In the excitement from the heavy radio play, Sam was anxious to see how Elvis performed before a live audience. They arranged to play two songs during the regular band's break at a popular hillbilly roadhouse. The crowd liked the music but was turned off by the performer's loud clothes and long greasy hair. Phillips, however, saw it as a positive. Not only did he sound different, he *looked* different.

Sam arranged for a promoter friend to squeeze Elvis in as a warm-up act for an all-star country package show at Overton Park, which accommodated over 4,000. When Sam arrived, Elvis was so nervous his face was pale and he could hardly talk.

"I – I – I – I just don't know what I am going to do," Elvis stammered. Sam patiently built him up, explaining "not to worry, you will do great." When it was Elvis' turn to sing, his knees were knocking together. Observers thought that his nervousness was causing his leg to shake. But as he launched into *"That's All Right,"* Elvis suddenly rocked up onto the balls of his feet, his body quivering all over. The crowd screamed for an encore. The band came back out to play another song. By then, Elvis realized what was happening and jiggled the leg on purpose as he saw how he could make the teenagers scream. It became an Elvis trademark the rest of his career. Guralnick, pp. 66-67.

Elvis Presley recorded for Sun Records 18 months. It was a fast ride. I was driving down a highway in my yellow Chevy convertible the night I first heard an astounding new country sound. I was listening to WCKY of Cincinnati, a 50,000-watt, clear channel AM station that played country music. I almost pulled off the road when I heard the old bluegrass song *Blue Moon of Kentucky* being sung in such an upbeat style so different from anything from the whining bluegrass high tenor on the original recording by Bill Monroe of Nashville's Grand Ole Opry. I listened carefully for the name of the singer: Elvis Presley. Strange name.

On August 2, driving his new pink Cadillac on the way to his second Sheffield performance on the highway passing through Cherokee, Elvis picked up two hitchhikers on their way to the concert. They were Bobby Knight, younger brother of *Tri-Cities Daily* News Editor Ben Knight, and Bobby Denton, who later become a popular regional singer in his own right, and subsequently a State Senator.

Elvis came back to Sheffield on November 15 for another two-hour *Louisiana Hayride* show, which happened to be the last day of the option Sam Phillips had given Colonel Parker and RCA to purchase the rights to Presley. The Florence Library archives microfilm of our article in *Times-Daily*, led off like a true entertainment promotion: "The King returns to the Shoals again...as the big man on the year's biggest All-Star Jamboree." We wrote that the third visit to the Shoals area followed a show when he took the limelight away from Webb Pearce, the nation's No. 1 country recording artist. Tickets at the door were $1 for adults, 75 cents for children.

On November 21, 1955, Elvis signed his first contract with RCA Records. RCA rereleased Presley's five Sun singles. The first recording, *Heartbreak Hotel*, took only five weeks to reach the top position in pop and country. When Elvis Presley moved to RCA in late 1955 the big recording company unsuccessfully tried every recording trick imaginable to create the slap-back effect that was Sun's trademark. Elvis was forced to use what he had learned from Sam to produce his own music.

Sam invited me to Memphis on April 4, 1957 for the weekend, highlighted by a show at Ellis Auditorium starring Johnny Cash, Carl Perkins, Jerry Lee Lewis, and Roy Orbison. He loaned me his light blue Cadillac with a dark blue top to pick up a date in Adamsville. The crowd exploded when Carl sang and bopped to his big hit *Blue Suede Shoes*. After the show, Sam explained that he had promised to give a new Cadillac "to the first Sun cat to sell a million records." He gave one to Carl for that record. After the Memphis concert, all the Sun performers met for a celebration at the Sun Records studio. It had been a great night for all of them, particularly Carl Perkins. When we visited, Perkins was warm and humorous and already well into the Early Times. Roy Orbison, the great balladeer, was low-key and genuine, one of the nicest entertainers I ever met.

I wound up spending a good part of the evening in conversation with a sad, sober Johnny Cash. He was preoccupied with the toll the tours were taking on his marriage. He sadly shared those concerns with me, a virtual stranger, perhaps because he knew I was a buddy of Sam Phillips. I vividly recall him saying, "I am trying hard but I don't see how I am going to be able to make it." Unlike many entertainers, Johnny Cash did not strike me as a woman-chaser, or heavy drinker, or anything other than a serious, young, eager singer. As her husband's fame grew, Johnny said his wife had often asked him if he was ever tempted by all the women his fame drew. He assured her that there would be no others, using the memorable words: "I walk the line for you." Those words became the inspiration for a song, *I Walk the Line,* which reached number one on the charts in 1956.

I enjoyed promoting horse shows, rodeos, and rock 'n' roll so much that I sometimes entertained the idea of pursuing a career in the entertainment promotions world. But it was obvious that long nights on the road, where the real money was made in that business, was a killer. Elvis Presley, Johnny Cash, and Carl Perkins ultimately sacrificed their health to the exhausting road schedules. Presley and Cash would become drug addicts and Perkins an alcoholic. Orbison, the nice man with the golden balladeer voice, would die early of a heart illness that he believed was triggered by a back-breaking road schedule. From the time we met through his remaining years at Sun, I remained on the Sun record distribution list---our basement filling with boxes of the little 45 rpm sample records with the bright yellow labels that were distributed to radio station for the hoped for play that would determine the destiny of a song.

Last Weekend with Phillips and Elvis' RedHead

My last Memphis visit with Sam was in the Summer of 1957. I hung out with him over that weekend, enjoying watching him work and listening to music afterwards in his den. The night before I caught the plane back to Muscle Shoals, Sam's assistant, arranged a blind date for me with a friend, a beautiful redhead, who was one of Elvis' host of girlfriends. During the evening, the red-head dialed Elvis on his private line, introduced me as the guy who had publicized Elvis' Sheffield shows, and handed the phone to me. It was a few minutes of friendly chit-chat, but I never experienced an extended conversation with Elvis like I had with Johnny Cash, Carl Perkins, and Roy Orbison.

That night we went out first to an outdoor drive-in restaurant, popular at the time among young people. In the next booth were the wives of the Tennessee Two, the guitar that led their music and the bass fiddle, which kept the band's tempo. We conversed with them like old friends, which Sam and his friend were. The next stop was the apartment of Sam's date. When time came to take them home, instead we decided to stay for the night at Sam's secretary's apartment. The sweet red-head and I slept together that night on a pallet, while Sam and the secretary slept in her bedroom.

Wrapped up with my own career pursuits, I failed to maintain contact with Sam after 1957. I learned later that he and his wife Becky divorced in 1960. Until his death in 2003, Sam lived with, but never married, his best friend and loyal assistant, Sally Wilburn. During that period, Sam and Becky remained on amicable terms and he maintained close relationships with his two sons. Sam had met Becky in the early 1940s while working as a disc-jockey at WLAY in Muscle Shoals, where older brother Jud was station manager.

In later life, Sam spent most of his time building radio stations in the Shoals area and collecting awards for his role in pioneering rock 'n' roll. The last time I saw him was in 1987 when he was inducted into the Alabama Music Hall of Fame at Huntsville's Von Braun Civic Center. With his thick wavy hair grown long, his face framed with a heavy reddish beard, he looked like an aging, still-handsome, hippie. Unfortunately, he had celebrated too much that night and his rambling, profanity-filled speech was embarrassing. As for me, I sat there and soberly reflected on my remarkable two-and-one-half-years association with a friend on his way to becoming a national treasure.

Johnny Cash, the 'Man in Black'

"If there had not been a Sam Phillips, I would still be working in a cotton field." ~ Johnny Cash

After Elvis Presley opened the door to Sun Records opportunities, several future stars found their way inside.

Johnny Cash, a former Arkansas sharecropper who sang with a deep, baritone voice, was one of those so determined to be auditioned that after several attempts at getting on the schedule, like Carl Perkins before him, intercepted Sam outside the studio. Sam said he was impressed with Cash's confidence and his unique voice.

John R. Cash had recently returned from military service and formed a band consisting of himself and two automobile mechanics. The band that made the first recording consisted of Cash, Marshall Grant, a guitarist recently converted to playing a stand-up bass, and Luther Perkins, chording one string at a time on a borrowed electric lead guitar. Luther's *tick-tack-tick-tack*, back and forth, alternating between two strings, one string at a time, created a *boom-chicka-boom-chicka* sound. Sam instructed Marshall to "slap hell out of that bass" so it could sound like a drum beat. He inserted a piece of paper on the neck of Cash's guitar, as some of Sun's black blues guitarists, that created a snare drum effect. That mix of new sounds, coupled with the echo effect of the studio, brought forth an original quality that had been lacking in country music for years.

Growing up in a sharecropper cabin near a railroad track, the sound of a locomotive remained with him as he wrote a poem centered on trains. That led Cash to write *Cry, Cry, Cry*, a song that began with:

"Everybody knows where you go when the sun goes down" and ending with

"I think you only live to see the lights of town

"I wasted my time when I would try, try, try

"When the lights have lost their glow, you're gonna cry, cry, cry."

When Sam Phillips prepared to release the record, he suggested the name "Johnny Cash" would have more appeal to young fans than J.R. or John. As Sam Phillips had said when he phoned to tell me Cash was being added the to the all-star cast for the August 2, 1955 Sheffield show, both sides of the record were attracting enormous attention in Memphis.

A Peek at an Exciting Pennant Race

Fascinated by a five-team pennant race in the American League, I proposed a bus trip to Detroit to visit relatives and write a few columns about that race. Our sports editor thought well of the low-cost trip and announced that I would be heading north for a weekend series between the St. Louis Cardinals and Cincinnati Reds in Cincinnati, then to Detroit's Briggs Stadium for series with the New York Yankees, Boston Red Sox, Baltimore Orioles, and Washington Senators. I rode a Greyhound bus, stayed at the same hotel with the Cardinals two nights in Cincinnati, then rode northward to Detroit. I was issued press box passes, which also permitted me to go on to the field before the game to mingle with the players.

My favorite childhood team, the Boston Red Sox came to Briggs Stadium to face the Detroit Tigers in late August. Always colorful, the Sox were sometimes bridesmaids but had not been World Champions since 1918. They called the Sox championship drought the "Curse of the Bambino" because it began with the Red Sox's sale of Babe Ruth to the rival Yankees. The Red Sox were still very much a part of the pennant race in August of 1955, only four games behind the Yankees, although some dubious Boston writers referred to them as "Ted Williams and the Seven Dwarfs."

The first game of the Detroit series dealt Boston a blow in its pennant quest. Billy Hoeft, a left-handed curve-baller who had become the fourth American League pitcher to strike out three batters on nine pitches, struggled most of the night. He yielded home-runs to Piersall and catcher Sammy White before achieving a personal thrill in the ninth. With the Tigers leading 5-4, the mighty slugger and future Hall of Famer, Ted Williams, came to bat.

Briggs Stadium was baseball's top hitters' favorite hitting park. When the tall and slender rookie was first called "the Splendid Splinter," Williams had become the first player to hit a home run over the roof at Briggs Stadium. That moonshot was a climbing liner that cleared the 120-foot barrier and bounded against a taxi company on the other side of Trumbull Avenue. It was another home run at Briggs Stadium that Ted Williams had called his happiest moment in baseball. Trailing 5-4 with two runners on and two out in the bottom of the ninth of the 1941 All Star game, "Teddy Ballgame" won the contest with a three-run homer. He said the contrast in lighting helped him pick up the pitch.

But on this dark and dreary Friday afternoon in 1955, mighty Ted struck out with the winning run on base. "That's the first time I ever struck him out," Hoeft said "I threw him nothing but curves in the ninth." Williams never took the bat off his shoulder. And the Tigers won 5-4. The large Boston press contingent of Williams skeptics drowned him in ridicule in their coverage.

Sunny Saturday was a new day. An even more dramatic game situation awaited. Before the game, on the first base side by the visitors' dugout stood the greatest pure hitter of all time, looking bigger than life, figuratively crowding out the sun. Teddy Ballgame. The Kid. The Splendid Splinter, The Thumper. With broad shoulders developed from constant practice swings, the former 165-pound skinny "Splinter" was now a powerful 210 pounder. He looked much like *Time* Magazine had described him that year:

> *"Ted Williams of the Boston Red Sox looked as fit as an Indian buck. After a winter out of doors, including a month of lazy fishing at the edge of the Florida Everglades, he was tanned to a light mahogany. His brownish green eyes were clear and sharp, his face lean, the big hands that wrapped around the handle of his 34-oz. Louisville Slugger, were calloused and hard...He expected, he conceded, to have a pretty good year."*

I walked cautiously up to Ted Williams and introduced myself. "Muscle Shoals, Alabama, huh?" Williams responded. "Great smallmouth fishing. A place I have always wanted to fish." This from the world's best-known sport fisherman, who once said he didn't brag much about his hitting but his pride in his fishing ability was different.

His friendly greeting was a serious contrast to his obvious mood, which lingered from the miserable previous day. His anger over striking out with the bat on his shoulder with the winning run on base was exasperated by vicious reporting by the Boston writers that Ted had choked in the clutch. He mumbled, "All curveballs the SOB threw me. Seven pitches. All curveballs!"

He stared at the writers sitting on the bench like a row of fat pigeons. Williams asked the small-town writer a rhetorical question: "Why are those guys in the dugout?" Just the week before I had observed for two days in a row a smiling Stan Musial in the midst of the beat writers, all buddy-buddy, sitting before the game on the dugout bench. Ted Williams rarely fraternized with Boston baseball writers for good reason. They regularly cut his throat in a town with too many newspapers.

"I don't want to talk with any of them," he roared. In words designed to be heard by the writers in the dugout, he said. "Come on out here to right field. I'll tell you about how I have always wanted to be a pitcher." I thought: RIGHT! WORLD'S GREATEST HITTER ALWAYS WANTED TO BE A PITCHER! GREAT STUFF.

Ted Williams went into great detail about the strategies he would use as a pitcher if only he had the chance: "Throw it inside, outside, up, and down. And be smart. I study all the pitchers because I'm always looking for an edge. Most pitchers are dumb. They don't study hitters like I study pitchers. But not guys like Whitey Ford or Eddie Lopat (Yankee Stars), or Bob Feller and Bob Lemon (Indians). They are all different the way they pitch, but they are smart as hell."

Why would Ted single me out for an exclusive interview? Obviously to poke a finger to the eyes of the beat writers. Also, likely because I was an 18-year-old fledgling sports writer and he was known for his fondness for kids. In most ways, he was still a big kid himself. It has been said that most baseball players are kids in big men's bodies. Ted would personify that description all of his life.

Williams strolled to the plate, hitless for the day. Tiger manager Bucky Harris brought in southpaw Al Aber to pitch to match power-on-power with the left-handed Williams. The Red Sox needed three runs to tie. Williams represented the go-ahead run. As the Thumper stepped in to hit, old-timers recalled the historic ninth-inning game-winning home run in the All Star game in this park 14 years earlier. Ted was focused on the lefty pitcher, determined not to take another curve ball over the plate for the final out. Nor was he thinking of hitting a single to continue the rally. It was home run or nothing.

The first pitch was wide for a ball.

Williams swung at the next pitch and fouled it weakly to first. One ball, one strike.

Third pitch low and outside. Two balls, one strike.

Ted Williams measured the next pitch. He ducked slightly, as always, to give lift to the ball. Aber's curve ball swept across the plate.

Ted's quick wrists snapped.

Wham! Then "A-a-a-ahh" from the stands. The white ball streaked toward the second deck of the right field stands.

I leaned forward in the press box with my cheap camera, squeezing the slow shutter as he swung. It was an amazing photo of the runners leaning to take their first steps while a white blur on the first base side of the pitcher steaked toward the upper deck.

Ted Williams was expressionless, like it was all in a day's work, when he circled the bases. He never lifted his cap nor smiled. But as he crossed the plate at full trot, the world's greatest hitter moved his hand slowly alongside his nose. His critics in the press box got the message.

This was the kind of heroics so rare that sports writers of the era referred to such rare feats as a "Merriwell Finish." The term came from the early Twentieth Century's fictional idol, Frank Merriwell. A "Merriwell Finish" was a dramatic and successful ending to a baseball game. In fact, the six words that Hal Middlesworth of the *Detroit Free Press* chose to lead his game story the next day were so perfect that they still ring clearly over six decades later: "Ted Williams was never more magnificent," Middlesworth wrote. "The Big Fellow, who thrives on pressure, delivered again Saturday---a dramatic grand-slam home run with two out in the ninth to give Boston a thrilling 4-3 decision over the disconsolate Tigers...No prima donna ever wrung more out of a scene than the Magnificent Masher..."

In wiping out the three-run deficit and tying the series, it was Williams' third grand slammer of the season and 14th of his career. The dramatic drive revitalized the fading pennant hopes of the Red Sox and all but slammed the door on the Tigers' chances. "I was just hoping we would get two or three runners on the sacks by the time it was Ted's turn to bat," said a jubilant Red Sox Manager Mike Higgins in the dressing room. "I didn't think it was possible that he could play four games here without lifting at least one into those stands. Ted made sure he got under that pitch. He didn't want to hit any grounders."

It was the second ninth inning shock for Tiger fans in four days, beginning with the Mantle and Berra back-to-back homer dramatics on Wednesday. I wrote in with my next *"Sports Chatter"* column of the greatness of Ted Williams, who had proven again in such a spectacular manner that there had never been a better hitter of baseballs.

Back to Summer Fun

The Greyhound bus from Detroit to Sheffield returned an 18-year-old giddy from such a thrilling experience. It was time to prepare for college at Florence State Teachers College with football practice beginning in less than a month. Elvis Presley would return in November for his third time that year and I would help promote the show. I finished the Summer by working part-time writing advertising spots for WLAY, the station in Muscle Shoals where Sun Records founder Sam Phillips got his start. The hardest job was making super market bargains sound exciting. The most fun was writing a 60 second commercial aimed at creating excitement about that week's movie at the Colbert Theater. On Friday nights, I worked in an analyst role supporting a team broadcasting Sheffield Bulldog football games. The team had two decent broadcasters whose names would become well known: Tom York, who would later become a Birmingham television personality and the father of the Alabama Sports Hall of Fame, and Sam Phillips' older brother, Jud Phillips, broadcasting the Sheffield Bulldogs. My job was to report the statistics at half time and provide an occasional comment during the game while also covering the games for the *Times-Daily*.

My choice of a college was easy. My varied work activities were based in the Muscle Shoals area. I commuted from our home in Sheffield's Cliff Haven to Florence State Teachers College. During freshmen orientation we were presented with purple and gold "beanie" caps, which looked so silly we avoided wearing them after the first day. I moved up from hanging out in front of the Sheffield Pharmacy watching the girls go by to hanging out in the news room of the *Times-Daily*, attending class, and working in a small office in a white house on the FSTC campus which was the home of the Public Information Department. I also found time for networking in the Little Drugs and dancing to rock 'n' roll in the Lions' Den.

Freshmen students learned from English instructor Nick Winn about novelist T. S. Stribling, a Florence native, who wrote about Southern heartaches during the Civil War restoration. In those classes I became aware of novelist William Bradford Huie of Hartselle, Alabama. One of our book report assignments was Huie's *The Revolt of Mamie Stover* (1951), about a World War II prostitute. History courses were most interesting. One professor singled me out as a reminder of his happy days writing sports, rambling on and on, which helped my grade in the class. My job as Assistant Sports Information Director that freshman year focused on covering practices for the *Times-Daily* and providing half-time statistics for game broadcasts.

FSTC Grad Harlon Hill, NFL's MVP

"Little Alabama Teachers College," was the constant refrain of National Football League television sportscasters as they raved over the feats of the Lions' most famous sports alumnus, wide receiver Harlon Hill. Harlon came from relative obscurity because FSTC ran the single-wing and rarely threw the ball. Their only pass play was called: 'Throw it deep to Harlon." Hill caught only 54 passes in four years with the Lions but they went for 1,020 yards and a school record 19 touchdowns. He was drafted by the Chicago Bears in 1954. His first year, Harlon Hill was named National Football League Rookie of the Year. The following year he was selected as the NFL Most Valuable Player.

After our season ended that year the legendary George (Poppa Bear) Halas, arranged a "Harlon Hill Day" and invited our team to the Bears game. It was December 11, 1955 against the Philadelphia Eagles. George Halas, known as the "Father of the NFL," hosted Coaches Self and Weeks and me in his office preceding the game. My small-town press credentials failed to get me inside the heated press box, so I sat shivering in an open press box as a bitter cold wind roared in from Lake Michigan. In retrospect, that was coldest I have ever been. I did talk my way into the heated press box at halftime.

Lions Basketball Team's Future Coaches

I traveled with the basketball team my freshman year. We could not win on the road. Part of the reason was that we traveled packed into vans, living off greasy hamburgers, and arrived at the visiting gymnasiums angry and demoralized. But the primary reason it was almost impossible to win on the road was the one-sided small college home-town officiating. We won most of our games at home. Our coach, Ed Billingham, was a sound fundamentalist but fell short as a motivator and had a lifetime losing record. Nevertheless, after graduation three players on that team would make their names in college coaching. Winfrey (Wimp) Sanderson of Florence and John Bostick of Winfield were assistant coaches at Alabama for several years. Sanderson moved up to head coach and led the Crimson Tide to 10 NCAA Tournaments and six trips to the Sweet 16---the only coach in Crimson Tide history to win 200 or more games in his first 10 years. He was the Southeastern Conference Coach of the Year in 1987, 1989 and 1990, and was the National Coach of the Year in 1987.

Wimp and I stayed in touch after graduation and during his coaching career played in the same group in the Huntsville Hospital Foundation golf tournament. He was a fierce competitor, even in scramble golf. Once, on a critical long approach putt, he chased the ball toward the hole on his hands and knees, begging it to drop in. But his ball hung on the lip. Wimp's antics loosened up the team.

He was known as the man in the "Plaid Coat" whose wry sense of humor increased with age. Sanderson resigned as Alabama's basketball coach 1992 after his longtime secretary filed a sexual discrimination lawsuit. The center on that team, Bill Jones of Lexington, became the Lions' head coach in 1974 after FSTC had become the University of North Alabama. Jones took UNA to six NCAA national tournaments, with five regional crowns and four Final Four appearances. Another player on that team, Don Shotts, had an unusually soft jump shot that seemed to either swish the net or sit quietly on the rim before falling in or dropping out. A few years later he was practicing dentistry when I moved to Huntsville. I had my choice between two old friends. Remembering those soft hands and hoping they would carry over to his dental techniques, I chose Don Shotts as my dentist.

A Golden Summer at Ole Miss

Academically, I yearned for journalism courses but the only one available at FSTC was taught by my boss. He held a master's degree from the prestigious Missouri School of Journalism, but came up short in the real newspaper world. He had not even learned that captions under photos were supposed to be brief. My friend *Times-Daily* News Editor Ben Knight had attended the University of Mississippi and was convinced Ole Miss had one of the best journalism schools in the country. That Summer of 1956 I took an interim position as Director of Public Relations for the University of Mississippi Extension at Oxford, Mississippi. Ole Miss' reputation was football and Faulkner, kudzu and coeds, the Lyceum Building, the Grove, and two future Miss Americas.

My parents followed me to Oxford in my yellow Chevrolet convertible on the Sunday that I moved into the dormitory. We stopped to eat a restaurant that was owned by a Greek. I chose the spaghetti, served by a stunningly-beautiful young blond waitress. I ate there several times that Summer, attracted by the blond beauty. I had moved on up from wanting a farmer's daughter to losing my virginity.

When I settled into the dorm, I was introduced to a traumatic phase of growing up. That was when I faced the transition from living at home for 19 years to living in a dormitory room. I had commuted daily to Florence State my freshman year, hanging out at night dancing in the Lion's Den or watching sports events on television in the men's dormitory. None of that prepared me for the abrupt shift from familiar family surroundings to being three hours from my hometown. The first full week I was at Ole Miss my roommate went home for the weekend. The more I stared at the walls, the more homesick I became. I began to appreciate why many students dropped out of school almost as soon as they enrolled in college.

As Acting News Director of the University Extension, I worked full time except for journalism and political science classes. I wrote news releases promoting conferences ranging from safety education to a majorette camp for high school students. The Extension was located in a modern building near the entrance to the campus where five years later riots would erupt as an angry mob of segregationists attempted to block the enrollment of a black Air Force veteran. What a perfect job for a 19-year-old. The highlight of the summer was the week that I was surrounded by hundreds of high school majorettes with absolutely no male competition. I dated two of them who lived in West Tennessee, one of whom was from Adamsville.

But the one I really wanted was the waitress from Mistilis Restaurant. I was running around with the son of a professor when one night a boy who was still in high school tagged along. I mentioned the blond and asked him if he knew her. He followed up introducing us. I was shocked nonetheless when that blonde and I began dating regularly that Summer. We were entertaining by ourselves. In those days they built Chevrolets that had plenty of room in the floorboard and my Chevy convertible was no exception. We didn't have to go in the back seat in those days.

The Ole Miss Rebels played decent football but its biggest winners in that era were Mary Ann Mobley and Lynda Lee Mead, two sorority sisters who became back-to-back winners of the 1959 and 1960 Miss America competition. On trips back home I turned the radio to 560 AM, WHBQ in Memphis, where Dewey (Daddy-O) Phillips mixed black blues singers with Sun Records artists singing rhythm and blues. A close friend of Sam Phillips, he was the first disc jockey to play "Blue Moon of Kentucky," the debut record of Elvis Presley, in July 1954.

Two important events changed my plans to stay at Ole Miss until graduation. At the end of the Summer the two best journalism instructors in the South left to accept large salary increases to revitalize the journalism program at San Jose State, California. The second event was a phone call from Florence State. My former boss, the professor with an advanced degree in journalism who wrote windy press releases and photo captions that required severe editing, was notified he would not be rehired for a second year. They invited me to return to the college and become the first student Director of Public Information. So, as the summer ended, I moved back home.

Serving as Sports Information Director and my assistant for the next two years was Billy Joe Camp, a sophomore from Hanceville. After a hitch in the Army following graduation, Billy Joe would later become Press Secretary for Governor George Wallace and subsequently be elected President of the Alabama Public Service Commission. I blamed Billy Joe Camp for getting me in trouble with my strict dad one Saturday night. We were drinking beer in Camp's room in the men's dormitory at 1 a.m. when Billy Joe stammered: "That man coming down the hall sure looks like yo' daddy." I was forced to follow my angry tee-totaler father back home to Sheffield. Billy Joe and I often recalled that incident during our days in Montgomery. The last time we relived the episode of my curfew problem night was 2010 when we celebrated dinner with our wives when the University of North Alabama Alumni Association presented plaques to us for public service to the state. Billy Joe always laughed harder at that story than I did. He and I remain friends to this day.

Heading Drive to Change FSTC Name

As the college's Director of Public Information, when Harlon Hill's pro football feats were bringing attention to our college it rankled me to hear network announcers constantly referring to Florence State Teachers College as "little Alabama Teachers College." What an image. How does one promote a football team at a *teachers'* college? FSTC's name, in fact, was a misnomer. The college had long since moved away from being primarily a teachers' college. Only 20 per cent of our students majored in education in the late Fifties.

But our college president was a former teacher himself who insisted on being called "Doctor" in spite of his degree being only honorary. He liked the existing name. Nevertheless, I stepped forward to spearhead a "movement" to change the name of the institution to delete "Teachers" from its name. *Times-Daily* News Editor Ben Knight became part of the effort, arranging contacts for me with his friends in the Legislature. The *Times-Daily* trumpeted the initiative with a front-page headline story and the *Birmingham News* ran an article and photo on its front page. That led to President E.B. Norton calling me into his office. The two front pages were in the center of his desk. "You won't get anywhere with this," he said bluntly. "The veterans tried that after World War II and if they couldn't get it done, you certainly cannot." "Well, I want to try anyway," was my response. "I have letters from several legislators committing to help, Governor Folsom is on the record for it, and I want to give it a shot."

In some institutions, they would fire an employee or expel a student for such audacity. I suspected that the only reason he did not fire me was the fear of retaliation from legislative supporters of the name change. The first legislator I visited, Representative Bert Haltom of Florence, turned me down when I responded truthfully to his question of whether President Norton supported the idea. I went back across the river to my home county of Colbert and met with our Representative and family lawyer, Jack Huddleston. He saw it immediately as making sense and agreed to sponsor of the bill.

Ben Knight and I drove to Montgomery to lobby for Huddleston's bill. The first evening, a couple of legislators suggested we go with them to the governor's mansion where the Governor was hosting a group of legislators. At past midnight, we walked into a colossal party attended by nearly half the Legislature. The Governor, well into the booze, was playing tennis. We decided to wait and go to his office to talk about the bill. When we saw him in his office, I reminded him of his campaign speech in Florence urging the college to think big and change its name. Folsom agreed for us to tell the legislators he supported the name-change.

Florence was one of four teachers' colleges in Alabama. When Huddleston's name-change bill was brought to the floor, representatives from the four other teachers' colleges in the state offered amendments also changing the names of their institutions to omit the reference to "Teachers." The bill passed both Houses without difficulty. College historians wrote later than this step symbolized the steady expansion of Florence State's academic offerings and mission. Ten years after that change, the Legislature created a Board of Trustees, which changed the name further, to Florence State University. E. B. Norton, thus held the distinction of being the only President to preside over three institutional name changes: Florence State Teachers College, followed by Florence State College in 1957, and, a decade later, Florence State University. In 1974, the newly-named University of North Alabama had grown from 2,000 when I was a student to 5,000.

That was my first taste of politics, far more exciting than being a senator at Boys State in high school. Politics became a love equal to journalism. At that point, Jimmy Hunt of Tuscumbia urged me to run for President of the Junior Class. We won without a runoff. I was having a great time in college, working more than studying, still able to find the time to meet people and play hearts in the Little Grill.

Two All-Americans and a Famous Guitarist

The players in the Sheffield Youth League that Summer included a couple of future All-American football players. Dennis Homan, was a quick little third baseman who became one of the Alabama Crimson Tide's great pass receivers, and George Patton, a power hitting outfielder, became a 210-pound Georgia Bulldogs star tackle. Another player in that league was Jimmy Johnson, a pudgy youngster who in a few years became one of America's greatest guitarists. During the next three decades as a producer, engineer, and backup artist he was a primary creator of the *Muscle Shoals Sound,* which earned the area recognition as the "Hit Recording Capital of the World."

Jimmy Johnson was head of a nationally-known rhythm section known as the "Swampers," a name affectionately bestowed on backup instrumentalists. From our state's adopted anthem "Sweet Home Alabama," the Lynyrd Skynyrd band recognized the Muscle Shoals Rhythm Section with this verse:

"Muscle Shoals has got the Swampers
And they've been known to pick a song or two
Lord, they get me off so much
They pick me up when I'm feelin' blue."

During the peak of his entertainment career, Jimmy Johnson's seats were near Brown Engineering's on the top row beneath the Legion Field press box. We frequently visited during half-time at Alabama Crimson Tide football games. Jimmy engineered The Rolling Stones' album, *Sticky Fingers* and provided supporting guitar for such popular artists as Wilson Pickett, Aretha Franklin,

Bobby Segar, Elton John, Willie Nelson, Rod Stewart, Simon and Garfunkel, Bob Dylan, Lynyrd Skynyrd, and Jimmy Buffet.

Artists from across America were attracted to the laid-back, funky sounds at Muscle Shoals, an unlikely place for a celebrity crowd. The nicest hotel on that side of the Tennessee River was a Holiday Inn and some stars slept in trailer courts.

Quin Ivy, a WLAY disk jockey and owner of Fame Recording Studio, produced songs by Percy Sledge of Leighton that were backed by Jimmy Johnson's band. Sledge's song reached No. 1 in the U.S. and was an international hit.

In its heyday in the mid-Seventies, the area was home to eight studios. Detroit rocker Bob Seger's *Old Time Rock 'n' Roll,"* my favorite dance song of all time was recorded there with Jimmy Johnson on guitar. But as much as I appreciated Muscle Shoals Sound music, I never heard Jimmy Johnson perform in a live show. I did hear Percy Sledge of Leighton sing his international hit song, *"When a Man Loves a Woman"*

A Frightening Experience on a Lovers' Lane

The golden age of lovers' lanes was in the late Fifties and early Sixties. From desolate river views or dirt roads in the middle of cotton fields and shady lanes, we parked to cuddle in our large cars. We called it "smooching." The gear shift was on the dash, making it easy to slide across the wide seat to be close to our dates. Drive-in theaters flourished in those days. Disc jockeys dedicated songs to us. Couples on double dates listened and slapped car seats to the beat of "Shake, Rattle and Roll" or "Brown-Eyed Handsome Man."

Police officers occasionally patrolled lovers' lanes to help assure our safety. Remembering that they had also been young, they tended to give notice by flashing their lights before shining search lights into the cars. Movies featured lovers' lanes as places where escaped convicts and rapists lurked but we never thought it could happen in our peaceful little four cities. Yet, in the autumn of my second year of college, the unexpected happened. I was parked in a wooded area outside Florence, late at night on a date with a classmate from Tuscumbia. All was quiet and the moon was shining as we lowered the windows to share the soft breeze. As the radio played rock 'n' roll, I scooted over next to my date. At that moment I sensed a movement outside. I whirled around to see the face of a middle-age white man peering through our driver's side windshield. I jumped and said, "Hey! What are you doing?" He said nothing. He was so close to the car I could not see if he had a weapon in his hands. I said, "Man, you scared hell out of us," in the calmest voice I could muster. He still said nothing. Just as suddenly as his face had appeared from the darkness, he was gone without a sound.

Author of 'Joe Must Go' Movement My Boss

In the fall of 1957, Leroy Gore, publisher of a new five-day-a-week newspaper in Sheffield named *The Muscle Shoals Morning Sun,* called to offer me a part-time job as Sports Editor. Merchants in Sheffield, which was less than a third the size of Florence, had formed a home town newspaper. The *Flor-Ala*, FSC's student newspaper, announced that I was concluding my tenure as Director of the Florence State News Bureau to become Sports Editor of the new *Muscle Shoals Morning Sun*. "When the *Morning Sun* goes to the public with its first issue Tuesday, October 15, Grainger will be the youngest sports editor of a daily newspaper in the state," the newspaper reported.

Muscle Shoals Morning Sun Publisher Leroy Gore was a former rural Wisconsin newspaper editor who initiated the recall movement of one of the most widely-feared political figures of his day— Senator Joseph R. McCarthy. The Wisconsin Senator was the face of the dark side of the Fifties, the term "McCarthyism" coined to characterize his demagogic and unsubstantiated accusations of Communists and Soviet spies inside the federal government. In the spring of 1954, Leroy Gore, the courageous editor of the *Sauk-Prairie Star*, launched a "Joe Must Go" recall campaign that helped fuel the fires that resulted in the U.S. Senate voting to censure McCarthy in 1954. Gore told a story of how McCarthy, a heavy drinker, appealed to Wisconsin dairy farmers by drinking milk on every campaign platform. "But," Gore smiled, "they didn't realize he had mixed the milk with plenty of scotch." Gore, soft-spoken and raspy voiced with a considerable mane of white hair, was a likeable boss. He was a liberal to the core. In the 1958 governor's race he endorsed the most liberal candidate of the 14, the candidate of the AFL-CIO unions.

Traveling Statewide in 1958 Governor's Race

In the Spring of 1958, I moved into the political arena. Ben Knight, Ed Mauldin, and other Colbert County leaders were supporting Agriculture Commissioner A. W. Todd of nearby Russellville for Governor. The Colbert County group offered to pay my salary if I would travel with Todd and handle his communications. It was not a hard sell because of my growing love for politics. I sat in the back seat of Todd's black Lincoln typing on my brown portable Royal typewriter with the dark green keys, bouncing along at break-neck speeds as we visited six to eight towns daily. Todd had an innate understanding of what was newsworthy. He would tell me what he planned to say of local interest at the next "stump speech." I would have the article written and ready for the local paper by the time we drove into town. Weekly newspapers published our write-ups because they contained matters of local interest, specifically what Todd promised to do for that community if elected. Other candidates depended on advertising and public relations agencies in Birmingham to circulate news releases each day, which were invariably dry, repetitious, and statewide in scope.

Because of the large and colorful field and unique campaign styles used by the candidates, the 1958 Alabama governor's race attracted national attention. *Life* magazine wrote, "Anything goes in Alabama as 14 candidates put on an election revelry with pitchforks, hillbilly bands, kinfolk and mules...Almost every candidate has a guitar, a group of hillbilly singers or a gag. Before a candidate and his entertainers come to town, a loud-speaker car usually precedes them, giving equal billing to the politician and his performers."

Candidates depended heavily on courthouse square "stump speeches" from flatbed trucks and rallies at county seat coliseums at night. Todd crowds were warmed up by up-beat gospel music sung by a young trio known as the *Sons of Song*. The beat sounded much like rock 'n' roll mixed with gospel lyrics as the exciting sound echoed from storefronts surrounding courthouse squares

The *Sons of Song* were headed by a handsome tenor, Calvin Newton. They were joined in major evening rallies by Wally Fowler and the *Chuck Wagon Gang*. Fowler, who was both a singer and music promoter, was the king of all-night gospel singing that was sweeping the South and much of the nation. The *Chuck Wagon Gang* was among the nation's top singing groups for several decades. A highly religious family group, the *Chuck Wagon Gang* drove to night rallies in a big Cadillac and departed promptly after the performance. Fowler and the youthful, teen idols, the *Sons of Song*, hung around signing autographs afterwards. As an eager young bachelor, I discovered that women often lingered after autographs had been signed, waiting to be asked out. Near the end of the campaign, Calvin Newton noticed me observing the scene with interest and invited me into their "circle." Cheatam, Russ. "Bad Boy of Gospel Music, The Calvin Newton Story." The University Press of Mississippi, 2003.

The only time since l958 that I saw Calvin was in the 1990s while having lunch at the Fogcutter Restaurant, my regular luncheon restaurant. He was dining with the entertainment editor of the *Huntsville News*, who called me over to his table. I could see the signs of fast-living on Calvin's face, but he otherwise was the same likeable guy I had traveled with 40 years earlier. In 2014 from his home in Chattanooga, Calvin, then 85, updated me with this email: "My wife and I celebrated our 50th anniversary last September, and both our children live here on Lookout Mountain very close to us. The latter part of my life is certainly much more fulfilling than the first part—thank the good Lord!"

Segregation: The Key to Election in 1958

In normal times A. W. Todd's message of support for agriculture and industrial development could have made him a serious contender. But 1958 was the first campaign when voters responded overwhelmingly to the person voicing the loudest noise desegregation. The segregation theme would dominate the next three elections. Todd was considered to be a moderate on segregation who appealed to "our Christian farm families" to enable him to move Alabama forward economically.

George Wallace underestimated the potency of race as an issue. Days after his loss, Wallace was said to have told friends like Seymour Trammel of Clayton: "I was out-nigguhed by John Patterson, and I will tell you here and now, I will never be out-nigguhed again."

During the campaign, I came to know and respect Leroy Simms, bureau chief for the *Associated Press* (AP) bureau in Birmingham. He would become my boss a year later when he became news editor for the *Birmingham News*. Later, he was my friend for two decades as publisher of the *Huntsville Times*. He was honorable and objective, a moderate Black Belt native, slow talking, and wise, who did not find it necessary to speak loudly. This was a time that the *Associated Press* was revered by journalists for its objective, timely reporting. Its yellow style book was the bible of journalism (avoid commas wherever possible and use lower case to make it easier for linotype operators to quickly type the words). AP was the organization that was always out front on fast-breaking news. Examples: the news bulletins coming across the teletype machines as AP reported the assassination of President John F. Kennedy in 1963. The most memorable symbol was Rex Thomas, the Montgomery AP bureau chief, who was a magician at converting news as it happened into short understandable sentences, dictating his words over the phone while flipping through a five-inch wide, loose-leaf notebook. AP writers of that era were conscientiously objective, permitting both sides of an issue to make their cases. (That made it all the more shocking decades later when AP had somehow morphed into an ultra-liberal opinionated shadow of a news organization.) My career was boosted during the Todd Campaign when Leroy Simms and his deputy, Jim Spotswood, told the *Birmingham News* editors that our campaign had 40% of the AP leads in coverage of the 14 candidates because we gave them something fresh every day.

After A Brief Beginning in Mississippi, a Call from the *News*

After the 1958 gubernatorial campaign, the *Birmingham News* put me on its list for the next vacancy in the news department. Following a call by Ben Knight to an old Mississippi acquaintance who was news editor of a new daily in Jackson, Mississippi, I was hired by the *State-Times* to write general news and feature articles.

My first interview was with former Governor James H. (Jimmie) Davis, a gospel/country singer, who popularized an all-time favorite song, "You Are My Sunshine." Frequently sporting a white western hat, he also acted in B-rated westerns and taught history and yodeling at a women's college before singing his way into the Governor's mansion in 1944. Our interview was in mid-morning when he obviously was still suffering from too much to drink the night before. The "Singing Governor" squinted through red eyes, responding poorly to questions about his future plans. I wrote that he obviously was moving around in preparation for another run for Governor of Louisiana. A year later, he gained the support of segregationist leaders and won in a runoff. His governorship was undistinguished but a few years later "You Are My Sunshine" was designated as the state song of Louisiana.

Jackson was known for its beautiful women, who out-numbered males by three or four to one because of the number of clerical jobs provided by state government and white-collar employers. This was the state which would have back-to-back winners of the Miss America contest. In 1959 the winner was Mary Ann Mobley of Brandon, Mississippi, and in 1960 it was Lynda Lee Mead of Nachez, Mississippi, both students at Ole Miss. Northern writers claimed Mississippi grew beauty queens like cotton. *The State-Times* sponsored beauty contests around the state and assigned me to report on and help coordinate those events.

I met a young lady on my first night in town. It was her first night too. She was from a town much smaller. I went back a second night and we went out. She was so shy that she fought me when I got too close. She would be saying "no" with such determination that I decided it best to wait for a third date. On the third night, she was saying "no" and crying with the same ferocity when I started to back away again. She reached down to show me her intentions were to continue. The protests were just noise.

Just three weeks later, the party ended. The call I had been awaiting came from the *Birmingham News*. A reporting vacancy had developed and I accepted.

Moving Up in Birmingham as the Civil Rights Era Loomed

Two weeks later I was in Birmingham. The job at the *News* was at the bottom of the reporting ladder. I was the night police reporter, working from 3 p.m. to 11 p.m., based in a press room at Birmingham City Hall. Since the local edition of the *News* did not come off the press until 10 a.m. the next day, the morning newspaper, the *Post-Herald*, had the break on wrecks, fires, and homicides that occurred during my scheduled shift. The daytime *News* police reporter had graduated from the night shift. Bud Gordon was infatuated with writing for police journals, a wannabee cop himself.

Without any guidance or orientation, I realized I was not impressing my bosses in my first few months on the job. Listening to much of the same stuff on the police radio and reading most of the same police reports was lonely, boring, and minimally productive. I began lingering at City Hall after hours, looking for news events that occurred after the *Post-Herald* had published its morning edition and its police reporter had gone home. I worked those extra hours without pay in order to be able to file stories in the afternoon that our readers had not already seen in the morning paper. The atmosphere in the early morning hours was less formal and police officers more open.

One night an officer told me about a man on Birmingham's Southside who had been arrested for shoplifting at a convenience store---for stealing milk for his infant son. I ran down the accused's address and knocked on his door. He invited me in and slowly related his story. He posed for a picture with the beautiful blue-eyed baby and his wife. The *News* ran the sad story on page one the next day. It created a groundswell of interest as readers sent donations to the newspaper for me to deliver to the family to buy milk and groceries. Sequels of events in that family's new life ran on the front page for three days. It was my first big break as a newspaper reporter.

As I came to be accepted, several policemen delighted in proving they had noses for news by passing along news tips. I grew especially close to the third shift sergeant, George Wall. He invited me to ride with him and his partner in the back seat of the police cruiser during the early morning hours. Tall, handsome, and highly intelligent, George Wall personified the image of a professional, respectable police officer. No one then could have portended the Birmingham racial disturbances just five years later when Sergeant Wall had risen to a higher level, that he was a marked contrast to his boss, the face of Southern demagogues, Eugene (Bull) Connor. He who had driven me around in a Birmingham police car was by then Police Chief.

I was not sufficiently ingrained in the culture of Birmingham in the Fifties to see black people as anything less than human beings. Without any on-the-job training, I had to learn for myself that the *Birmingham News* did not consider events involving black people to be particularly newsworthy. Police reports identified victims by sex and race. When I saw a homicide on the police blotter, I assumed it was worth at least a few paragraphs without regard to race. But I got the message when the copy desk reduced my articles regarding black homicides to a sentence or two, identifying the victim as a "black male" or "black female." Black on black crimes received scant attention in major Southern newspapers at the time. A single page entitled *"What Negroes Are Doing"* ran regularly in the Sunday paper; that was the extent of the *News* coverage of the minority community. But a black murder or rape of a white woman was almost always Page One news, and a ticket to death row in many cases.

I went to Homewood city hall when I learned that police had captured a young black male suspected of breaking into the home of a white woman and raping her. He was found hiding in Shades Valley High School in the early morning hours after a day-long manhunt. Shortly after they brought him to the Homewood jail, they allowed me to interview Ernest C. Walker, a 23-year-old black man. He tried to disguise his fears, but his expressions showed that he sensed the eventual outcome. Southern black men did not rape white women and expect to live long lives in those days. Walker's attorneys contended that he was mentally retarded but an all-white jury sentenced him to death. At a clemency hearing, Walker confessed and apologized but Governor John Patterson declined to intervene. He was executed at 12:14 a.m. December 4, 1959 in Kilby Prison's "Yellow Mama" electric chair. *Birmingham News*, Associated Press, Dec. 4, 1959, P. 1.

Suspicious Death of Bessemer Tot Still Bothers Me

The news story that frustrated me most that first year was my inability to get to what my instinct told me was the real truth of the death of a three-year-old Bessemer child that was burned to death in the family's backyard. The Bessemer authorities stonewalled the case, giving out no details beyond their finding that the death had been accidental. I wrote an article that ran on Page 2 of the *News* reporting what little the police disclosed.

The next day I went to the tot's house. The family showed me a burned spot in grass in the back yard about the size of an automobile steering wheel. Several curious neighbors crowded around us. After several attempts, I could not get any of the adults or the tot's playmates to explain convincingly what had happened. The grass was burned solid black. I suspected one of the older children had soaked the tot in gasoline and set it on fire. But no one who knew the real story would talk about the real facts. I shared my suspicions with a close friend Bill Berry, a Birmingham fire department captain and inspector who specialized in arsons. Bessemer is a separate city, 17 miles from Birmingham, so Bill had no jurisdiction. As a favor to me, he went along on his off-time on an unofficial basis and maintained a low profile when I went to the house a second time. We could get nothing further from the family. Neither of us could substitute for law enforcement officers whom we believed were not doing their jobs.

Black Baby Born Outside While Nurses Looked On

I walked blindly into a situation that led to a shocking realization about racial attitudes in the "Pittsburg of the South." A daily stop on my "police beat" was the city's largest emergency room at University Hospital. One Saturday afternoon I learned that a black baby had been born late the previous night in the gutter just outside the Emergency Room entrance while medical personnel stood by and watched.

When I asked why they had not helped, they said it was against hospital rules to treat indigents who did not produce their government identification cards. The mother could not locate her card. As the pains of childbirth attacked, the young mother made it as far as the desk at ER before she was turned away. She sat down on a wet curb outside the entrance and delivered the child.

I turned in my "copy" about the incident at 6 p.m. on Saturday night. Our process called for us to type our stories on manual typewriters on pages with two carbon copies attached. One copy was sent by a pneumatic tube to the *Associated Press* bureau, located around the corner on the same floor as the news desk. AP transmitted the story on the newswire shortly thereafter. Attributed to the *Birmingham News*, the story was circulated by the AP wire service across the nation.

Soon, as I sat at my desk, all hell broke loose at the City Desk. When hospital managers and community leaders heard the news on the radio, they began phoning Executive Editor Vincent Townsend at home. What on earth did the *Birmingham News* mean painting the hospital and our great city as a place where poor pregnant mothers were treated in such an inhumane fashion? Townsend, who was considered by city leaders as the unofficial Chamber of Commerce's image master, immediately ordered the editor on duty to "kill" the story.

So, my story was omitted from the *Birmingham News'* Sunday paper. But even Vincent Townsend, arguably the most powerful man in Birmingham, could not put the genie back into the bottle. Once transmitted by the Associated Press, it was on its way to appearing in Sunday newspapers worldwide. No one ever criticized me directly, but the message was that I was working for a newspaper whose management believed they were making plenty of money without printing controversial news that would disappoint their advertisers and damage the image of their city.

Joe Henry Johnson Executed for Murdering an Elderly Woman

I had an assignment to go to a rural community in northern Limestone County where a murder had been reported. As I was driving on the narrow road in the darkness of the early Winter morning my headlights picked up a car with its rear bumper wedged into the metal rail of a one-lane bridge. A man in shirt and tie was shoving a young black man in handcuffs into the police vehicle. "I'm Coroner Buddy Evans," he said as I got out of the orange company car. "I lost control when this fellow tried to escape and my car ran into the guard rail." Evans said he was returning the accused to the scene after taking him to his office in Athens for tests. Evans finally locked the prisoner in his car and the two of us succeed in prying his bumper loose from the guard rail.

The prisoner , Joe Henry Johnson, a 17-year-old black farm hand, was arrested and confessed to raping and killing a 62-year-old white woman in the barn of her Limestone County farm. The Johnson family lived in a tiny dwelling on the farm. She was raped, murdered, denuded of her clothing, and beaten to death with a blunt instrument. Shortly thereafter, Johnson entered the woman's home, severely beat her 89-year-old mother and ransacked the house.

I covered Joe Henry Johnson's trial. It was alleged that the crime occurred when the victim caught the young farm hand molesting a cow in her barn. On the first day of the trial, Johnson's lawyers entered a plea of guilty to the first-degree murder charge. The question for the jury thus became the degree of punishment. Would the twelve white men hand down the death sentence to a 17-year-old black teenager for raping and killing a white woman? After hearing the evidence, the jury returned a death verdict. One of the saddest photographs I ever made was a closeup of his young mother, tears streaming down her face, as she heard the jury's verdict. That dramatic photograph did not appear in the *Birmingham News* but made its way into my scrapbook. I just looked again at that picture. Joe Henry Johnson's mother's tears were so big they brought tears to my eyes looking at her as she witnessed the verdict.

Joe Henry Johnson was executed in the "Yellow Mama" electric chair on November, 24, 1961. His attorneys argued that he was young in years and had been intoxicated and mentally impaired at the time of the crime. Circuit Solicitor (District Attorney) George C. Johnson, a fiery orator, countered that Johnson had committed a cruel adult crime. The judge sustained objections by defense lawyers to a statement by Johnson in his closing arguments: "We want to file in the archives of Alabama, and give notice to the Southland that we are going to protect the womanhood of Alabama." *JOE HENRY JOHNSON v. STATE of ALABAMA, SUPREME COURT OF ALABAMA, 8 Div. 33, June 22, 1961.*

Death at a Dangerous Highway Crossing

I was sent to a rural train crossing at Fackler in Northeast Alabama in early 1960 to report on a tragic school bus-train collision. A freight train knifed through the Jackson County school bus, spilling screaming children alongside the tracks and killing four students. The driver said the bus brakes failed. After interviewing survivors and family members, I wrote about a scene littered with bloody text books. In-depth coverage of that terrible accident resulted in my first news-writing award, the Associated Press' Spot News Award, hastening my ascension to the assignment of political writing, the position to which I had aspired so desperately.

Sister Crowns Sister as Labor Day Queen

I took a company camera with me when I went home to Sheffield for the Labor Day weekend in 1958. My youngest sister, Linda, was among the beauty contestants for the "Miss Labor Day" crown that highlighted the annual festivities at Tuscumbia's Spring Park. When the contestants paraded across the platform Linda was so glamorous she sparkled. The skinny little sister of previous years had filled out in the right places. She was beautiful. She won!

When it came time for the previous year's winner to crown the queen, the 1957 winner was running late so they went back to the 1956 winner, and guess who crowned the queen? Her beautiful sister Joyce had won the title in 1956. Now I had a picture the *Birmingham News* would no doubt feature---sister crowning sister. Some of my so-called "friends" in the audience hooted---"Who's the ugly photographer up there?" The photo and story were prominently featured on the front page the *News*. The local daily, the *Tri-Cities Daily,* ran two shots of the coronation.

CHAPTER 4

The Sorrowful Sixties

America transitioned from a time of innocence and hope in the Fifties to a time of anger and violence in the Sixties.

The decade began with a tide of hope: the election of a charismatic young President, but ended in bitterness fostered by a counter-culture ignited by an unpopular war. The President inspired an exciting air of "Camelot" across most of the nation before falling to an assassin's bullet in Dallas, Texas.

I was a young political reporter who stood amongst the anger and hatred of the mob at the Montgomery bus station when some of its members attacked the Freedom Riders on a sunny Saturday in May of 1961. Two years later, almost to the day, I hosted President Kennedy when he flew into Muscle Shoals for the 30th anniversary of the Tennessee Valley Authority. That Summer saw him lay down a historic marker for civil rights which Congress passed as a memorial to him. Before the end of the 1960s two other Americans had died, also by the hands of assassins: Robert F. Kennedy, the immediate younger brother of the 35th President, and Dr. Martin Luther King. Walsh, Kenneth T., "The 1960s: A Decade of Promise and Heartbreak," U.S. News, March 9, 2010. Gatlin, Todd. *"The Sixties: Years of Hope, Days of Rage,"* A Bantam Book, November, 1987.

The 1960 Presidential Campaign

The summer of 1960 was a happy time for me. I was assigned to write about my favorite subject, politics.

In the May Democratic primaries Alabama voters chose eleven candidates for the Electoral College, five pledged to the Democratic nominee and six free to vote for anyone they chose. Those six were called Unpledged Electors, States Righters or Dixiecrats. The Unpledged Electors were supported by the White Citizens Council and other segregationist factions opposed to the pro-civil rights stances of the probable Democratic nominee, John F. Kennedy, and the certain Republican nominee, Richard Nixon. Thus, the Fall election would be to see if Alabama's 11 electoral votes would go to Nixon or five votes to Kennedy and six to segregationist Democratic Senators Harry F. Byrd of Virginia and Strom Thurmond of South Carolina.

Democrats emphasized that they supported the Kennedy-Johnson ticket in Alabama, although this did little to assuage the Dixiecrats. With Patterson teaming with the Alabama Congressional Delegation, the Democrats waged a united campaign that Fall.

It was a fun campaign. I had an occasional lunch with Republican Claude Vardaman and ran their press releases, the bulk of the organized campaign came from the Democratic side in Alabama. The Governor and all 11 members of the Alabama Congressional Delegation traveled to major night rallies where all spoke so briefly it was hard for me to come up with newsworthy quotes for all eleven. Particularly difficult was attempting to translate to understandable English the thrust of long rambling sentences uttered in rapid fire by U.S. Rep. Frank Boykin of Mobile. One of the reporters covering the campaign wrote one sentence: "Congressman Frank Boykin also spoke." Boykin, owner of thousands of acres of Southwest Alabama timberland, sported a slogan, "Everything is made for love." Those rallies always ended on a humorous note with Sen. Lister Hill condemning Vice President Nixon for a litany of political transgressions. In his deep Southern drawl, Hill would call Richard Milhous Nixon, "Reechard Meelhous--- Treeecky Deek---Neex-on." And the crowd would roar.

Nixon in Alabama with "Broad Grin and Ready Handshake"

Nixon came to Birmingham in August, the only Presidential candidate other than President Dwight D. Eisenhower to visit Alabama in 30 years. I met him at the airport and traveled with his motorcade for his speech at Woodrow Wilson Park. I led the article with: "Richard Milhous Nixon touched down into this historically Democratic state today with a broad grin and a ready handshake." And ended it with: As the huge motorcade headed downtown, a policeman saluted him, women flung kisses, applause, and confetti---1,000 pounds of it. Signs carrying such slogans as "Two Parties for the South" and "Nixon for President" were waved by teen-agers who ran in front of the parade."

On civil rights he said: "I recognize that this is not just a southern problem. Bu it is a problem in my State of California, and in New York and in all the States of the Union as well. It isn't going to be solved by demagoguery, but it's going to be solved by men and women of good will, sitting down and working out these complex problems." Peters, Gerhart, and Woolley, John T. Richard Nixon: "Speech of Vice President Nixon, Woodrow Wilson Park, Birmingham, AL," The American Presidency Project. August 26, 1960.

The Democrats countered by bringing former President Harry S. ("Give 'em hell Harry") Truman to Decatur. In spite of Southern opposition to the 1948 civil rights platform plank, most voters in the progressive Tennessee Valley respected Truman's commonsense leadership and plain talk. A large crowd came to hear the white-haired ex-President "give Republicans hell." Dave Langford and I covered the visit. We captured several Truman nuggets, including:

- "Either party will integrate. It's the law."

- "Nixon doesn't live or act on principal and my friends you ought not to vote for him...He never says the same thing in any two parts of the country.

- "If we'd had somebody with guts (in the White House), we wouldn't have this trouble in Cuba."

- "Anybody in the Tennessee Valley who votes the Republican ticket will be in a hell of a fix...TVA has always been opposed by the Republicans. They tried to keep it from being built and they are still trying to wreck it. Remember Nixon, Dixon, Yates and when they tried to give the TVA to the special interests."

Capital Press Corps in action. Rex Thomas was the dean and I was the youngest member for this press conference in 1961.

Dave Langford's Colorful Writing Flair

By 1961, I had become one of the *News'* two full-time political reporters, covering the Governor's activities, state government, and the state Legislature. I was in the *News* office on May 5, 1961 when Dave Langford rushed in with the panicked look of a reporter with a really big story. His story was headlined, *"Fliers from city gambled lives, lost in Cuban attack."* The article was the first hint of Birmingham involvement in the failed "Bay of Pigs" invasion, the nation's lowest point in the five decades of the Cold War. The *News'* editors must have had no inkling of the importance of Dave's story or someone from the federal government had convinced Vincent Townsend to downplay the story "in the national interest." It ran, not under an eight-column front page banner headline, but was inconspicuously located under a headline in a small font on Page 2.

Dave had learned that a Florida lawyer was in Birmingham notifying next of kin that four Birmingham airmen were missing. Langford wrote that the four all worked at Hayes International and were Air Force veterans. It would later be reported that the four were also members of the Alabama Air National Guard Birmingham wing.

As the invasion date drew near, and President John F. Kennedy had assumed office, it became obvious that Castro was not likely to be defeated by the resistance movement alone. President Kennedy worried that such a well-organized plan would have the United States' fingerprints all over it. He ordered the CIA to scale back the operation. Kennedy barred intensive bombings of Cuban airfields, which permitted fast-flying Cuban fighter planes to shoot down the lumbering B-26s. All the men recruited to train the Cuban exiles had received aliases and were warned that if they were captured or killed the U.S. would deny any association with them. Dave was a public information officer in the unit and had heard rumblings that something was going on. There was no way the CIA could keep the mission secret. President Kennedy later acknowledged America's involvement but denied that American military personnel had entered Cuban territory. Not until 1987 did the U.S. reveal that eight Air National Guard members had indeed flown into Cuban airspace.

Twenty-five years after breaking the story, Dave Langford looked back on the Alabama airmen's involvement in the Cuban invasion in a news feature he wrote for the Associated Press. He portrayed them as "mostly laid-back, beer-drinking sons of Dixie" who were "led by "a bullish general with Andy Rooney eyebrows... eager to kick Castro's tail." It was 17 years before the CIA declassified critical documents and posthumously awarded the agency's highest award for bravery to the four Birmingham airmen who lost their lives fighting for freedom in Cuba.

Dave Langford and Paul Hemphill had finagled appointments to the Reconnaissance Wing of the Alabama Air Guard to avoid the draft after college graduation. They were Public Information Officers during the deployment. They explored the jazz clubs and literary hangouts in Paris together. Since the unit's deployment was little more than a show of force, they had plenty of time for reading. Hemphill, the sports addict, began reading serious literature. He examined the writing styles of Ernest Hemmingway, William Faulkner, and John Steinbeck. At that point, he decided that there was more to write about in life than sports.

They returned to Birmingham in late Summer, 1962. I had moved on in June to Tuscumbia to edit the *Valley Voice*, so I missed their "war" stories. Dave was still in Birmingham in 1963 when the civil rights movement focused its protests on Birmingham. After child demonstrators helped face down Bull Connor's fire-hoses and police dogs, Ku Klux Klansmen dynamited the Sixteenth Street Baptist Church. Dave later characterized the turning point in the Birmingham demonstrations as when "a torrent of public outrage rejuvenated Martin Luther Kings civil right movement like a thunderstorm on a parched cotton field."

We last saw Dave and his wife, Roye, when Mary and I were attending the 1980 Democratic Convention in New York City as delegates pledged to Jimmy Carter's reelection. Dave still retained a disarming smile and the Mississippi Delta accent.

After he retired from AP in 2003, I learned from Paul Hemphill that Dave was diagnosed with cancer. Dave moved to Tupelo to be near his son, the managing editor of the *Tupelo Daily Journal*. Paul called in October, 2004 to tell me Dave had lost the fight with cancer at age 69.

Paul Hemphill, a Leading Southern Author

Paul Hemphill left sports writing to become a street-prowling chronicler of life in Atlanta. Paul wrote about real Southerners, the "good ole boys," the truck drivers, baseball bums, sheriffs, bootleggers, country singers, evangelists, and stock car drivers. Hemphill wrote columns for several months from Viet Nam, exposing his readers to the blood and mud and fear. After returning, he applied for a Nieman Fellowship at Harvard University. By 1970, the daily grind had taken its toll. So, he quit the *Journal* to write books.

Paul had decided at age 15 that his fate was to play professional baseball. It became an obsession. He attended baseball camps, looking for opportunities to find a place at the bottom rung of the professional ladder. He thought he had found a spot in spring camp as the only second baseman on the Graceville Oilers team. It was a Class D (lowest professional level) team in a tiny town across the Alabama line in North Florida. But he struck out all four times he came to bat in his first exhibition game. The manager was forced to "let the kid go."

In the early 2000s, after he wrote a novel, *Nobody's Hero,* he encouraged me to join other friends in sending comments for the feedback section of the Amazon book department. In language not comparable to Hemphill's deathless prose, I tried to help him sell the book by writing: "Paul Hemphill is one of a very, very few writers who can craft a realistic novel meshing Southern racial transition into a delightful sports story. His success is no doubt because Hemphill knows the South. He has made a career writing about the South's best and worst of times. Moreover, he has an uncanny grasp of the emotions of human beings. And as a former athlete and sports writer, describes sports so you feel the sweat of the locker room and the giddy excitement under the lights."

Our last communications were in 2007 when he was fighting throat cancer after years of smoking unfiltered cigarettes. The email below was his announcement to a list of friends that he had won an important battle against cancer:

From: Paul Hemphill [mailto:pahemp@msn.com]
Sent: Friday, June 22, 2007 3:10 PM
To: jones; Silverman; Jack Simms; dwayne cox; Debbie Shaw; allen; Betsy Robertson; William Starr; roy blount; don; Elliott Brack; bob brown; charles grainger; cjackson; jay orr; tucker; kindred; bobby; Thomas; Wayne Flynt; Wayne Greenhaw; david; isen; jack crouch; grimsley; joe mcginniss; cullen; chapin; stratton; Lois Langley; David McMullen; Melissa Fay Greene; meta larsson; Corinne McGrady; david; Garner; don rhodes; Reid J. Epstein; johnson; ken; Museum Lovelace; sam swindell; Maria Saporta; schu; Scott Blusiewicz; bill; smiley; Alan and Susan Smiley-Height; Oney; Marian Asbury; J. Thomas Chaffin; William Verigan; Virginia Parker; Michael Webb; Jonathan Yardley

Subject: cancer survivor

Friends.

When my last radiation session ends at about 8:45 Wednesday morning, I'll qualify as a cancer survivor. Not all of you know that I was diagnosed with throat cancer a couple of months ago, my legacy to the chemists in the big house at Winston-Salem NC. The nightmare of treatment is over. I haven't eaten real food in six weeks, shrinking my frame to 119 pounds. I'm hallucinating about cheese omelets and French fries at the Stage Door Deli, ribs at Dreamland, doughnuts at Krispy Kreme. In due time. If there's to be a second act, now it begins.

Paul Hemphill

Paul died two years later. The *New York Times* obituary, led with this: "Paul Hemphill, who brought a lean journalistic style and a sharp ear for dialogue to essays and novels devoted to the blue-collar South of stock-car racing, football, country music, evangelists and wayward souls, died Saturday morning in Atlanta. He was 73..." His capacity memorial service, characterized as a different kind of service, opened with a steel pedal guitar, fiddles, and **Hank Williams** yodeling the old spiritual, "I Saw the Light."

I met his widow, Atlanta Magazine writer Susan Percy in 2019. She wrote me a nice note when she reviewed this piece and we agreed to meet for coffee and talk about Paul and his buddy, Southern writer Pat Conroy.

Alabama and the Civil Rights Revolution

Racial tensions had begun to mount in Alabama in the mid-Fifties. On December 1, 1955, Rosa Parks, an African American seamstress, boarded a city bus in downtown Montgomery and sat one row behind the whites-only section. As the bus filled with passengers, the white driver ordered Parks to surrender her seat to a white man. Parks refused, prompting the driver to summon the police, who arrested her for violating the city's segregation ordinance.

In the 1950s and early 60s, Birmingham became known in some quarters as "Bombingham" as Ku Klux Klan bombers responded to integration efforts. Martin Luther King called it "the most segregated city in America." At the center of this violent time, and standing at opposite ends, were Reverend Fred L. Shuttlesworth and Eugene "Bull" Connor. From his pulpit and on the streets, Shuttlesworth sought racial equality while Commissioner Connor fought to retain segregation. They sparred in City Recorder's court during my days on the police beat.

News Executive Editor S. Vincent Townsend was Birmingham's image-master. With his influence with both daily newspapers and a television station owned by our parent company, he avoided personal public attention while having the last word on most important community and state matters. Over the next half-dozen years, the Civil Rights Revolution's focus on Birmingham provided dramatic opportunities for successes and failures in Vincent Townsend's management of the community's worldwide image. Townsend was a big, pot-bellied man who instilled fear in his subordinates and public officials alike. He seldom laughed but had a disarming smile when he wanted to use it. He always treated me with respect, and I admired his leadership, but suspected that his wheeling and dealing would someday have its limits. Mr. Townsend never criticized me for the story about the birth outside the University Hospital emergency room although it was obvious to everyone who had killed it and why. Once after racing through Northeast Alabama behind lawmen in an all-night chase of a kidnapper, I pulled over to a pay phone and dictated the story to another reporter before deadline for the statewide edition. When I returned later that day an envelope from Mr. Townsend was waiting in my mail slot. Hand-typed on his Underwood, he commended what he called "real newspapering." Enclosed was a bonus check for $25.

In 1961, the Congress of Racial Equality (CORE) organized racially integrated groups called Freedom Riders to ride public buses through the South to test new court orders that prohibited segregation in interstate bus terminals.

A large mob of white Klansmen and news reporters were waiting for them when they arrived at the Birmingham bus terminal on Mother's Day. Freedom Riders and some reporters were beaten viciously with metal bars, pipes and bats until the police finally arrived. Shortly after the bus had left Birmingham, the *News* City Hall reporter Bud Gordon called me in a panic. The City Desk had reached him to say they had lost touch with Tom Lankford, the reporter assigned to cover the Freedom Rider trip to Montgomery. When Gordon, a wannabe cop, picked me up on the way he was dressed in suit and tie---plus a holstered .38 pistol on his belt. Here I was in our standard dress of coat and tie. At the time, all reporters, businessmen, and politicians wore suits daily with starched white shirts that were stiff in the neck. Working in Birmingham I always ended the day with a distinctive ring of soot around my collar as a reminder that this was a steel mill town.

As the Greyhound bus entered the Montgomery city limits and state police escort peeled away Public Safety Director Mann was on the phone with Montgomery Police Commissioner to reconfirm that the Montgomery police would be on duty at the terminal. But when the bus rolled in to the terminal at 10:23 a.m. a motorcade of policemen sped away, leaving the terminal unprotected. A mob of several hundred waited as the Freedom Riders stepped from the bus. Attackers swarmed over them, women in the mob screaming *"Get the niggers!"* They attacked with baseball bats, broken bottles, and lead pipes. Freedom Riders and six white reporters were beaten and their cameras smashed while the few remaining policemen calmly directed traffic.

I reported in the *News* the next day that the first incident we saw when we arrived was Public Safety Director Floyd Mann, pistol drawn, holding off a group of whites who sought to beat a television photographer and a Negro. Mann also rescued another Negro from his attackers, warning, "I'll shoot the next man who hits him."

Bud Gordon grabbed a pay phone to give the reporters in Birmingham a running report on what we were seeing. He conspicuously pushed his coat back to advertise the fact that he was armed, giving the appearance of a police detective. I was trying to hang close by when we became separated in the melee. When it was apparent that angry ruffians were paying particular attention to me, I spotted my friend Floyd Mann in the parking lot about 30 feet away. I walked quickly toward him. Floyd Man put his hand on his pistol just as two of them converged on me. In that fleeting moment, I saw young men wearing khaki pants splattered about the cuffs in red mud, sidestepping me the instant I stuck out my hand to greet the armed state lawman.

The tense white mob lined the streets waiting for victims to appear. I had never witnessed anything like the feeling that emanated from that mob and have never been able to adequately describe such an eerie scene. There was absolute, frightening quiet. Not a sound. I saw in real life the mob hysteria I had always heard about, with men and women behaving like wolves waiting for the kill, poised to attack anything that moved. Off to the right a young black person tried to flee from two teenaged boys waving garbage cans overhead as weapons. The mob howled with blind fury. The young white thug bolted forward and knocked the black youth unconscious by crashing the heavy metal garbage can on the back of the victim's head.

But Floyd Mann, a law and order professional, was clearly the hero of a day, an exception among cops who clearly were in sympathy with the assailants.

Segregation and the 1961 Birmingham Mayor's Race

In the 1961 mayor race, Police Chief Eugene "Bull Connor's candidate, former FBI agent Art Hanes, ran second of seven candidates behind Tom King, a young moderate former district attorney, reached the runoff. Vincent Townsend and the *Birmingham News* endorsed King. Hanes kicked off the runoff campaign by going on television while the returns were being announced and to make sure the voters knew King had carried the black-dominated Legion Field boxes. Two *News* reporters who were Connor confidants played a leading role in sinking Townsend's candidate. According to author Diane McWhorter's account, *News* reporter Tom Lankford snapped a photo from a third-floor window of Tom King shaking hands with a black man whom Lankford's *News* colleague Bud Gordon paid $20 for the favor." Hanes distributing the photo, claiming King was "Washington's candidate" and won by nearly 4,000 votes. McWhorter, Diane. *"Carry Me Home," Simon and Schuster, 2001.*

I covered the Birmingham city elections that Spring. One candidate who stood no chance tried to give me a set of cookware as a "present."

I declined that, as I would two other attempts at influencing my coverage during that period. One was in a thick envelope that magically appeared on the table while I was having lunch with a party leader during the 1960 presidential campaign. I casually slid the envelope back across the table and assured him he did not need to pay to get fair coverage by this reporter. The other happened a year later when I was riding in the car with the campaign manager for a candidate for Governor who slid a roll of bills across the seat that he called "expense money." I politely declined by saying, "No thanks, the *News* covers all my expenses." Serving in the Legislature years later, even when serving on the powerful Ways and Means Committee, no one ever tried to buy my influence. I joked, "Which is the most influential? A news reporter or a legislator?" In fact, my peers at the newspaper said it had not been many years since reporters were poorly paid and politicians were accustomed to subsidizing them. I was aware of rumors that a political reporter had owned two state-leased liquor stores, a patronage plum governors reserve for their strongest supporters.

Alabama's Quickie Divorce Mill

The Birmingham News and other newspapers concerned about the state's image wrote for 25 years about the evils of Alabama as a "quickie divorce mill." Celebrities and common folk alike flocked to the state where a couple could decouple in as little as a day rather than the normal six months for a divorce. Between 1945 and 1970, divorces became a gold mine as Alabama churned out more divorces than Nevada, the other state with lenient divorce laws.

Among the prominent people who sought out the service was Tina Onassis, who hastily divorced her husband, Greek shipping tycoon Aristotle Onassis, in South Alabama, in 1960. (Onassis married former First Lady Jacqueline Kennedy in 1968, five years after President John F. Kennedy was assassinated). Flowers, Steve. "We were once divorce capital," Andalusia Star-News, Nov. 20, 2013.

97

During the 1961 session of the Legislature, two legislators stopped me in the rotunda to ask if I had heard about the quickie divorce granted to the son of S. I. Newhouse in Marion County. Newhouse was President of Newhouse Newspapers, the largest chain of newspapers in the nation, which owned the *News*. "Since your newspaper is always writing about the evils of quickie divorces, are you going to print this story?" I dutifully called the news desk and relayed the challenge to the frantic editors who said they would take it from there. They verified that the young Newhouse's spouse had indeed been granted a divorce that day in Marion County, the territory ruled by former State Senator Rankin Fite. I checked the first edition the next day beginning by looking at the front page. Nothing there. This crusading newspaper which invariably ran front page exposes about celebrity divorces in Alabama chose to give the story four paragraphs in the classified advertising section under a small one column headline.

A 1961 effort to reinstate the year's residency requirement for divorces failed to pass the Legislature but the Alabama Bar Commission added to its code of ethics a section prohibiting attorneys from taking part in quickie divorces. The practice was halted entirely in 1970 when two Alabama circuit court judges and seven others were indicted for taking part in a quickie divorce scam.

1961 Legislature: Reapportionment, Redistricting, and Ultimate Change

In a Sunday story writing about what was expected to happen in the upcoming session of the Legislature, I summarized the key issues with two "R's"---state legislative reapportionment and congressional redistricting. The entire session would turn out to be consumed by those two issues. The regular session would end in a flurry of fist fights without passage of either reapportionment or redistrict bills and, for the first time ever, failure to pass the budget bills to keep schools and state agencies operating. It was close to 2 a.m. on the 36th day but the Senate clock had been unplugged at midnight. A special session a few days later was required to pass the budgets and a stop-gap Congressional redistricting bill. Six years later, the Legislature was reapportioned by order of a Federal court. On the way to the wild ending, something truly historic for Alabama occurred late in the session. In an emotional moment on the Senate floor, the "Black Belt-Big Mule" coalition that had held the state in a political stranglehold throughout the Century blew apart.

Alabama Press Conferences on Sunday TV

Alabama Press Conference appeared on WAPI-TV, an NBC affiliate owned by Newhouse Newspapers, which also owned the *Birmingham News*. Since it was a *News*-produced program, as the writer covering the Legislature, I became host and moderator in the Summer of 1962. Like NBC's format, we invited two visiting newsmen each week to join us in questioning that week's guest, an office-holder engaged in newsworthy events of the week. My style was to throw mostly soft pitches, working in a high hard one when a guest evaded important facts. One Sunday two House members on opposite sides of the Legislature's congressional redistricting fight were the invited guests. When the sponsor of the anti-Roberts bill dodged a question regarding the controversial genesis of the bill, I followed up with a high hard one. Remembering he was on TV---"in front of God and everybody"---the spin stopped and the facts tumbled forth. After the program, we went to a gourmet restaurant for a *News*-sponsored meal where, as said in the South, fun was had by all.

Background of the Infamous "Chop-Up Jefferson" Bill

Several North Alabama members joined those from Roberts' District in opposing the Ferguson-Givhan bill. As it began to appear that the bill was stalling, legislators from Roberts' East Alabama District were looking everywhere for an alternative that would save their district. They found their compromise with the Ferguson-Givhan supporters with what became known as the "Chop Up Jefferson" bill. The idea of those "chopping up" the state's highest population county was met with alarm and consternation by Jefferson County leaders. Their leader became Vincent Townsend and the *Birmingham News.*

Opponents conducted a filibuster in the House, offering numerous amendments, before debate was shut off after 21 hours before the anti-Jefferson County bill was passed as a substitute for Ferguson-Givhan. I wrote that it was largely representatives from more populous North Alabama counties who had stood with Jefferson County. Albert Brewer of Decatur in a floor speech welcomed Jefferson County "into its true geographical area---the political alliance of North Alabama." He called the Black Belt-Big Mule alliance "sixty years of marriage of the Imperial Queen and a scoundrel." Grainger, Charles. *Birmingham News*, Aug. 16, 1961, 1 and 3. *Birmingham News*, August 20, 1961, 1 and 6A.

When the bill moved to the Senate on the 26th of 36 legislative days, Black Belt senators' strategy was to delay Congressional redistricting to protect South Alabama congressmen while keeping legislative reapportionment from coming up for a vote. I happened to be standing in the rear of the Senate talking with E. O. (Big Ed) Eddins of Demopolis, a hulking, intimidating senator and Black Belt planter, when Sen. Larry Dumas of Jefferson County walked to the podium with arms filled with papers. Dumas offered an amendment to that day's special order calendar, to place three bills to reapportion the Legislature at the top of the calendar. Eddins suddenly stood erect as he realized what was happening. In his mind, the Black Belt was being betrayed by its long-time ally, the Big Mule senator from Jefferson County. He ground his teeth and shouted, "That does it! The SOB has double-crossed us. We will get even!"

Neither Big Ed Eddins nor I realized that---at that moment---the 60-year alliance between the Black Belt and Jefferson County's Big Mule interests had come to a permanent end. Eddins moved around the Senate floor, huddling with small groups of senators, pulling together a solid majority to "chop up" Jefferson County's congressional district. Dumas saw he was badly out-numbered and reacted with the only weapon at hand. He started a filibuster that became a 72-hour, around-the-clock marathon. Dumas was joined by two young senators, Ryan deGraffenried of Tuscaloosa and Bert Haltom of Florence. Each stood at the microphone and wearily talked for an hour, then handed off to the next one. They got no more than a semblance of rest with the third hour coming around so soon. As a defense, their frequent quorum calls made it almost as tiring for the majority, a majority of the Senate answering the roll to avoid automatically ending the session for the day. Cots were brought so senators could nap between quorum calls, and doctors frequently examined the health of the three filibusterers.

In the final week of the session, the majority wore down the three filibusterers, passing the bill overwhelmingly. But the Governor immediately vetoed the bill when a motion to over-ride the veto came before the Senate. The filibuster had doubled in number with two more Senators from North Alabama and a Senator from Mobile taking an hour at a time at the microphone.

As the 35th of 36 legislative days drew toward an end, with pressure building and nerves tightening, the "chop-up" forces attempted to beat down the presiding officer with a series of angry motions. They accused Lieutenant Governor Albert Boutwell of Birmingham of aiding the filibustering senators by refusing to recognize "point of order" motions designed to halt the filibuster and permit the issue to be brought up for a vote. When a South Alabama senator accused Boutwell of violating his constitutional duty in order to save his congressional district, the presiding officer broke down and wept openly from the tension. The angry senator again shouted for recognition while Sen. Haltom was speaking. Haltom refused to yield the floor, saying he had an hour to speak and wished to use every minute of it. The South Alabama Senator shouted louder and louder for recognition, nearly 30 times within 10 minutes, but Haltom kept the floor.

An Historic, Chaotic Ending on Final Day

As the filibuster continued on past midnight and into the final day, Jefferson County leaders brought in former Lt. Gov. Jim Allen, a strong parliamentary leader to sit at Lt. Gov. Boutwell's side to bolster him with whispered advice as the majority hammered away at him with parliamentary efforts to break the filibuster.

As the session was grinding to an emotional end, I was at the press table in the center of the Senate floor between the two podiums, directly in front of the presiding officer's chair. A few feet behind me House members crowded the aisles. Order deteriorated when the Governor's executive secretary said something that offended a giant House member who connected with a wild swing to his jaw. Then the session ground to a chaotic close with senators and reporters utterly exhausted. So, the Legislature fizzled out its 1961 session in the wee hours of this morning, leaving Jefferson County's congressional district intact but the state without a redistricting or a general appropriations bill. The filibusterers who had fought for 96 hours to keep Jefferson from being chopped up to redistrict the state's congressional districts had won. It was midnight, the chop-up bill was dead.

The outcome was the strategy of most senators the final days: kill the general appropriations bill to force the Governor to call a special session to keep the government operating so a redistricting bill could be reconsidered. As they picked up the pieces from the chaotic session ending, a consensus developed for an "agreed-upon" bill, which was called the "Nine-Eight Plan." It was now the only redistricting plan with enough support to pass that would avoid unlimited at-large congressional elections. After polling legislators to be assured the budget and the "Nine-Eight" Congressional redistricting bill would pass in a special session, Patterson called the legislators back into special session the next week. The "Nine-Eight" plan zipped through. Far from perfect, but the only bill that could pass, this odd-man-out plan remained in effect for the next two primary elections.

The big loser in the session was the Black Belt-Big Mule alliance. The winners were the growing counties who had sought so long for proper allocation of state legislative seats. Frustrated at the continued refusal of the Legislature to reapportion itself, late in the session a group of Birmingham residents had filed a class action suit in Federal court. The suit asked that all members of the legislature be elected at-large until the legislature abided by its constitutional mandate to reapportion itself. The following year the U.S. Supreme Court handed down the *Baker v. Carr* landmark decision that held that citizens could find reapportionment relief in Federal courts if state Legislatures failed to act. As in other areas in which the state failed to solve major problems on its own, the Federal brought about reapportionment of the Alabama Legislature.

Wallace Dominates Alabama, Has Appetite for National Run

I sat behind my desk during the early stages of the gubernatorial primary of 1962, editing press releases and working the phones for fresh coverage. The last three weeks was the thrill of the Century for a young political writer. I alternated each week riding between campaign stops in the backseat of sedans carrying the three main contenders: former Gov. James E. (Big Jim) Folsom of Cullman in North Alabama, who in the mid-1900s was the most popular governor ever to be elected; State Senator Ryan DeGraffenried, a handsome, eloquent lawyer who was a poster child for a New South concerned about its image, and former Circuit Judge George C. Wallace, known as "the fighting little judge" for his attacks on the federal judiciary. Folsom and DeGraffenried rode in the passenger side of the front seat on those campaign swings. The hyper Wallace sat fidgeting sitting alongside me in the back seat. He rummaged through his pockets past the cigars and scraps of paper to find an envelope to make notes for his next speech. He wrote down the same short reminders before every speech.

On the drive up the mountain to his "stump speech" in Arab, I thought: "This restless little man with the darting eyes, heavy eyebrows, and ducktail haircut is the most ambitious politician I have ever met---constantly wooing those who he thinks need to be won over to support him." He was likeable, even charming. We kidded each other. I called him "Wallace." He called me "Cholly," in his thick Black Belt dialect.

I said, "Wallace if you don't stop targeting me in your speeches, you're gonna get me killed."

"Aw, don't worry, Cholly, they won't hurt *you*," Wallace said with a reassuring smile. I was not so confident. His idea of "protecting reporters" was remindful of Arkansas Gov. Orval Faubus during the hot days of school integration at Little Rock. Faubus would pick out a Yankee reporter for ridicule during a speech, then later assure him he had meant "nothing personal" by it.

I had grown to dread the part of Wallace's campaign speeches where he made me the butt of his joke (or target of his wrath, in the minds of some of his listeners). The line was designed as an indirect reference to Folsom's liquor drinking while poking fun at the daily newspapers. Midway through his speech a campaign aide was instructed to pass a cup of ice water up to the perspiring speaker. Wallace would look around until he spotted the reporter from the big city newspaper, point at me, and drawl, "Now for the benefit of Mr. Grain-guh of the *Bum-ingham News*, this is ice wattah I'm drinking." Most of the crowd would chuckle, but as the campaign intensified smiles aimed in my direction were becoming fierce glares.

On this hot day in late April, the "fighting little judge" was on a roll. Perspiring, shirt sleeves rolled up, hips moving as he rocked back on his heels, his finger stabbing downward, the microphone ringing from his staccato voice, he flailed away at the perceived enemies of our "Southern way of life." As the time for the ice water routine approached, I quietly slid along the truck bed, facing the crowd, until I was directly below him. "Now for the benefit of Mr. Grain-guh of the *Bum-ingham News...*" he growled. I held the cup below his waist, forcing him to stoop for it. He resumed, "This is ice watttuh..." For one of the few times in his public life George Wallace was speechless. It took his tired mind seconds to realize it was me. "You sonofagun!" he sheepishly mumbled while I laughed heartily. The Klansmen-looking Wallace supporters could only assume this was an inside joke between two friends and withdrew their threatening glares.

Wallace began looking for excuses to split with the governor when an incident occurred that made a clean break with Folsom convenient. Adam Clayton Powell, a flamboyant black Congressman from Harlem, came to Montgomery to speak to a group promoting black voter registration. Folsom invited him to visit the Governor's Mansion and sent his limousine to pick him up. Powell bragged to the media that they had chatted about race relations while enjoying a scotch and soda. It was a public relations disaster. Whites saw it not as Southern hospitality but a violation of Southern racial conventions. Folsom tried his usual method of defusing controversies with humor, saying, "Ya'll know ol' Big Jim don't drink scotch." Later, he confided to allies, "Adam Clayton Powell is one son of a bitch I wish I had never met."

As segregationist voters turned on Folsom following the Powell controversy, Wallace drove to Montgomery and announced to everyone in earshot at the Jefferson Davis Hotel that he was separating permanently from his old friend because he was fed up with Folsom's "drinking and entertaining niggahs in the Mansion."

News City Editor Fred Taylor reviews election results with author, 1962

One of Wallace's closest friend when he attended the University of Alabama was Frank Johnson, a hardworking law student from Winston County. Late one night Wallace drove to Montgomery to request his former friend to jail him for a short time, which would help him politically. The judge told his former friend that if he defied his order, he would send him to jail "for as long as I can." Wallace found a way to avoid jail. He claimed victory, insisting throughout his 1962 campaign that those who said he backed down were "integratin', scalawaggin', carpetbaggin' liars." And his audience would go wild.

Big Jim: His Preachments of "Peace in the Valley" were Strikingly Ill-Timed

When in my rotation of traveling with the major candidates I joined Big Jim's campaign for the last week. A campaign staffer drove the orange *Birmingham News* vehicle to permit me to ride in the car between stops with Folsom. The tired but friendly candidate sat in the right front seat while I sat directly behind him. Sheriff Jim Clark of Selma drove the big Lincoln. I learned that Clark and Sheriff Fred Holder of Scottsboro had been hired by the campaign leadership to alternate as drivers with the primary responsibility to keep him safe AND SOBER.

On the way to Nauvoo, less than ten miles away, Folsom pulled a flat half-pint flask of Early Times and took a deep sip without a chaser. I looked at Clark, to see if he would attempt to dissuade Folsom from falling off the wagon. The Dallas County sheriff, who had been appointed to the office by Folsom, simply looked straight ahead at the highway. "They're tearing down my signs," Folsom said to me. "Who, Governor?" I asked. "You know who, the Ku Kluxers. They're doing it for George Wallace." How ironic it was for Big Jim and me to be talking about the evils of the Ku Klux Klan when Jim Clark, the man driving the car that day, would form a horse-mounted posse of

MY JOURNEY THROUGH A CHANGING SOUTH

violent thugs to oppose the voter registration campaign in Selma just three years later.

Later that day, after we arrived at the courthouse square at Scottsboro, an excited old man ran up the sidewalk to intersect Folsom, who was briskly moving along shaking voters' hands. "How, are you, boy?" Big Jim said as he shook the gap-toothed old man's hand. As Folsom moved on, the old fellow beamed and proudly said to bystanders, "See, I told you he'd recognize me. He calls me 'Boy' every time I see him."

It was an exhausted Folsom who showed up early that evening at the television station. What was telecasted statewide that night was an outrageous event that would have been comical had it not been so sad. Television cameras tended to magnify mistakes and appearances. (See Richard Nixon, 1960 Presidential debate). As he introduced his family, when he got to one son he mumbled, "Now which one are you?" Back in Birmingham watching the telecast, I was not surprised at that point because he frequently used lines like that as humorous ways to show off his large family.

As Folsom talked about his plan to provide free textbooks, he thumped loudly on a stack of books. The sound boomed loudly from TV sets throughout the state. Like a broken record, he became stuck on the claim that other candidates were imitating his free text book program. "They're just 'me-too" candidates," he slurred. He gazed into the camera and made cooing noises, repeating in a sing-song voice, "Metoo!...Metoo...mee tooo, meee, toooo!" for what seemed like several minutes.

In their homes, Folsom supporters grew anxious, antsy. Some of those depending on his election for a third term to resume doing business with the state evolved from concern to panic. Two brothers with heavy investments in the campaign watched together at their home near the Florida line. One was a pessimist, the other an optimist. The pessimist said, "Rex, I believe ol' Big Jim has been drinking." The optimist said, "Aw, Big Jim wouldn't do that to us. He'll be okay." Whereupon the eight-year-old son of the optimist burst into the room shouting, "Dad, look on TV! Big Jim is on television drunk!" The brothers threw up their hands.

The "Cuckoo Bird" television performance was the end of the Folsom era in Alabama, but I submit Wallace would have won the election anyway. These were not times for "moderate, law and order" candidates. When the votes came in the next day, Wallace was in the lead, DeGraffenried was a distant second, with Folsom making a strong run for second. Wallace handily defeated DeGraffenried in the runoff.

DeGraffenried, a Political Role Model

I traveled with Ryan deGraffenried several days during the runoff. The Tuscaloosa senator spent the first week, calling courthouse politicians across the state to warn them they were being watched in case Folsom supporters tried to steal enough votes before the official count to put him into the runoff. But some of the old-line Folsom supporters responded that if they were tempted to steal votes it would be to keep Folsom out of the run-off because they knew he could not beat Wallace. What was left of DeGraffenried's campaign unraveled when Folsom endorsed his candidacy a few days before the run-off election. The pro-Wallace *Montgomery Advertiser* labeled him "Big Jim deGraffenried," suggesting his election would mean a continuation of "Folsomism," which the paper said meant crony corruption, intemperance, and racial moderation. Wallace won the run-off by the largest vote in state history: 340,730 (55.87%) to 269,122 (44.13%).

The 1962 campaign was the first step toward George Wallace's unrivaled domination of Southern politics for more than two decades. A lion was now in the streets. In spite of losing the runoff, the 36-year-old DeGraffenried had momentum, running first in several urban areas. With Wallace's term limited to four years, the handsome Tuscaloosa senator looked like a sure-fire winner in 1966 when Wallace would be constitutionally prohibited from serving a second term. Traditionally, candidates ran for governor in order to become known well-enough to win the next time around.

When I began covering the Alabama Legislature for the *Birmingham News* in 1961, the state senator who most impressed me was Ryan deGraffenfied. A young, energetic, powerfully-built, dark-haired handsome man, his booming baritone voice dominated Senate debates. The dynamic young Senator from Tuscaloosa captured the hearts of Jefferson County leaders in the last-ditch fight that avoided the chopping up of Jefferson County's congressional representation. He filibustered a full hour every three hours for three days to save Alabama's largest county from being left with no direct congressional representation.

Ryan also became a personal friend and role-model for this young reporter during that session. When I became concerned about how to handle constant invitations by lobbyists to expensive dinners, I chose to seek advice from a person considered to be completely honest. He looked directly into my eyes and said, "Charlie, if they think they can buy you for the price of a steak, let them keep thinking." The other piece of his advice that I followed was to read the book that had helped him understand Alabama politics. It was V.O. Key's *Southern Politics*. The title of the chapter about Alabama, was *Alabama: Planters, Populists, "Big Mules."* After all these years, a yellowed copy of that book remains in the center of my office bookcase.

After Dr. Wernher von Braun's memorable speech to the Legislature requesting seed money for research, DeGraffenried was the senator who introduced the constitutional amendment to fund the research institute at the University of Alabama Center in Huntsville.

I was not surprised when Ryan ran for governor. He stepped without hesitation into the 1962 gubernatorial race against heavyweights Folsom and Wallace, both well known to voters from previous races. While Wallace appealed to the base emotions of the violent segregationists and Folsom sang "peace in the valley," DeGraffenried advocated sensible leadership. He was coming up fast behind Wallace and Folsom so that when Folsom sang his "cuckoo bird" song the night before the election Ryan edged into the runoff. Fresh off the runoff loss to Wallace, he prepared for the next election.

With incessant energy and determination to win the grand prize the second time he ran, Ryan had made 680 speeches in the four years since his 1962 campaign when he officially began his second campaign early February, 1966.

Ryan DeGraffenried was the candidate Wallace most feared in 1966, characterizing him as having the charisma of a Southern version of John F. Kennedy. In his autobiography, Wallace wrote that deGraffenried had conducted a spirited campaign in 1962, was a good speaker who drew large crowds, and was "a very worthy adversary." When he discussed it with me, I knew Wallace had not been seriously concerned about any other candidate, even former Governor Patterson. Editorial writers saw Ryan as the candidate who as governor would have been dedicated to bringing restraint in the face of popular demand for excess, who would appeal to reason when unreason was in vogue, and would be dedicated to the higher destiny of the state when murmurs in the crowd called for incitements to base passion.

As I was leaving Ryan's funeral outside the church in Tuscaloosa, Wallace saw me and came over to say he knew I had lost a great friend and he was sorry. When I saw him a few weeks later, after his wife Lurleen qualified to run to succeed him, Wallace started the conversation by saying, "Charlie, she would not have run if Ryan had not gotten killed." He correctly saw Ryan as the candidate Wallace most feared. He correctly saw DeGraffenried as having the charisma of a Southern version of John F. Kennedy. In his autobiography, Wallace wrote that DeGraffenried had conducted a spirited campaign in 1962, was a good speaker who drew large crowds, and was "a very worthy adversary."

John F. Kennedy, My Favorite President

President John F. Kennedy, 1963

On May 14, 1963, I was among 25 newspaper editors from Alabama invited to the White House for a luncheon meeting with President John F. Kennedy. Although Birmingham's racial turmoil was attracting worldwide attention, our meeting had been scheduled weeks earlier, before the racial turmoil began, as one of a series of meetings with newspaper editors from various states. The timing of the meeting portended a serious discussion with the President, who would urge us to work in our communities to bring together moderate blacks and whites lest extremists dominate. Dr. Martin Luther King had begun civil rights demonstrations in April. Viewers of television news world-wide were shocked by scenes of demonstrators being met by fire hoses and police dogs. Following the dynamiting of

King's brother's home in Birmingham on May 11, a mob of angry rock-throwing blacks was met by state troopers swinging clubs.

Editors sipped cocktails in the Blue Room while we awaited the President. I was focused on the large painting of George Washington. Our first President stood tall, extending the right hand of a leader lightly, always in command, a serious expression, rosy cheeks, white hair curled above his ears. Bright red drapes and silk table covers portrayed unmistakable royalty and majesty. "He was the most important of all the Presidents," I mused to myself. He and he alone was the difference in maintaining a government with a democratic leader versus a heritage and inclination on the part of many to revert our fledgling government back to an English-type monarchy. The full-length painting by Gilbert Stuart was the first work of art acquired for the President's House in 1800. While I was gazing at the massive portrait, President Kennedy slipped into the room without fanfare, mingling in the knots of editors. Meeting him was a majestic moment. The overpowering first impression was the bronze tan which strangely mirrored the first impression I had eight years earlier when I met baseball slugger Ted Williams, who, ironically was not only my sports hero but also President Kennedy's. JFK was soft-spoken in conversation, thus ending the Williams comparison. Appearing well-exercised and under 45, in slight contrast was the slight fatigue of face from two and a half years in what has been said to be the world's most stressful job. I found a way to work into our conversation that my first son had been born on the same day as his had in 1960. After lunch he would write on my gold-leafed White House luncheon menu, featuring rack of lamb as the entree and peach melba as the desert: "To Chuck. Best from John F. Kennedy. May, 1963."

In the next issue of *The Valley Voice*, I wrote:

"I left the palatial house-you-read-about secure in the knowledge our country is led by a man with qualities of greatness---but with a nagging insecurity at a point he made.

"That was the apparent direction Negro leadership is headed.

"That direction could be smeared with the ugliness and mobs and bombings and bloodshed and Federal troop-occupancy of American communities, North and South.

"John Fitzgerald Kennedy, sun-tanned and as cordial a host as you'll ever see, let it be known to us he is worried about the civil rights battles that lie beyond the horizon.

"Those could make the Birmingham's, the Oxford's, and the Little Rock's look like tame scrimmages."

This was the way I led off my report of our meeting at the White House.

I noted that President Kennedy's point was that King's non-violent approach, which most in the South regarded as provocative, would be challenged by angry rabble-rousers like Malcolm X, anxious to achieve their ends by any means necessary, including violence. He and Vice President Lyndon Johnson stressed that cities could not erect walls to avoid outside agitators of whatever persuasion, but the influence of outsiders could be overcome by community leaders of goodwill. Ironically, two years later Malcom X was assassinated.

At the conclusion of the two-and-one-half hour luncheon discussion, President Kennedy told us Attorney General Robert Kennedy would like us to drop by his office to chat further. Before I left the White House, I sat down with White House Press Secretary Pierre Salinger to discuss the President's scheduled visit to Muscle Shoals four days later to celebrate the thirtieth anniversary of the Tennessee Valley Authority. I explained that our Legislature was having difficulties agreeing on a congressional redistricting plan and we in the Muscle Shoals area were fearful that we could lose our Congressman,

Bob Jones, who had run next to last in the previous statewide election. Salinger knew that Jones was both a close political and longtime personal friend of the President. I suggested that they permit a receiving line of state legislators and other local dignitaries. He said White House Advance Man Jerry Bruno would coordinate those details with me in my office within two days.

But by far the most potent element of the Kennedy legacy was the one that associated JFK with the legend of King Arthur and Camelot. According to Mrs. Kennedy, the couple enjoyed listening to a recording of the title song before going to bed at night. JFK was especially fond of the concluding couplet: "Don't ever let it be forgot, that once there was a spot, for one brief shining moment that was Camelot." President Kennedy, she said, was strongly attracted to the Camelot legend because he was an idealist who saw history as something made by heroes like King Arthur, "There will be great Presidents again" she said, "but there will never be another Camelot."

He was my favorite President. He was charismatic, he was the father of a son born on December 5, 1960, as was I, and his No. 1 sports hero was Ted Williams, as was mine.

JFK, FDR and the 30th Anniversary of TVA

"Thirty years ago today, a dream came true. President Franklin Delano Roosevelt—in the presence of TVA's two great defenders, George Norris of Nebraska and Lister Hill of Alabama—signed his name to one of the most unique legislative accomplishments in the history of the United States. And, in reality this act of signature was only the beginning." --JFK remarks at Muscle Shoals 30th Anniversary celebration of TVA, May 18, 1963

When President John F. Kennedy's helicopter whirled to earth near the Tennessee Valley Authority administration building, he greeted smiling TVA officials, members of the Alabama congressional delegation, and a tense Alabama Governor George C. Wallace. Wallace greeted Kennedy with a wave of his hand and later a handshake. Together they walked the 100 yards to the outdoor speaker's platform. Men cheered and women and children shrieked with delight when the President waved at them. They also yelled when Wallace raised both hands above his head in greeting.

On his way to the outdoor podium, Kennedy shook hands along the receiving line of local leaders which Advance man Jerry Bruno and I had invited. I was at the head of the line, alongside my two *Valley Voice* owners, Attorney Howell Heflin and farmer-ginner Ed Mauldin. Heflin was elected to the U.S. Senate 15 years later and for the 18 years he served featured prominently in his office was a black and white picture in a black frame taken by the *Voice* photographer. It showed JFK meeting Mauldin, with the hulking Heflin close by on the left, and me introducing my partners from the right.

I wrote in the next edition of *The Valley Voice*:

"Muscle Shoals made the sun-spangled Saturday its biggest since Franklin D. Roosevelt came here in the Big Depression. He was on his way to assuming office. People were desperate. They came from miles around to see a man who they hoped would be the country's savior.

"Times were different Saturday when JFK came.

"The area was prosperous, largely because of the TVA facilities he came here to salute.

"Sitting a few feet to his right on the red-white-and-blue bedecked speaker's platform was the man who has set himself up as the

President's chief civil rights adversary. Alabama Governor George C. Wallace, who later rode with the President on the high-powered presidential helicopter to another speech at Huntsville's Redstone Arsenal, was tense and mostly unsmiling.

"The perspiring crowd...cheered JFK time again. He began with these words:

"Thirty years ago, today a dream came true. President Franklin Delano Roosevelt—in the presence of TVA's two great defenders, George Norris of Nebraska and Lister Hill of Alabama—signed his name to one of the most unique legislative accomplishments in the history of the United States. That simple ceremony which took only a few minutes ended a struggle which had gone on for a decade. It gave life to a measure which had been vetoed twice by two preceding Presidents—Calvin Coolidge and some said it couldn't be done...But today, 30 years later, it has been done. They predicted the Government was too inefficient to help electrify the valley. But TVA, by any objective test, is not only the largest but one of the best managed power systems in the United States."

At both Muscle Shoals and Huntsville, the President avoided references to his differences with Wallace, but he talked directly with the Alabama governor during the 35-minute helicopter trip to Huntsville in a conversation characterized as "not unfriendly." U.S. Senators Hill and John Sparkman and Congressman Robert E. (Bob) Jones were sitting with them in what Jones later described to me as a frank talk. What Jones heard his old congressional pal say was reasoned argument, but also something similar to a parent quietly lecturing a misbehaving child. "Governor, do you know what you are doing to your state?" Jones said Kennedy asked Wallace at one point as they winged their way to Redstone Arsenal, where America's space program began and now flourished.

117

Press Secretary Pierre Salinger wrote a memorandum summarizing his version of the conversation between Kennedy and Wallace. "The subject of Birmingham came up after the helicopter had been in the air for 15 minutes," Salinger wrote. "The president asked Wallace about the current situation in Birmingham. Wallace replied the situation was quiet and he felt the law enforcement contingency of around 1,000 would be able to maintain order. The president replied that the situation would remain tense in Birmingham as long as no progress was made...that progress had to be made there to avoid future trouble...

In his speech at the Marshall Space Flight Center on Huntsville's Redstone Arsenal, he said, "I know there are lots of people now who say, 'Why go any further in space?' When Columbus was halfway through his voyage, the same people said, 'Why go on any further? What will we possibly find? What good will it be?' I believe the United States of America is committed in this decade to be first in space. And the only way we are going to be first in space is to work as hard as we can here and all across the country." President Kennedy's farewell to the Tennessee Valley turned out to be his final adieu. He said "I leave this valley, this state, this region, in which I arrived only few hours ago, realizing once again what a strong, great people we are, and we are determined to keep it so."

The May 22, 1963 edition of the Redstone Rocket, noted "While the President hobnobbed with John Q. Public, a babe in arms touched him and squealed, a graying grandmother shook his hand and gulped..."

The next confrontation between Kennedy and Wallace came quickly. At his press conference on May 22, the president was asked about Wallace's announced intention to block the integration of the University of Alabama. He said he would be reluctant to use troops and marshals and did not believe the governor wanted the federal government to send in marshals, but he had no choice but to enforce the order of the courts — popular or not.

The President federalized the Alabama National Guard four hours later after his representatives had agreed, in the spirit of avoiding violence, with a request by Wallace to make a final statement. Alabama National Guard General Henry Graham marched to the spot Katzenbach had stood, saluted, and said, "Governor, it is my sad duty to ask you to step aside, on order of the President of the United States." Alabama troops were asking their Governor to lawfully obey a federal court order.

The Governor stepped aside and drove back to Montgomery and the ceremony of futility was over, more a show than a historical moment. But Wallace's career entered a new political dimension. After Wallace stepped aside and the University of Alabama was peacefully integrated, on that evening of June 11, Kennedy gave his famous civil rights address on national television and radio, launching the initiative for civil rights legislation that would provide equal access to public schools and other facilities, and greater protection of voting rights.

President Kennedy was assassinated in Dallas, Texas, on November 22, 1963, while on a political trip to Texas to smooth over frictions in the Democratic Party. As I type these words, I glance at the wall in my office at JFK's personally autographed portrait to me "with best regards" and the *Valley Voice* photographer Bill Jenkins photo of the receiving line at Muscle Shoals' 30th anniversary celebration of TVA while I introduced the handsome JFK as he looked directly into the eyes of equally tall Edward Mauldin. I think of him along with my other hero, the Thumper, Ted Williams. Ironically, Ted Williams was John F. Kennedy's hero also.

After President Kennedy's death, Milton Cummings and I were recruited by Kennedy staffers to help raise funds for the construction of a Kennedy Memorial Library in Boston. After it was built, one of the photos displayed there was a newspaper photo of two 29-year olds, Ted Williams and JFK, posing in the Red Sox dugout in June, 1946. That was one of the few years the Red Sox won the American League pennant and was the same year Kennedy was first elected to Congress.

Wernher von Braun's Powerful Speech

"Let's be honest with ourselves about it: It's not water, or real estate, or labor, or power, or cheap taxes that brings industry to a state or city. It's brainpower. Nowadays, brainpower dumped in a desert will make it rich... Dr. Wernher von Braun, June 20, 1961 speech to the Alabama Legislature advocating funding for a Research Institute in Huntsville.

Dr. Wernher von Braun, Huntsville's leading citizen, known worldwide as the Father of Rocket Science, displayed a demeanor so calm it totally masked his anxieties as he stood to address a joint session of the Legislature in the well of Alabama's historic House of Representatives. Though JFK would be assassinated in Dallas on Nov. 22, 1963, just over eight years after his speech, on July 20, 1969, NASA's Apollo 11 mission would win the Cold War Space Race against the Soviets by landing the first humans on the moon. Von Braun's anxieties were based on a stirring of concerns that this was a large audience of unknowns. WWII had ended just 15 years earlier. On this sunny June day, as I sat in the back of the Chamber with the Capitol Press Corps, covering the event for the *Birmingham News*, I would later learn that Alabama's most famous immigrant was worrying about how he would be accepted in this deeply conservative setting.

Never had a more charismatic speaker appeared before the Legislature. Nor had there been a more powerful, or more memorable speech, at a more appropriate time. Alabama was just recognizing its role in the exciting space program. "The university climate brings the business," he said, totally grabbing the legislators with the line about brainpower dumped in a desert making it rich.

I led my article that appeared in the *Birmingham News* the next day with this:

Von Braun Speech Arouses Legislature
BY CHARLIE GRAINGER, News staff writer

"MONTGOMERY, Ala., June 21---An aroused Alabama Legislature is slated to receive an opportunity Friday to answer a challenge by Space Scientist Dr. Wernher von Braun for an immediate boost in the state's educational research programs.

"Sen. Ryan deGraffenried of Tuscaloosa announced during a Senate filibuster last night he will introduce legislation that would meet the rocketeer's request for $3 million for a newly-opened research institute at Huntsville.

"The senator told upper house members his proposal would be a general obligation bond issue that would be voted upon in a statewide referendum.

"Von Braun's frank call to the joint session of the Legislature for funds immediately left lawmakers astir---with many later indicating they would seek the $3 million as fast as possible...

"Milton Cummings, Huntsville businessman and Democratic Party leader who accompanied von Braun here, said he later talked with Gov. John Patterson about the possibility of meeting the request. "The Governor did not commit himself," said Cummings, "but I am deeply encouraged by his attitude toward our meeting this need...""

After the speech, I was invited to a one-on-one dinner with Mr. Cummings. He was a successful cotton broker who had moved into the space age by buying a majority of the stock and taking over the leadership of a local company, Brown Engineering Company. He impressed me with his sincere, straight-forward elaboration of the merits of von Braun's request. Cummings would later head a statewide campaign for approval of the $3 million bond issue. It was overwhelmingly supported by Alabama voters.

It was the first time Milton K. Cummings and I met, and it would be a turning point in my career. I would go to his ante-bellum home in Huntsville the next year for a reception for Congressman Bob Jones' re-election where we retreated to the kitchen and chatted pleasurably. In 1963, he sent an emissary to my newspaper in Tuscumbia to invite me to Huntsville to talk about coming to work for him as his executive assistant. That led to a 36-year career in management and government relations at Brown Engineering. I would also later come to know von Braun, when I was a member of the Legislature where I served as his escort when he addressed a joint session following the lunar landing in 1969.

As a member of the Legislature, I wrote a resolution praising the U.S. moon lunar landing success in 1969, which was displayed for several years in the Von Braun room at the U. S. Space and Rocket Center, a national facility the rocket scientist had convinced the Legislature to fund.

Research Park: A Product of Visionaries

While they were working together to promote funding for the Research Institute at UAH, Dr. von Braun suggested to Cummings that Huntsville needed a central research park for the emerging space and defense industries. Cummings tasked Vice President Joe Moquin to find the right site for Brown Engineering to buy enough acreage for its own facilities as well as to sell at cost to other companies.

At the time, Brown Engineering was in the Huntsville Industrial Center, or HIC building. "It was a renovated cotton mill and they immediately began campaigning for a different facility. No windows. A very unattractive building and Moquin was concerned about the potential of the future of the company. He couldn't see how we could attract science and engineering personnel, a fundamental part of our business." Proximity to Redstone, Marshall Space Flight Center, major roads and what was then a branch of the University of Alabama, now the University of Alabama in Huntsville, was "important to the people we'll be hiring for our future," Moquin recalled that he and Cummings used as basic criteria for the location.

The vision of its founders has been transferred over the years to community and city leaders who have picked up where Cummings left off. Moquin had retired and was serving on the CRP Board when I became its Chairman. Over two decades later, I was still Chairman of the Board. I reminded attendees at numerous ground-breaking ceremonies over the years that the founder's vision created a park where "success succeeded success, where leading space and defense companies congregated and where aspiring start-up companies aspired to locate. We saw our job over the last quarter century to keep their dream alive by maintaining the high quality that led CRP to become one of America's economic crown jewels. His legacy, the Cummings Research Park, once a patchwork of old cotton fields, now contains 220 companies employing 25,000 people, most of whom provide support for Army and NASA missile and space programs. It is second only to North Carolina's Research Triangle as the United States' largest research park.

Milton K. Cummings, A Leader for the Last Half of the Century

I eased my car into the driveway of the stately white-columned home of Milton K. Cummings on a September Saturday afternoon in 1963. He had sent an emissary to my office in Tuscumbia to ask if I would come over to Huntsville to discuss my becoming his executive assistant at fast-growing Brown Engineering, where he owned most of the stock and was Company President. I looked around the massive, ante-bellum home with unforgettably enormous columns along its front. Here was

Milton K. Cummings, Company President, 1956-67

where the Cummings family had hosted Senator John Sparkman and family when they spent the night listening for election returns when he was the Democratic nominee for Vice President in 1952. It was where Lily Flagg, a 950-pound Jersey cow world-renowned as the top butter producer in 1892, was feted at an elaborate party that attracted guests from across the nation. And in this house a year earlier I had visited with Milton Cummings and Bob Jones when they hosted a party for the famous actress Tallulah Bankhead, a Huntsville native.

Nobody seemed to be home. Suddenly a black car drove up. "Hey, I'm Bob Harris, Director of Administration at Brown Engineering. Mr. Cummings called and asked me to come over to let you know he played an extra nine holes but is on his way."

When he arrived, we maintained the excellent chemistry we had in previous chats. I was not a hard sell. Managing eight mostly part-time employees as Publisher of the weekly *Valley Voice* in Tuscumbia, I had come to realize that management excited me more than writing editorials or selling ads. When he got around to talking salary, I gulped. This job sounded so much like fun I would work for practically nothing. For negotiating purposes, I threw out a number above what I expected. "OK, that's fine," Mr. Cummings responded. No negotiations. He had made up his mind. "When can you be here?" he said. "As soon as we can sell the newspaper," I said.

We sold the paper to a Northport publisher within a few days and I reported to Brown Engineering to work for Milton Cummings in October. I started by handling public relations, filling in for the boss in meetings, and working on the side handling communications for our district Congressman, Robert E. (Bob) Jones. During a statewide race two years earlier, I had come to appreciate Bob Jones. This Congressman found the money to build highways, power dams, and to support a vigorous space program. Because he was a major advocate of the government-supported Tennessee Valley Authority, he was viewed in South Alabama as a North Alabama liberal. Frank Boykin, the wealthy Mobile area congressman was the only Congressman to receive fewer voters than Jones in the 1962 "9-8" low-man-out elections. The flamboyant Boykin, whose slogan was "Everything is made for love," was later convicted of conspiracy and conflict of interest, but was pardoned by President Johnson. In 1964, Jones was reelected by a comfortable margin.

I had the time of my life working closely with Milton K. Cummings. In many ways he was like my own father, certainly my closest friend. Joe Moquin and Bob Jones called him by his first name, but he was 26 years older than I was, so I always called him "Mr. Cummings." Mr. Cummings' life story was awesome. He succeeded first as a cotton merchant and stock trader, then as primary owner and president of a home-grown company whose history became synonymous with the dramatic successes of Huntsville's space and missile programs. He was a giant among New South business leaders, a humanitarian, personally unassuming, and a brilliant businessman. We had so many mutual interests he frequently took me to his home where he entertained at lunch.

He was also a great prankster when among friends. One incident that particularly stands out was at our wedding in Knoxville in 1967. As Mr. Cummings was coming through the receiving line, he put a condom in my hand. Shocked, I quickly dropped it on the floor before the next person could shake my hand. One of the ring beares picked it up, wanting to know what it was. Fortunately, someone else dealt with that issue!

Another story, when the tables were turned, was several months later when he was visiting Mary and me at our home. As we were enjoying our cocktails, our male poodle, Lafayette, began sniffing at Mr. Cummings leg, (which I knew but Mary did not know) was artificial. As he hiked up his leg, Mary ran across and grabbed him, trying to avoid the inevitable. But it was too late! Both of us were terribly embarrassed, but Mr. Cummings laughed heartily!

He was a child of Huntsville's mill village culture. "I'm just a lint-head (a somewhat pejorative term for children of the mill villagers)," he would sometimes say. After suffering osteomyelitis, at age four doctors amputated one leg just below the knee. It was the crutches that caught the eye of the man who would become his boss and benefactor. When he graduated from high school, Mr. Fletcher offered to send him to Harvard Medical School or wherever he wanted to go. The offer was tempting but he turned it down in favor of helping care for his family. Fletcher gave him a $75 a month job as a clerk. After his benefactor died, Cummings went into the cotton business for himself at the age of 25 in the middle of the

Great Depression. He soon became the most successful cotton merchant in the area.

By 1953, a year after the defeat of the Stephenson-Sparkman Democratic ticket, he had decided that neither President Eisenhower nor Agriculture Secretary Ezra Taft Benson understood the agricultural problems of the day. So, he got out of the business. He confided to me years later that those were the darkest days of his life, that he sank into a depression that dragged him into thoughts of suicide before his friend Bob Jones realized what was going on and found ways to bring back the sunshine.

He was managing his investments in the stock market with highly satisfactory results when in 1957 Cummings was invited to invest in a new stock issue for Brown Engineering Company, a small, near-bankrupt contractor supporting the missile program on Redstone Arsenal. Brown Engineering was operating from leased engineering and manufacturing areas in the Huntsville Industrial Center (HIC) building, a former cotton mill manufacturing complex. What Cummings believed the company needed was the right management and a significant capital infusion. By 1958, he provided both, pouring more than $1 million of his own money into the struggling business. The Board asked him to serve as President for 90 days to get Brown Engineering on its feet. During that period, he saw the company's great potential, enjoyed the excitement of supporting America in the Space Race, and decided to remain on a permanent basis. Though he felt comfortable making the business and financial decisions in 1959, Cummings began to look around for an executive vice president to manage the company's engineering and technical operations.

Exactly one month before my first day at Brown Engineering, on September 9 at 8:30 a.m. four black students integrated Huntsville's Fifth Avenue School, becoming the first students to integrate Alabama's public schools. State troopers were sent there by Governor George Wallace ostensibly to keep the peace but in actuality to prevent blacks from enrolling. Over the weekend, an angry Huntsville business community and police chief sent a clear signal to Wallace to keep his troopers outside Huntsville.

Mr. Cummings took the lead in galvanizing Huntsville's government contractors to take positive action to provide equal opportunity for employment of minorities. When the then Vice President, Lyndon Johnson surveyed government contractors regarding employment of blacks, Cummings brought together 15 contractors to develop a plan to take positive action to provide equal employment opportunities. The very moment President Kennedy was assassinated on November 22, 1963, Cummings was in Vice President Johnson's office discussing his 30-page action plan with the Vice President's staff.

When President Johnson declared "war on poverty," in 1964, Cummings again took the lead in Alabama. He founded and served as president of the community action program in Huntsville. Huntsville attorney Robert Sellers Smith and I wrote the developmental grant that opened the doors of the new agency in 1965. Cummings served as the first chairman of our anti-poverty organization, the Huntsville-Madison County Community Action Agency which evolved into the Community Action Partnership of Huntsville/Madison & Limestone Counties. Cummings believed the cycle of poverty began with a lack of educational opportunities in the preschool years. The antipoverty agency's mission was, and remains, to alleviate poverty and social deprivation, beginning with child development and pre-kindergarten programs.

Following passage of the Civil Rights Act of 1964, former Florida Governor LeRoy Collins became the first director of the Community Relations Service. The organization was designed to facilitate orderly integration through biracial efforts at the local level. Collins asked Cummings to become one of the first members.

In Selma, blacks were demanding the right to vote through peaceful protests, planning to march to Montgomery to dramatize their demands. At nearby Marion, a demonstration had been disrupted by troopers at the courthouse. A young black man fled the scene with his mother to hide in a nearby café. A state trooper followed them into the café and fatally shot the son. Alabama justice took care of the trooper. A jury gave him six months in jail.

On Sunday March 7, which came to be known as "Bloody Sunday," troopers attacked and beat marchers, halting the march. President Johnson dispatched LeRoy Collins to Selma to seek out local leaders to attempt bi-racial cooperation. Collins asked Cummings to join him in meeting with Selma business leaders. We flew to Selma on a twin-engine charter. When we drove downtown for the meeting the tension in the air was indescribable. When we returned to the airport for the return flight to Huntsville the pilot carefully inspected the plane to look for any indications that someone had sabotaged the plane. When he found what appeared to him to be sugar around the gas tank, the shaken pilot said he would not be willing to fly us until he checked the plane further. He suggested that we rent a car and drive to Tuscaloosa, 80 miles to the north. We drove on, worrying all the way about the nervous pilot test-flying the airplane. But two hours later he picked us up at the Tuscaloosa airport. He had found nothing further to substantiate his fears.

By 1966, Brown Engineering Company had matured to become a viable player in the space and defense industry. The quiet influence and leadership of the team of Cummings and the operational and technical expertise of Executive Vice President Joe Moquin and his top staff positioned the Company to obtain vital support roles with NASA MSFC. Brown Engineering also was on the ground floor of emerging Army intelligence and missile defense efforts. Offices and subsidiaries had been opened in several locations in the South and Northeast. Total employment exceeded 3,300. Although the lunar landing was still three years away, the giant rocket had been developed and work in Huntsville had begun to descend. Our stock, listed on the American Stock Exchange, became stuck in the low teens, with light traded. Cummings and Moquin decided that continuing vitality would require entering new, more diversified markets. They began looking at possibilities to gain a national presence by acquiring, merging, or being acquired.

After eight years as President and CEO, Cummings stepped down in April 1966, remaining as Board Chairman. Interest on both sides was developing when Mr. Cummings' Atlanta stock broker suggested he look at Teledyne, Inc., a fast-growing company in Los Angeles. which was experiencing spectacular stock growth through acquisition of companies in a wide range of fields. Teledyne had grown from a tiny electronics company in 1960 to 293rd place on the Fortune 500 list in just six years. It was headed by two former Naval Academy roommates, Dr. Henry Singleton, as Chairman, and Dr. George Roberts, as President. The company became Teledyne Brown Engineering, Inc. (TBE), a wholly owned subsidiary of Teledyne, Inc. A TBE board was maintained, which was advisory in nature, and Mr. Cummings became less and less active.

In the early 1970s, he fractured a shoulder, taking him away from the golf course and restricting his activities to watching the tape at his local brokerage house and dropping by the Elks Club for drinks after lunch. I was busy carrying on my work with the company while also serving part-time in the Legislature, which kept us from spending long hours together as we had when we he was active. He had served as a state senator himself, filling a short-term vacancy, and was immensely proud when I was elected. One of my greatest regrets was the fact I became so busy working two jobs that I saw Mr. Cummings less frequently during his few retirement years. It was like a member of my own family had died when I received a page at the Montgomery airport on March 7, 1973 to tell me Mr. Cummings had died of a self-inflicted gunshot wound. I could only conclude that the depression that had caused him to threaten suicide during the dark days of the Eisenhower Administration had returned with the boredom of retirement.

Joseph C. Moquin, Who Ran Company Next Two Decades

Major General John Bruce Medaris, the tough, impatient commander of the Army Ballistic Missile Agency during the 1950s, was rarely at a loss for words.

"You what?" he asked his visitor. "You want my best management guy?"

TBE President Joe Moquin, center, with author
and Senator Richard Shelby, 1996

131

"That is exactly who I want," said Milton K. Cummings, President of Huntsville's fast-growing, home-grown engineering and manufacturing company. "You have asked us to quickly develop broad industrial support for missile and space programs. Now I need you to help me take the next step. I'm asking you to let your best management guy come over and help support your missile programs as our operations manager, as my number two person in charge of technical operations. I need the best and brightest engineering manager possible to run that side of the business so I can spend my time finding the money to recruit the best engineers and scientists from all over the country."

"But my best man, without a doubt, is Joe Moquin, and I don't know how we could do without him," the general said. Medaris thought for a few minutes, then conceded this unusual step was important to Huntsville industry being able to quickly provide engineering and manufacturing support to the emerging missile programs.

That, as Milton Cummings recounted so often I can still repeat the story virtually verbatim, was how Joe Moquin joined Brown Engineering as Executive Vice President in 1959. Under the Cummings-Moquin leadership, the company would grow to more than 3,000 employees by the mid-1960s when Joe succeeded Mr. Cummings as President. The company merged with Teledyne, Inc. in 1967. When Heflin was first elected to the U.S. Senate in 1978 Joe and I met him at the Huntsville Airport on his first trip to D.C., where he would discuss committee appointments with the Senate Democratic leadership. We had done a comprehensive analysis of the economic impact on Alabama of space and defense compared with agriculture, heavy metals, and other indices. From that, Joe Moquin argued that space and defense were the most important areas of interest for a senator from Alabama. Heflin served as ranking member of the committee that authorized funding for NASA but never was able to work his way onto the most important committee in the Senate, the Appropriations committee. Instead, he carefully advised Senator Richard Shelby when he was changing parties in the 1990s which gave the Senate majority to the Republicans.

When Moquin retired as TBE Chairman in 1989 he was honored by 700 people at the Von Braun Civic Center with tributes that included a telegram from President Bush, flags flown aboard the Space Shuttle, and a street in Cummings Research Park named in his honor. I was master of ceremonies. U. S. Senator Howell Heflin characterized Joe Moquin as "one of the most informed and knowledgeable people in the defense and space industry and one of the first people I seek out for advice in these areas." One of the least known but most significant contributions Joe Moquin made over the years was his chairmanship of the Chamber of Commerce's Federal Agency Task Force, an ad hoc group formed in 1976 to support Huntsville's federal agencies, which functioned into the 1980s An informal group called the "Bubbas" functioned in the 1990s and the current Federal Agency Task Force was formed in 2000 as an independent support group to assist Huntsville's Federal Agencies. Following his retirement from TBE he provided transitional leadership to two important community institutions, serving as interim President of the University of Alabama in Huntsville and interim Director of the Space and Rocket Center for several months each.

Robert E. Jones, Jr., Our
Congressman for 30 Years

"The Tennessee Valley of North Alabama has blossomed over the past 40 years; and no individual deserves more credit for the transformation than Congressman Bob Jones" From the Huntsville Times, 10 February 10, 1976.

"I do not know how you would classify men who have served in a representative capacity in this country, but I am sure that if you

picked the upper 5 percent of this generation, of all generations, Bob Jones name would be high among them." Former U.S. House Speaker Carl Albert.

Robert Emmett Jones Jr., an Alabama Democrat was our Tennessee Valley congressman for 30 years, and frequently called "Bob the Builder" and "Mr. TVA." As the moving force on the House Public Works Committee he built highways, public buildings, and inspired legislation affecting navigation, floor control, and clean water. He was a major moving force in the creation of the Interstate Highway System, hailed as the greatest single public works project in history. The Rayburn House Office Building and Kennedy Center for the Performing Arts were among the public buildings constructed under his leadership. He steered through Congress the Clean Water Act of 1972, which established the basic structure for regulating pollutants discharges in the United States. He was the Tennessee Valley Authority's constant champion.

He was first elected to Congress by special election in 1947 when Congressman John J. Sparkman of Huntsville resigned the seat after being elected to the U.S. Senate following the death of John H. Bankhead II. When I became closely involved in his 1964 reelection, on several occasions he responded to my questions by recounting that memorable campaign. I had read about that campaign in V. O. Key's book, *Southern Politics in State and Nation* (1949), a microscopic state-by-state examination of Southern politics. This was the book State Senator Ryan deGraffenried had recommended to me in 1961 as must reading for those seriously interested in the real workings of politics in Alabama and other Southern states. The Alabama chapter found the 1946 special primary provided an extreme illustration of localism, the powerful impact of voters supporting friends and neighbors. Each of six of the district's seven counties was represented by at least one candidate. Each hometown candidate led the voting in his home county. Jackson County's turnout for Bob Jones was a record, 97.5 per cent. Colbert

County had two candidates, Tuscumbia attorney Jim Smith and publisher-writer Bradley Twitty. (Jim Smith was father of one of my best friends, known as "Fuzzy," who served as a circuit judge; Twitty was the Northport publisher and author of the 1954 biography of Big Jim Folsom, entitled *"Y'all Come,"* who bought the *Valley Voice* in 1963 when I was preparing for a new career in Huntsville.) Smith polled 62.1 per cent and Twitty 30.1 per cent, 92.2 per cent of the total votes in Colbert County. District-wide, Jones led with 22.7 per cent; Smith ran second with 19.5 per cent.

Thus, Bob Jones and Jim Smith, two of the most common of American names, were pitted against each other in the primary runoff. They had become best friends in law school. That congressional campaign put their friendship to a test. In 1964, Bob Jones proudly recounted to us his recollection of the uniqueness of that race: "I had strong support in my home county and Jim ran well in the west part of the district, and the two of us made the runoff. We were both running on a shoe string. So, to save money, we decided to share a hotel room, most of the time in Decatur in the center of the district. Neither of us ever had an unkind word to say about the other. And we have been close friends ever since."

Bob Jones may have even exceeded George Wallace in his ability to remember the names of constituents. He associated people by families. We retold a story that was perhaps only slightly embellished during the 1964 campaign: Once Jones was campaigning in Paint Rock when a young man decided to test the widespread belief that Bob Jones knew more people in his district by their first name than any politician ever. "I bet you don't know who I am," he derisively said to Jones. The congressman responded, "No, I don't recall your name but I knew your dad, Bill Young, who raised cotton, and your older brother, Sam, who mostly raised cattle." The skeptical young man became a Jones supporter.

I had become closely acquainted with Bob Jones during the 1962 "9-8" or "low man out" Congressional elections, which I was covering for the *News*. Campaign workers for Jones and the other North Alabama congressmen formed a loose alliance that singled out Boykin as the name to leave off their ballots. This was particularly true in Jones' district and the district bordering it on the south, represented by Jones' close friend Carl Elliott from Jasper. After the June primaries, I returned to Jones' district to edit the *Valley Voice*, and we maintained frequent contact.

I had moved to Huntsville to become Milton Cummings executive assistant in October 1963 when Jones asked for advice on strategies for his 1964 reelection. Once again, the Legislature had been unable to pass a congressional redistricting plan. After the session ended, a delegation of national Democrats were concerned about losing valuable seniority in the congressional delegation from Alabama. They requested a meeting with Governor Wallace to request him to call a special session of the Legislature to focus on the issue. The group was headed by Milton Cummings and AFLCIO President Barney Weeks, neither of whom had ever supported Wallace. Through his staff, Wallace blew them off with the message that he had no interest in meeting with them. As Jones planned for the "9-8" re-run, advice was to bolster his public image in his own district, where he was to be opposed by a state senator from Huntsville, then to do what came naturally---announcing the funding of public works projects for other parts of the state. He had two full-time writers on his staff who wrote project announcements, but they were from other states and needed local help from a political perspective. I agreed to support them as time permitted.

When Jones began serving in Congress, he was assigned a two-room suite office in the Old House Office Building near another freshman, 29-year-old John F. Kennedy of Boston. Jones and Kennedy, similar in sunny personalities and considered moderates within the Democratic Party, became close friends from the outset. Jones later joked that their relationship was such that when Jones was on the House floor, Kennedy, a bachelor who partied most nights, would sneak away from his office to the big black leather sofa in Jones office for an afternoon recovery nap. Their relationship continued to grow over the next 16 years until President Kennedy's assassination on November 22, 1963. Jones' staff contact in the White House during the Kennedy and Johnson administrations was Henry Hall Wilson Jr. of North Carolina, who served effectively as Congressional Liaison for both presidents. It was Wilson that Jones called often in the "9-8" runoff in 1964 to expedite major projects for Huntsville, Mobile, and Birmingham.

He survived the primary opposition without difficulty, then entered the statewide campaign by pushing projects in other districts. In the early morning hours of late May, the week before the "9-8" runoff, Jones and Billy Hamilton, Birmingham Mayor Albert Boutwell's assistant, worked out the details with Henry Hall Wilson that permitted the announcement of a long-sought modern Post Office for Birmingham. *The Birmingham News* headlined the story and conservative business leaders responded to Hamilton's early morning calls by heaping heavy praise on the North Alabama Congressman. It was probably the largest project in South Alabama history---twin tunnels under the Mobile River connecting with a new interstate system. *The Mobile Press Register* devoted most of page one for two days to the enormous project.

Jones and Elliott stayed in regular contact to be prepared to have their forces circulate sample ballots in their districts in the last few hours of the runoff campaign. The nominee their ballots would leave off was former State Senator John Tyson of Mobile, who had won the first primary competition for the seat vacated by Frank Boykin. Elliott wrote in a 1992 autobiography that ten days before the June 2 election a group called the United Conservative Coalition held a meeting at the Jefferson Davis Hotel in Montgomery. "This outfit was the core of the old-line Dixiecrat states' righters, a reactionary think tank, part of the heartbeat of the George Wallace (team)," Elliott wrote. He said the meeting was for the express purpose of deciding whether they wanted to target Bob Jones or him for defeat. Elliott was identified with both the Kennedy and Johnson Administrations and as an opponent of George Wallace. Three days before the election the coalition distributed ballots throughout most of the state bearing the Wallace slogan "Stand Up for Alabama," listing the names of all the Congressional candidates---except Carl Elliott. He wrote that he was bothered by being targeted by the segregationist organization but what hurt worse was he found out that his old friend and ally Bob Jones had been registered in a room at the same hotel that night.

Elliott ran a poor ninth and was eliminated from Congress. John Tyson ran eighth and Jones seventh. When I was in Washington a few weeks after the election Jones was troubled that his old friend seemed to be blaming him as one of the reasons for his defeat. Knowing that I always visited Carl when I was in town, he asked me to see if I could explain to him that our district had carried out its end of the bargain in dropping Tyson in order to help save Elliott. Jones' campaign organization passed out blue sample ballots with Tyson's name omitted. I showed Carl the county-by-county numbers and emphasized that our congressional district dropped Tyson by a greater percentage than Elliott's. But that did not seem to convince him. It was like we had not done enough. It was nearly 30 years later when he published his autobiography that I realized that Elliott particularly blamed George Wallace and his followers for his defeat but also felt betrayed by Jones being in Montgomery the night before the Conservative Coalition voted to target Elliott for defeat. It may not have mattered. 1964 was the year the Republican Party nominated a majority to Congress.

Interstate highway Plan Altered to Include Fast-Growing Huntsville

The Interstate system did not direct interstate access to Huntsville in its Interstate 65 plan. A major improvement was a 26-mile spur from the North-South Interstate eastward through Huntsville. It was approved in 1969, but the state was slow in finding its ten percent of the funds, and local political issues delayed construction until 1987. By that time, Huntsville was said to be the most populous city in the contiguous United States without a freeway connection to the Interstate Highway when the Interstate Highway System was first laid out during the mid-1950s. Interstate 65 was routed on a north-south bee line connecting Nashville, Tenn., with Birmingham, Ala. Huntsville was a small town about twenty miles east of I-65. However, during the latter Fifties and through the Sixties, Huntsville underwent massive population growth due to the establishment of the U.S. Army Missile Command at Redstone Arsenal, and the new NASA Marshall Space Flight Center. Jones made the case with his colleagues on the Public Works Committee in 1969 that the first addition to the nationwide system should address this issue. This brought about I-565, the spur connecting Huntsville to I-65, which was opened on October 26, 1991. As Chairman-elect of the Chamber of Commerce, I was on the platform when the freeway was finally opened. The State Highway Department coordinated the ceremony. The governor at the time was Guy Hunt, Alabama's first Republican governor since Reconstruction. I knew that Hunt and his highway director were highly-partisan, viewing loyal Democrat Bob Jones as the enemy. So, in the abundance of caution I checked with the Huntsville mayor's office two days before the dedication and was assured that Jones' name was on the list of dignitaries invited to participate in the dedication. But the father of the project was not only not invited to speak about the project's genesis, he was not even invited to the ceremony. The state highway department claimed they simply slipped up and omitted his name when the final list was prepared. During his remarks, Huntsville Mayor Steve Hettinger referred to Jones' signal role in creating the project, but neither the highway director nor governor could bring themselves to share credit with Bob Jones.

For years the moving force on the House Public Works and Transportation Committee, Jones moved up to the chairmanship in 1975. He had served in the House for 30 years when he voluntarily retired in early 1977. He died 20 years later. I was honored to be a pallbearer, helping carry his casket up the rocky hill to his grave in the Scottsboro cemetery. There was an enormous outpouring of friends and supporters saluting a World War II veteran who went from life in a small town to being recognized as the national leader in building highways, public buildings, and waterways.

John J. Sparkman, the 'Cherub' of the Senate

U. S. Senator John J. Sparkman sparked the extraordinary growth of the Huntsville region during 42 years in Congress. In an era when members from both parties found ways to work together on important issues, he was called the "cherub of the Senate" because of his happy disposition. He was both gentile and intelligent. He was always an insider, voting with the liberal majority most of his career except on civil rights issues. I came to know him when I was covering the 1960 Presidential campaign. We became closer after I moved to Huntsville as executive assistant to his close friend and finance chairman, Milton Cummings.

Congressman Bob Jones later enjoyed recounting the details of how he and Sparkman worked together to bring the German rocket team from Fort Bliss to Huntsville in 1949. Jones and Sparkman believed that a major job-creating prize, an Air Force jet engine test facility, was awarded a few months earlier to Tullahoma, TN rather than Huntsville because of the influence of Tennessee Senator Howard McKellar, powerful chairman of the Senate Appropriations Committee. The "consolation prize," the historical understatement of our region in the Twentieth Century, was the relocation of the Von Braun team to Huntsville. By the early 2000s the Arnold Development Center employed a few hundred while Redstone Arsenal was the employment center for several thousand.

Sparkman worked closely with Alabama's senior Senator, Lister Hill of Montgomery. They became recognized as among the Senate's most effective combinations. They were Southern segregationists, ardent New Deal supporters, and liberal populists on economic issues. Hill was the House sponsor of Senator George Norris' bill creating the Tennessee Valley Authority in 1933. Unlike Sparkman and Jones, who were not known as orators, Hill entertained campaign crowds with old South style oratory. The line they laughed at most in the 1960 Presidential election was when Hill, in the deepest of Deep South drawl, spat out the words, "Richard Meeee-house Neeeex-on" when ridiculing Republican candidate Richard Milhous Nixon.

DeGraffenried Offered Chief of Staff Post

The year preceding the 1966 governor's race, Ryan deGraffenried called to ask me to drive over to Courtland where he was spending the night at the home of a supporter. We sat outside on the front porch of a large white ante-bellum house. I swung in a white wicker swing while he rocked in a wicker rocker, listening to the crickets and talking about the upcoming election. If anything, our relationship had strengthened as he cheered on my involvement in the 1964 statewide congressional races and stayed in close contact. That night he was confident he would be elected. He said he wanted me on his team to lead Alabama forward---specifically as his chief administrative staff person, later to be known as Chief of Staff. I said that would be the only thing I could imagine that would entice me to take leave from my new career in Huntsville.

DeGraffenried had begun his campaign a few days earlier, already on a break-neck speaking pace, rushing from town to town, mostly by air. As I went to bed, I noticed severe winds buffeting my apartment. During the night I was awakened by a call from my friend, Dave Langford, Editor of *the Huntsville News*. "Charlie,

Ryan deGraffenried's plane is down!" Dave said. At that moment, a light plastic-coated ceiling tile banged against the ceiling as a result of heavy winds forcing their way into the attic. I knew Ryan was campaigning in Fort Payne, in mountainous Northeast Alabama, and that the airport sat alongside a tall mountain. "Dave, Ryan must be dead. I can't imagine a plane clearing that mountain in winds like these." Sadly, the next morning that prediction was confirmed.

Close Call in a Private Plane

In late 1963, I was at the Alabama Bar Association meeting in Mobile laying networking for Congressman Bob Jones' statewide campaign for reelection traveling with Jyles Machen, Jones' district staff coordinator. Harry Pennington, the judge in the case of a kidnapped child that I covered for the *Birmingham News* in 1959 and a future colleague in the Legislature, had flown down with his wife in his single-engine plane. He had two extra seats in the back and invited us to return to Huntsville with them. I was wary of Harry's lack of flying experience but Jyles accepted for us before I could think of an excuse to decline. Harry was a typical businessman who owned an airplane yet had only rudimentary piloting experience. He went through the checkout routine before boarding, thinking he had doublechecked everything just as he had been taught.

We had barely cleared the runway on takeoff when the oil began showering the windshield. Harry grabbed the radio and began shouting the international distress signal "Mayday" as he tried to see around the oil covering the windshield. As he frantically circled around to try to make it back to the runway, my view of the cows in the pasture below was so clear we must have been no more than 500 feet above the ground. I had forgotten to breathe, time was moving incredibly slowly, and all I could do was to slowly pick which group of cows we were certain to crash into. With Harry peeking through the side window, still trying to see the runway, we bounced our way in for the landing. Harry, a pal of our segregationist governor, George Wallace, chewed out the negligent maintenance man, a black man, for failing to tighten the oil cap. They cleaned oil off the windshield for 20 minutes. And we took off again. Only to become lost halfway home. There was a temporary directional glitch leaving Mobile County, but Harry had recovered and was flying smoothly on a slightly Northeast course until we had flown slightly northeast of Tuscaloosa. There we encountered a giant, solid black thunderstorm directly ahead. Harry made a sudden U-turn. After that none of us knew where we were. When we finally flew out of the clouds, I recognized a lake near my former home at Cahaba Heights. "Harry, Harry I recognize that lake. I used to live there. We are south of Birmingham and that is the Cahaba River!" So, he made a left turn heading north. Whereupon, we found ourselves lost again. Thank God for Guntersville Dam and the Tennessee River. It was a highly visible landmark. "Harry, that is Guntersville Dam down there, so follow the river until we get to the bridge to Huntsville and turn right," Jyles submitted. The Huntsville Airport runway was located just north of a deep rock quarry filled with deep water. More than one pilot had almost landed inside the quarry at night. But Harry glided us over the deep pit and made a perfect landing. This time Evelyn and I came very close to actually kissing the ground in joy and relief. I silently mouthed, "Thank you, God."

Oldest Son Caught up in Rip Tide

My oldest son, Chuck, was about 13, swimming by himself on a beach at Destin, Florida. He found a sand bar about 50 feet into the Gulf of Mexico where he bobbed up and down with the waves, pushing up each time a wave came in, smiling and shouting to me as I watched from the beach. He was having so much fun, bobbing up and down, I thought he was kidding, not clear what he said above the roar of the surf, when I realized that his smile had turned to a look of terror. "Dad, I need help!" he shouted as I saw a wave burst over his head. A young man in his midteens saw me throw my wallet on the ground and ran down to beach to help. As I started to plunge into the water, he shouted, "No, wait, let me get him," he shouted. "I'm a licensed lifesaver." He flashed by me, swimming toward Chuck. His skill in lifesaving was a thing of miraculous beauty. He brought Chuck ashore just like the lifeguards did it in the movies. "Thank you, God, and thank you, son," was all I could say.

State Legislative Candidate in 1969

When my apartment-mate John David Snodgrass was appointed Circuit Judge half way through his first term in the Alabama House of Representatives, we decided I should run for the seat. John David argued that I had the perfect credentials for the position. I agreed that being a member of the youth movement that had taken over the state Democratic Party governing body, which would appoint the nominee, could be an advantage. With my background as a former political reporter for the *Birmingham News,* Judge Snodgrass thought I would begin serving better informed on the Legislature's rules and inner-workings than many members. I agreed that the fact that I had lived in Huntsville only five years should not be a disadvantage because it was a cosmopolitan city; most of the voters were also newcomers.

First, I would have to get past the Chairman of the local Democratic Party and longtime George Wallace campaign manager, Alvin Blackwell. This was the man I barely defeated two years earlier when we competed for a position on the State Democratic Executive Committee. Blackwell, a Huntsville business leader and Lurleen Wallace's campaign leader when she swept the state in 1967. *Huntsville Times* staff writer Hugh Merrill described me as typifying the "new-breed" of politicians emerging with the advent of the Kennedys in national politics. Merrill saw me as being in the mold of Bob Vance, the young Alabama Democratic state chairman and described me this way: "Young, likeable, a tightrope walker, and reasonably quiet." I was 31 at the time, while. Blackwell was a year older than my mother. When the state committee selected me by a 44-6 margin, he was shocked. He had first assumed the county Democratic committee, which he chaired, would make the nomination. But a legislative seat is a state office, so the nomination for the Legislature would come from the state party, of which I was a member. He had also assumed the Wallace forces would deliver the nomination at the state level. But most of the members closely identified with Wallace voted for me because I took the time to contact committee members of factions. It was a meaningful reminder of the old dictum: The best way to get someone to vote for you, is to ask them directly.

In the general election I was opposed by a Republican and two candidates representing the extreme right and left. The Republican nominee was clearly the chief competitor. He owned the billboard company, so he had all the color billboards, and was a native Huntsville establishment candidate. Late in the campaign the Republican Party circulated a sample ballot to 30,000 households referring to several of us candidates as "Humphrey Democrats" in an effort to get Wallace supporters to split their tickets. Since I was host to Vice President Hubert Humphrey's visit to Huntsville 17 months earlier, I probably came as close as anyone on the list to being a "Humphrey Democrat." My response to a reporter's question was that I as a member of the state party governing body supported the Democratic ticket from top to bottom. Running on that ticket were Wallace's presidential electors; fiery segregationist Eugene (Bull) Connor, seeking reelection to the Alabama Public Service Commission; Congressman Bob Jones, whose congressional seniority depended on his loyalty to his national party and was regarded in South Alabama as a liberal national Democrat. One of the appeals of the Democratic Party of Alabama in those days was that it was a big tent, large enough to cover candidates holding a broad range of philosophies.

Education was the issue all four candidates publicly agreed would be the Legislature's priority in the next session. I campaigned to get the support of those most involved in education: the teachers, principals, and school administrators. After interviewing the four candidates, they endorsed me. We won the House seat over three opponents by a margin of over 7,000 votes cast and went to Hamilton at the end of the week to the home of the House Speaker, where he administered the oath of office.

When the regular session of the Legislature convened in February, 1969, at age 32, I became the third youngest member of the House. From my experience of covering the Legislature as the *Birmingham News* reporter eight years earlier it appeared that success in the House comes from following the management theory known as the 80-20 rule, which meant 20% did the work of the other 80%.

The Alabama capitol building was so remindful of its rich history that it grabbed first-time visitors, and first-time legislators. From my seat on the aisle of the second row in front of the press tables I looked up to the raised platform where the House Speaker towered over proceedings. Above his head was a large marble plaque that read:

IN THIS HALL

The Confederate States of America was organized on February 4, 1861 and Jefferson Davis of Mississippi was elected first President of the Confederacy February 8, 1861, *Tablet erected by United Daughters of Confederacy, Ala. Division*

With the secession of Alabama and six other deep south states and subsequent formation of the Confederacy in February 1861, the building served as its first capitol until May 22, 1861. At the main entrance to the building in the center of Corinthian columns highlighting its Greek Revival architectural style a commemorative brass marker in the shape of a six-pointed star is set into the marble floor of the front portico at the precise location where Jefferson Davis stood on February 18, 1861, to take his oath of office as the first President of the Confederate States of America.

The House chamber was constantly crowded during sessions, with constituents filling the third-floor galleries. Outsiders frequently slipped past the elderly doormen to stand in the rear of the chamber during proceedings. The marble lobby separating the House and Senate chambers was so packed with lobbyists and others anxious to talk to legislators that when it was necessary to go across the rotunda to talk with our Senator, I found myself navigating an obstacle course.

The same month I became the newest member of the Legislature a school bus lost control carrying Huntsville students down a steep grade on Monte Sano Mountain, killing one student and injuring 21 others. Earlier that year four children had died across the Tennessee River in Morgan County. Another was killed in Lauderdale County in Northwest Alabama that year. All three tragic accidents were caused, at least in part, by faulty brakes, compounded by driver error. I discovered first that the Alabama law relating to school transportation was woefully weak. School bus safety was left basically to individual judgments of local school systems. All that was required to drive a school bus was to be 21 years old and possess a basic driver's license.

At the national level, studies were suggesting seat belts on school buses were impractical and costly. But it seemed to me and school transportation people I consulted that it could be critical to a driver's ability to retain control of a bus that had lost its brakes if he was buckled in with at least a lap belt. I learned that Alabama lacked standard inspection and driver training programs and 25% of the local systems lacked persons assigned as transportation supervisors. Early in the regular session of 1969 I called a person I had learned was among the South's most knowledgeable persons regarding school bus safety issues. When I was in college at Florence State College Dr. Houston Cole was President of our arch rival in football, Jacksonville State College. I called him in Johnson City, Tennessee, where he had become President of East Tennessee State College. He agreed not only to provide advice but to drive to Montgomery to meet with a small group of us, including those within the State Department of Education involved in student transportation. At that meeting we developed the framework of a comprehensive school bus safety bill that would become a national model. It would require regular inspections of school buses, especially focused on assuring reliable braking systems; special training and licensing for drivers; a requirement that all drivers must wear seatbelts while driving a school bus, and a requirement that each system have competent transportation supervisors. With the help of Senator Jack Giles of Huntsville, the Senate adopted the House-passed law.

When he signed it into law, Governor Albert Brewer described it as "the most progressive legislation on behalf of school-bus safety in the history of the state." The Legislature followed up by passing a resolution designating Act No 281 as the "Grainger School Bus Safety Act." I was deeply honored when I realized how few laws are named in honor of their author. Toward the end of his speech summarizing the Legislature's educational achievements, Governor Brewer paused, looked over at me in at my desk on the second row, and smiled. He told the Legislature and statewide television audience the comprehensive legislation would serve as a model for the entire country.

After fifty years of relatively safe school bus transportation, the words of the School Bus Safety Act continued to appear verbatim in Alabama's school transportation manuals. There had been "dramatic improvements" in safety over that period, Kevin Snowden, the Alabama Department of Education's program coordinator of transportation, reported in 2015. Interview with Kevin Snowden, August, 2015.

Ironically, the greatest blemish to that long run of school bus safety occurred in a catastrophic event in my home town of Huntsville in November, 2006. A Lee High student racing alongside a school bus, apparently distracted while playing kids games with students on the bus, clipped the contractor-operated city school bus on a city interstate connector. The collision caused the bus to swerve and go over the edge of the interstate. Four girls, riding in the first two rows, were killed. The driver was not wearing his legally-required seat belt. A three-year investigation by the National Highway Traffic Safety Administration determined that the teenage driver lost control of his car while attempting to pass the bus and his car veered into the bus. The out-of-control bus climbed the interstate guardrail, before plunging nose-first to the ground thirty feet below. In the months following the accident, the contractor was not retained by the city school system. My intent in requiring drivers to wear seat belts was that the drivers being securely in their seats would enhance the chances of their being able to retain control of buses in emergencies.

Governor Brewer, A Business Leader

I was proud to be a friend of Albert Brewer and a strong supporter in his campaigns for governor in 1970 and 1978. For three years after he ascended to the position following the death from cancer of Governor Lurleen B. Wallace in 1967 he provided professional, dedicated, positive leadership that had been lacking for so long in Alabama. The 1969 Legislature was known as "the education Legislature" and Brewer took pride in being a full-time governor. He presented a positive face of Alabama leadership to the rest of the nation, the only opportunity since Ryan deGraffenried's fatal airplane crash in 1966.

His bitterness after the election when former Governor George Wallace ran the dirtiest campaign in Alabama history against his former ally was apparent. Wallace won decisively in the runoff. That disappointment clearly carried over to Brewer's unsuccessful campaign in 1978. As his primary fund-raiser in North Alabama I observed first-hand a candidate reluctant to campaign among people, such as going with his campaign workers to the Madison County Cattle Auction. For many years we continued to be friends, seeing each other occasionally. Once he called and I agreed to serve on the Alabama Public Affairs Council, a think-tank bipartisan organization, he was chairing while teaching law in Birmingham. But over time we were in separate orbits, which did not prepare me for the man he became in old age.

I was surprised and disappointed with the new Albert Brewer who in the 2000s blew me off at a wedding in Huntsville. When I happily greeted him, he mumbled something about my son being "mixed up with all those Republicans." That meant he had become a deeply partisan Democrat with no patience for other views. He must have hastily read a newspaper article that led him to conclude that my son Chuck was advocating Republican politics when he was fired as chief counsel of the Secretary of State's office. Actually Charles E. (Chuck) Grainger Jr., a 17-year state employee serving in a non-partisan, career position, was fired in 2003 by the newly-elected Democratic Secretary of State, Nancy Worley, because he refused to advise her that her efforts to fire another employee were legal. Grainger testified at a Personnel hearing that the day he was fired he formally removed himself as legal counsel advising Worley regarding her layoff plan, because the Alabama Bar Association advised him to recuse himself because he would be covered personally by the decision. He testified Worley indicated his job was at risk if he didn't provide her with a legal basis to fire the head of Office of Voter Registration. Worley claimed she was joking when she said Chuck Grainger's job was at risk. Associated Press. "Worley's former lawyer fighting to get job back." The Decatur Daily. March 30, 2004.

The state later paid Chuck $50,000 in a settlement after he sued her for illegal layoff tactics and for instituting policies that violated employees' religious freedom. While he went on to establish a law firm specializing in business law in Montgomery his former boss failed to impress. She was defeated seeking reelection for a second term. One of the issues voters appeared to remember was her greed in purchasing a luxury SUV at tax-payers' expense for her own use at a time when her budget had been cut back so deeply, she was forced to lay off employees. Worley was indicted by a Montgomery County grand jury in 2007 on charges of shaking down her employees for financial support during her unsuccessful re-election campaign in 2006. In 2012, she pleaded guilty of a misdemeanor count and paid a small fine. She then served two years as head of the Alabama Education Association, which by then had become an active union, with all the money that came from automatic dues checkoff, and was viewed as an unofficial arm of the increasingly liberal State Democratic Party. She was elected to lead the Alabama Democratic Party in 2015. Her Christmas message to her membership and political followers that year included a long-winded tale that drew attention to her large size. Scher, Brent. Washington Free-Beacon. "Alabama Dem Chair Got Stuck on Her Toilet, Told Everybody About it for Christmas" January 8, 2015." Whitmire, Kyle. AL.Com. "In holiday message, Alabama Democratic Party chair describes getting stuck on the toilet," January 06, 2015

VP Humphrey Flies to Town
on My Birthday in 1967

Vice President Hubert H. Humphrey flew all the way to Huntsville, Alabama on May 22, 1967 to wish me a happy thirtieth birthday. Not really. As head of the National Aeronautics and Space Council, he actually came at the request of Alabama Senator John Sparkman to review future plans with managers of the NASA/Marshall Space Flight Center and to attend a community dinner tribute that evening. At Sparkman's suggestion, Humphrey's staff called to ask me to coordinate the visit.

An overflow dinner crowd attended, enthused by Humphrey's optimistic approach to issues. Here was the Minneapolis mayor who led the successful fight at the 1948 Democratic convention to insert a plank in the platform that demanded civil rights for African Americans, including the abolition of state poll taxes in federal elections, an anti-lynching law, and desegregation of the armed forces. Alabama Governor Jim Folsom and future Governor George Wallace were two of the few Southerners who stayed in the convention hall when the issue erupted. Half the Alabama delegation and all of the Mississippi delegation walked out in protest. Alabama electors that year supported a Dixiecrat ticket headed by South Carolina Senator Strom Thurmond. I remembered as an eleven-year-old hearing my dad and granddad complaining that they were unable to vote for President Harry Truman because the Dixiecrat ticket had replaced Truman electors on the Alabama ballot.

When the Vice President visited Huntsville, none were seeing him as a liberal Devil incarnate. This audience had accepted integration earlier that decade. Without directly differing with President Lyndon Johnson, Vice President Humphrey extolled the virtues of adequately financing the space program, just two years before Americans began landing on the moon. Two years earlier, Johnson and Congress were asking NASA, "What can we do for you." Now they were asking NASA managers how they could get by with less in order to pay for an unpopular war in Viet Nam and costly Great Society social programs. Dethloff, Henry C Suddenly, Tomorrow Came: The NASA History of the Johnson Space Center. 2012, Dover Publications, p.191;

To the surprise of our dinner attendees, HHH did not look like the round-faced, Humpty-Dumpty-type character they had seen on television. He was taller, slimmer, rather handsome, exuding contagious happiness. After the dinner, the Vice President learned that we were celebrating my birthday in the restaurant downstairs and dropped by our group's table to offer his congratulations and appreciation for our hospitality.

Legislative Experience Helps Avoid Opposition After First Term

I experienced the most exhilarating experience all office-holders can hope to wish for: I was unopposed in my bid for election to a second term, this time for four years, in 1970. I went to political rallies with a broad smile and message of appreciation for the honor, in a speech brief in its content for that era.

I fared better than the Legislature as a whole, which wound up being ranked 50th among 50 Legislatures by a national citizen's group due to its lack of independence from the executive branch and lack of space and resources. The Senate suffered a scandal when a Fraternal Order of Police lobbyist accused a Senator from Prattville of soliciting a bribe for his support of a law enforcement bill. He was forced to resign his seat but was ultimately acquitted of the charges. This would kindle the desire for an ethics law to govern the behavior of legislators and lobbyists.

Author and Mary at his desk, listen to Governor
Albert Brewer address, 1969.

The Legislature also failed to pass an air pollution control bill at a
time when Birmingham residents were complaining loudly about
soot and smog from coal and steel industries. I could identify with
the smoggy surroundings seven years earlier when I worked for the
Birmingham News. Reporters wore suits, ties, and starched white
shirts. Every evening when I drove across Red Mountain to return to
my little house in Cahaba Heights, I arrived home with my starched
white shirt collar blanketed in black soot. With that in mind, I
became a leader in the fight for a far-reaching consumer dominated,
air pollution control bill in the next term of the Legislature. On
the positive side, that Legislature responded to Governor Brewer's
ambitious education initiative by passing perhaps the greatest
education reform packages ever passed in the state. State support
was increased in numerous areas, teachers' pay was raised in line

with other Southeastern states, and an Alabama Commission for Higher Education established.

In 1969, our legislative delegation and community leaders realized that the University of Huntsville campus, which was proudly labeled the "MIT of the South," was rapidly progressing in spite of limited support from the main campus in Tuscaloosa. When funding increases intended by the Governor and Legislature for research programs at UAH were rerouted to Tuscaloosa programs, the Madison County legislative delegation met with Huntsville Chamber of Commerce and economic development leaders to discuss alternatives. Strong arguments were made for the Huntsville campus to declare its independence from the University of Alabama system. On a 13-12 straw vote, the group voted to recommend to our legislative delegation that we remain a part of the U-A System. I thought it best to remain in the U-A system and took the lead to assure that cooperation. In the next session of the legislature, I was a member of the powerful Ways and Means Committee, and the the newly-independent Legislature had begun a process of earmarking appropriations. Later that year UAH was made an autonomous university by the Board of Trustees of the University of Alabama. Occurring within weeks of the moon landing in July of that year, 1969 was a momentous year for Huntsville.

Nationally, a growing desire by legislators to increase the effectiveness of their legislative bodies had led to the creation of a bipartisan National Conference of State Legislatures. The group set out to evaluate deficiencies in operations, procedures, and independence in the 50 legislatures. Alabama ranked 50th, based on the Conference's ratings of functions, accountability, and independence. In Alabama we looked for ways to correct the most glaring deficiencies that frustrated conscientious members, beginning with autocratic leadership of the House and dominance by the executive branch. *Strengthening the States: Essays on Legislative Reform*, 1971—Donald G. Rosenthal, (ed), Alan Herzberg, (author)

Toward the end of the 1969 session we created a Legislative Reform Study Committee, chaired by reform-minded Senator Richard Dominick of Birmingham. Serious and hardworking, Dominick himself was a product of legislative reapportionment. Court-ordered reapportionment had increased the number of senators representing Jefferson County, the state's most populous county, from a single Senator to seven. The county's Senate representation jumped from one-35th to one-fifth. Reapportionment set in motion the change to a more independent Legislature in 1971 when we began finding ways to improve the process. By far the most important step forward was to change Speakers to someone less blatantly autocratic than Rankin Fite. This was essential to Alabama having its first House in memory that would be independent of control by Governor George Wallace's Executive branch.

CHAPTER 5

The Soaring Seventies

The 1970s was widely known as a troubled time in American history. Richard Nixon's presidency was fatally flawed by Watergate, the scandal leading to his resignation short of his second term.

The Vietnam War took until mid-seventies to end. In the wake came the election of a Southerner whose campaign slogan contained the simple promise: "I'll never tell you a lie." Jimmy Carter was liked by Mary and me when we each served as Carter delegates at the Democratic Convention.

In Alabama, we gained legislative independence. I ended one career, moved up the ladder in another.

Experienced Legislator Takes Control

Our delegation chairman referred to me as "the best man I have" when people asked Harry Pennington how I was doing in my first term. That was because he welcomed a member who would pitch in and provide the grunt work required for passage of routine legislation.

Author delivers speech in House, 1973

As the 1970s dawned, I then experienced the most exhilarating experience all office-holders wish for: I was unopposed in my bid for election to a second term, this time for four years, in 1970. I went to political rallies with a broad smile and short message of appreciation for the honor. I kept the speeches short and smiled a lot. The crowd invariably applauded loudly with approval.

I was elected chairman of the five-member Madison County delegation. Pennington, who lost the Senate election to Gene McLain, was appointed chief of staff by Gov. Wallace later in the administration. McLain and I, representing Pennington's home county, happily gave the vote of approval to the veteran lawmaker when called to Montgomery.

Author leaves Capital, 1973.
Photo by Tommy Giles

Author receives Distinguished Alumnus Award from
UAH President Ben Graves. Senator John Sparkman,
left, and Congressman Bob Jones observe.

I became a leader in the fight for a far-reaching consumer dominated, air pollution control bill. The Legislature also responded to Governor Brewer's ambitious education initiative by passing perhaps the greatest education reform packages ever passed in the state. State support was increased in numerous areas, teachers' pay was raised in line with other Southeastern states, and an Alabama Commission for Higher Education was established.

Sex Scandal Hits Legislature
Shortly After Session Ends

A few days after that session had ended in 1969, the Legislature dodged widespread embarrassment when only one newspaper in

160

the state chose to print a front-page article about a so-called "sex scandal" at the capitol. The *Birmingham Post-Herald* reported under a one column headline midway down the page that Montgomery police arrested a teenage assistant House clerk for allegedly soliciting male customers at the Holiday Inn near the capitol. I was not a guilty member. Though I'll be the first to add, I did commit the sin of lust when she would utter tantalizing words when she was serving coffee or running errands.

She looked a lot older than the 15 she turned out to be when she was arrested on solicitation charges. And she was gorgeous. Thinking it would help get her out of her predicament, the young lady reportedly gave the authorities a list of married legislators she claimed she had dated during the legislative session. I knew she was telling the truth because a member of our delegation who had succumbed to her temptations told me about it when it was going on. And he knew close to a dozen other married men whose names he rattled off to me that went out with her.

I could not recall a member who lost his seat because of that specifically. However, several were voted out because they had not worked hard enough or the voters voted against them because, for whatever reason, they wanted to try a different model.

This, of course, was in an era preceding the Watergate scandal where investigative reporting by two *Washington Post* reporters helped force President Nixon to resign. The fame it brought the reporters, including a popular movie glamorizing their role, led to aggressive media reporting in future decades.

America Wins the Race to the Moon

America won the race to put a man on the moon, fulfilling Wernher von Braun's childhood dream and President Kennedy's challenge for men to land on the moon, then return safely to Earth, during the decade of the Sixties. On July 20, 1969, Commander Neil

Von Braun speaks to farewell crowd at Huntsville "Splashdown" before transferring to Washington. Governor Brewer and author applaud.

Armstrong became the first man to step on the surface of the moon, uttering the historic words, "That's one small step for a man, one giant leap for mankind."

Von Braun rode on the shoulders of Huntsville officials at a community Apollo 11 "Splashdown celebration" on July 24, 1969. I sat beaming with Governor Brewer and others on the Courthouse platform at the Courthouse. The following week, the Legislature hosted a victory speech by the space pioneer. I was in the honor guard that escorted him into the House chamber. As he had done in his historic speech to that body in 1961 that launched UAH's research institute, von Braun mesmerized the legislators by citing "the enormous implications of the lunar journey...we are reaching out in the name of peace...and while we take pride in this

American achievement we share it in genuine brotherhood with all nations and all people." In his office, I presented him with the Legislature's resolution honoring the achievement. Hanging in my office still today there is a picture of the adjective-filled tribute. He signed it with the words, *"To Representative Grainger, with grateful appreciation for the resolution you introduced."* Wernher *von Braun.*

NASA leaders convinced von Braun to transfer to NASA Headquarters in Washington to chart a future course for post-lunar space in 1970. In a downtown farewell celebration, he provided these words of inspiration to the citizens of his adopted city: "My friends, there was dancing in the streets of Huntsville when our first satellite orbited the earth. There was dancing again when the first Americans landed on the moon. I'd like to ask you, don't hang up your dancing slippers." R. J. (Bob) Ward, *Dr. Space, The Life of Wernher von Braun*. Naval Institute Press, 2005.

Wallace and the Independent Legislature

The first stage of the transformation of American state legislatures toward more independence and improved efficiency had begun. It was precipitated by the reapportionment revolution, the decisions by the U.S. Supreme Court in *Baker v. Carr* (1962) and *Reynolds v. Sims* (1964). Legislative districts were redrawn on the basis of population to conform as closely as possible to the "one person, one vote ideal." *Reynolds* was brought about as a result of the suit filed by young lawyers in Jefferson County.

Governor George Wallace with Senator Ted Kennedy at Decatur
July Fourth celebration while author looks on, 1973.

Speaker Fite's raw use of power was sometimes comical, at least to those of his cronies who were not particularly serious about passing legislation. His loyalists were mostly pro-Wallace members from rural areas. Frequently the Speaker would avoid using his gavel to permit noise and confusion to envelope the chamber early in the day. Out of that melee few noticed when a slow-talking legislator on the back row of the east side rose and quietly requested recognition from his desk. "Mr. Speakah, av've been looking out the winder and I see a bad storm coming. It's time we went home. I move we adjourn." Before most members understood the motion, the Speaker called for a voice vote, then rammed through the motion with a thundering blow of the gavel. After this happened a few times we were on the lookout for that member's motions, making sure to shout "no" louder than the "ayes." But the Speaker always ruled that the "ayes" had prevailed and the session was adjourned.

His favorite tactic was to ridicule and to embarrass his opponents---to the merriment of his good 'ol boy gang. I remembered that during the time I was in college, Fite and two of his colleagues from Northwest Alabama had slipped through the House a bill of local application that abolished my home county of Colbert. That's right, they abolished the county. The bill introduced by the member from Franklin repealed an act in the late 1800s. It was the act that had originally peeled off a section of Franklin and created Colbert. Of course, our member had not read it. No one read local bills from other counties. But the Speaker and his cohorts had a merry old time at the expense of our legislator. The local newspaper gave it a headline as though it was serious and made a hero out of our Senator for killing the bill to repeal our county. The senator, of course, was a part of the plot. He had moved to Colbert after growing up in Fite's county of Marion and after his one term in the Senate he sat by Fite on the throne when he was Speaker and served as his primary arm-twister threatening us reluctant legislators. Our legislator from Colbert, the member who that year responded to my request to offer a bill to change the names of Alabama's teacher's colleges, was not reelected the next time around. He was not the first victim of the Speaker's effective use of humor.

By far the most important step forward was to change Speakers to someone less blatantly autocratic than Rankin Fite. This was essential to Alabama having its first House in memory that would be independent of control by Governor George Wallace's Executive branch. To prepare new members in advance for the regular session, we instituted the practice of holding a new member orientation conference for all members before the beginning of the regular session. The first conference, in late 1970, turned into an opportunity for reform-minded legislators to begin laying plans to bring independence to the House.

As the time in January neared for the Legislature to organize itself, Wallace was hearing from some veteran members and numerous freshmen that he needed to take seriously the Legislature's desire for legislative reform. Always quick to sense political change in the making, Wallace anxiously raced to the front of the parade by announcing his support for legislative independence at a press conference. He communicated directly to legislators an open invitation for legislators to have "walk-in" privileges to meet with him on short notice, without an appointment if necessary. Few believed he really meant it, while some saw it as a way for him to let someone else do the heavy lifting while he focused on the more important challenge of running for President. He would demonstrate in many ways during the next four years that his interest in affairs of state was far exceeded by his hunger to campaign and deliver fiery speeches.

Wallace leaders reluctantly bowed to the independent Legislature movement as a majority of us serving on the tax-writing and budget-appropriating Ways and Means Committee began offering amendments to the Administration budget that earmarked appropriations bills, rather than leaving them to the governor to selectively dole out funding based on his own priorities. Or in the case of universities, still unhappy with University of Alabama leadership maneuver in 1969 that captured for the main campus funding intended for the University of Alabama in Huntsville we specifically earmarked UAH funding for the next four years.

In the 1971 session, members of the Ways and Means Committee divided up the package of bills the Governor's office had sent upstairs to be introduced. I was asked to offer a bill requesting $10 million for junior colleges and Alabama's two traditionally black universities. One of the those, Alabama A&M University, is in Huntsville. Wallace always supported A&M and Alabama State in Montgomery because their presidents had long ago learned that he had a soft spot for support from pro-Wallace presidents of predominantly black colleges. That had begun when he was a freshman legislator himself, introducing bills providing funding for all-black Tuskegee University. Customarily, when a funding bill like this was enacted the Governor would allocate the funding, showing a strong preference to those institutions whose presidents were his political friends. It hit me quickly that since it was an Administration bill, I needed to ask Governor Wallace for his priority list.

When we met in his office, Wallace was gracious, but he declined the request to provide his priorities for allocation of the funds. "No, Cholly, you earmark the money," Wallace said. He had the Finance Director there to witness the conversation.

"But Governor, this is your bill. I am handling it because I am on the committee and have a traditionally black university in my county. These institutions are accustomed to you deciding the priorities for your bills."

When it became apparent that he was serious I told him I would instead ask the State Superintendent of Education to construct a priority list based on need. "That sounds good. You go ahead, Cholly, and if any of the college presidents pushes back you tell them you have my support." I wondered if he was being serious, delegating such a responsibility to a legislator who had joked with him and befriended over several years but who was never willing to support his racist politics. I later concluded George Wallace realized the Legislature was going to earmark the distribution of the funding anyway and he simply didn't want to get that involved. And something told me in his manner that he trusted me to do the right thing. The meeting with the Junior College Presidents was memorable. Most of them had been appointed due to their allegiance to Wallace. When I went down the list of proposed allocations the State Superintendent had developed based on need, not politics, the President of Baldwin State Junior College in South Alabama exploded.

"You can't do this!" he bellowed. "I'm going to see the Governor right now and straighten this out."

I had prepared for that response. "Please go on over and see the Governor as soon as possible," I said. "I am confident he will tell you what he told me. And after that please communicate with the rest of this group because Ways and Means is meeting at 10 tomorrow morning. Be sure to explain to your legislators that your school may not get everything you expected, but it will just get worse if this bill dies this year." The junior college and trade school leaders responded quickly. The bill was approved unanimously the next day. It ultimately became law.

In 1973, Wallace had become the front-runner in the Maryland Democratic presidential primary, when he was shot four times at close range at a campaign rally in Laurel. He became a wheel-chair bound paraplegic, and ultimately abandoned his Presidential aspirations. His interest in gubernatorial duties, already declining before the shooting, nose-dived afterwards.

During the next four years state issues became more compelling and Wallace was increasingly focused on running for President. As complex issues such as federal court involvement in property taxes emerged, it became convenient for him to yield to the reformers, letting the new "independent Legislature" have several of those responsibilities. After he was grievously wounded, Wallace lacked the strength and motivation to provide significant leadership in the 1973 legislative session.

Alabama Legislature Takes Lead in Pollution Control

In the period leading up to the 1971 session of the Alabama Legislature, I worked on a House-Senate interim committee that wrote the comprehensive air pollution law proposed by a small coalition of members.

While the state board controlling such standards had been dominated by polluting industries, our bill excluded membership from polluting industries. Our bill prevailed in the House after we successfully tabled a weaker bill offered on behalf of the Associated Industries of Alabama that would have continued representation on the board by polluting industries and would have prohibited citizen law suits. The competing bill was offered by Rep. Joe McCorquedale of rural Clarke County in southwest Alabama, a silver-tongued orator and Wallace floor leader. He implied that Governor Wallace supported his bill.

"No," I said from the proponents' microphone. "Governor Wallace stood right here at this microphone yesterday and told a press conference he would sign the strongest air and water pollution control bills the Legislature sends to his desk. Ours is clearly the strongest bill. Therefore, he favors our bill." House members howled with laughter as McCorquedale changed the subject. – Casson, Barbara, "House Oks Strong Pollution Bill," *the Birmingham Post Herald*, July 28, 1971.

The Clean Air Commission created by the act later selected me as the recipient of the Governor's Air Pollution Control Award. In presenting the award, Governor Wallace noted that I had also sponsored the supplemental appropriations bill providing funding to enforce the law and a separate bill to establish salaries for environmental health workers, which would permit the agency to recruit and retain highly qualified personnel. --"Alabama Air Pollution Control Commission, Legislator and Businessman Receive Governor's Air Pollution Control Awards," The Sunburst, November-December 1973.

I had tapped John Daniels, the young lawyer who provided the legal expertise in the preparation of the clean air bill, to use his brilliant drafting skills to finalize the water pollution control bill I introduced in the House.

Congressman Bob Jones also made it possible for me to draw from the small army of experts working in Congress on what would become the Jones-sponsored monumental federal Clean Water Act of 1972. It, like the federal Clean Air Act of 1970, was the product of a bi-partisan Congressional coalition at a time when members of opposing parties often worked together to address significant national issues.

In the committee process, I brought the Alabama Wildlife Federation, Alabama Conservancy, and Bass Angers Sportsman's Society before the Conservation committee for testimony. They made it clear which of the two bills being considered by the Legislature was favored by clean water proponents.

When the Senate took up clean water bills before we could get it to the top of the House calendar, Senator Aubrey Carr of Guntersville, the center of some of the most beautiful lakes in America, offered my House bill as a substitute for a weaker Senate bill. Through his skillful efforts it passed the Senate first, then easily cleared the House after we beat down a bill drafted by the AIA which its sponsor had difficulty explaining.

While the bill was on its way to the Governor for his signature, Senator Carr offered a resolution in the Senate designating the bill as the "Grainger Water Pollution Control Act" which was passed by both houses. It could have been aptly named after Carr as well. His role in its passage was critical.

When he signed it into law Wallace described the bill as "a strong, sound bill---one of the finest in the nation." Pointing out that the law prohibited representatives of polluting industries from serving on the board, Wallace said, "This will mean that the people of this state can be confident that they will be represented on the commission by persons without conflicts of interest, people who are capable of making impartial decisions." Because of the passage of the clean air and water bills and other conservation measures, Wallace said "this Legislature has distinguished itself as one of the most conservation-minded legislatures in the history of the state."

One afternoon in 1973 when several wives were in town for the legislative session, incompatibility, as the basis for divorce, was brought up for a vote in the House. Previously, one side in a divorce case was required to prove mental or physical cruelty. Changing the law to avoid the need to find the innocence or guilt of either party---a no-fault divorce---, and can be based on "incompatibility" of the parties without proving one spouse is at fault. I was in the balcony talking to visitors from home. Often times members would reach across to click the yes or no vote on a member's voting machine when a member was in the chamber and signaled a thumb up or down for yes or no. Mary was sitting at my desk on the House floor. I signaled a thumb up, and she voted to send it on its way to the Senate and the Governor to join other states with no-fault divorce laws. I jokingly told my visitors that I hoped I would not live to regret allowing my spouse to make it easier to file for a divorce in Alabama.

Seizing Control of the Money Committee

While we had taken a major step forward toward legislative independence, legislative leaders continued to be appointed by the Wallace-backed Speaker of the House. As the senior member of the delegation from Madison County, the third largest delegation in the state, I had been one of 15 members appointed to the powerful Ways and Means Committee. Wallace loyalists served as chairman and vice chairman of the committee. Joined by the former speaker

Rankin Fite, they had only three votes but controlled the flow of legislation. In the 1971 session they pushed projects to their home counties while the rest of us, the committee majority, fumed over how little we had to show for being on the Legislature's most powerful committee.

One afternoon I was in Birmingham for a meeting when I called my good friend, Jabo Waggoner, to invite him to meet me at my hotel for a refreshment. "Jabo," I began, "are you satisfied with the level of funding you are getting for the University of Alabama in Birmingham? Or anything else in your county?" Our chairman, Pete Mathews had gotten so much for his university at Jacksonville that they named the baseball field in his honor. "Hell, no, I am not satisfied," Jabo answered. And Jabo was a loyal Wallace supporter. "I have been doing the math," I said, "and 12 of us on the committee, practically all of whom are Wallace supporters, are being dominated by the committee chairman, vice chairman, and Rankin Fite in spite of the fact that we are in the majority."

We called Tom Stubbs of neighboring Shelby County, another member who had gone on the road to campaign nationally for Wallace. He met us at a restaurant in Hoover. The three of us developed a concept to gain majority control of the committee. It would take courage and commitment but we believed others on the committee would see it our way. We assure a majority on issues important to our group by asking each member to identify a priority that he wanted in that session, then the rest of us would agree to vote to make it happen during that legislative session. The next week in Montgomery we developed the plan further, agreeing to meet each week on Tuesday evenings in the room of a freshman member from Coffee County to plan for the Wednesday committee meetings. We agreed to work together on issues important to any of us. Coordination would be critical. The group, now up to 11, chose me as the group's chairman. We agreed that if issues came up that required caucusing, I would move to recess---regardless of the time of day.

The opportunity came soon when the committee bogged down in a debate over local vs. state control of mental health programs. A Huntsville group was making the case for the local initiative versus the budget proposed by the governor. I saw we were about to deadlock and moved to recess. That surprised the chairman, who had always unilaterally determined when the committee recessed or adjourned. The chairman and vice chairman were livid. When we returned, they had gotten the Speaker to sit on the front row next to the committee dais. If anyone thought this was going to be easy, they could now see that we were playing with fire. This was the first time the speaker had ever attended a committee meeting. It was a clear threat that he was considering removing the dissident majority from the committee. We were betting he would not risk taking on that many of us. The chairman was white-faced as he lectured us about our irresponsibility. The Speaker sat with a disapproving look on his face when he attended our committee meeting the next time we met. If he was about to take our committee appointments away, he didn't say so to any of the young mavericks on the committee. In retrospect, he probably calculated that as too much of a gamble. And he sat there while we voted, in an attempt to sway our votes. So, he didn't try any severe retribution against any. If he had chosen to do so I, as the chief organizer of the rebels, would be the first member punished.

The hard part came when the appropriations bill was brought to the floor. The committee chairman summarized the bill as was customary. Then he shocked me by recognizing "the gentleman from Madison to explain the committee amendments to the bill." It caught me utterly by surprise. After I caught my breath, I stumbled down to the microphone with a panic stricken look on my face. The price of leadership or some would say, the Wallace Administration's punishment for crossing them. The clerk passed a copy of the bill over to me. I gradually collected my wits and began explaining the bill. I talked rather rapidly in explaining the justification for the $1 million conditional appropriation for the University of Alabama in Huntsville, Jabo Waggoner's $600,000 for the UAB nursing school, Doug Easter's $300,000 for the Elba Airport, and down the line.

While I was explaining that the UAH appropriation was based on its growth, a large threatening figure came up from behind and bumped me. He literally bumped me with his shoulder while I was standing at the microphone speaking to the entire House. My tormentor was a racist bully, a former outstanding football player from Jacksonville State and a legislator in his second term, Rep. Ray Burgess. Burgess must have thought our university was getting money that could have gone to his university. He must not have realized that the chairman of Ways and Means was vice chairman of that university board of directors. "You SOB," he growled. Just loud enough for me to hear, and not loud enough to be heard by other members. "You need to worry about what I will do to you." I could almost see the steam rising from between his angry jaws. It was unimaginable, a member threatening another while he was addressing the House. Yes, he was an angry racist and a Wallace administration stalwart supporter.

He was better known for what happened a few days later. As a newly-elected black member, Rep. Thomas Reed, approached the microphone, the bully took the microphone opposite. Reed was one of two blacks who had recently been elected from Tuskegee County, home of the predominantly black Tuskegee University. They were the first since the Reconstruction period after the Civil War to win election to the state's lawmaking body. I don't recall now what the issue was that was being challenged but Reed won the debate with humor. He made reference to Burgess' opposition, by saying when they finally agreed upon a point, that they were drinking out of the same dipper. After that they had several other exchanges at the microphones, all after other references to what they were drinking from, when old-fashioned laughter raced across the floor of the chamber.

Burgess' life came to a tragic end a few years later when in a moment of rage against his wife she shot him in an eye. He laid at the point of death for several days before succumbing. Authorities concluded her act was in self-defense and no charges were placed. Reed also met with an unhappy career ending a few years later. He was convicted and served a brief term in prison and blamed his prosecution on his efforts to bring down the confederate flag as a symbol of what the NAACP, which he chaired, opposed so strongly. He was able after serving a brief sentence to be reelected to the State Legislature.

Ending of Political Career, Acceleration of Another

At the age of 36 I became an elder statesman, which is to say I lost the 1974 election to the Alabama State Senate. Forget my dream of being elected to the U.S. Congress. I had missed that train. The political express would reboard just two years later when our powerful Congressman, Bob Jones, retired after 28 years in office. One had to be at the peak of his/her career to be in the right place and right time to be elected to Congress. Like every two decades or so. So, wrong timing for me. End of six-year career as an officeholder.

Afterwards I ultimately found the bright side from a career perspective. The new turn in my career meant I could get off the breathtaking merry go round of public office to spend more time with my lovely wife, two adolescent sons, and precocious four-year-old daughter who thought daddies spent most of their time going to meetings. And I could devote full time to my job at Teledyne Brown, which with me focused on it would grow from a Directorship to a Vice Presidency in four years. That position included a myriad of managerial responsibilities, the most important continuing to handle the company's governmental relations. That meant I interfaced with Congress on a regular basis, focusing on increasing funding for Redstone Arsenal's space and defense activities. A portion of my responsibility included union prevention. I first insisted on managers following the Golden Rule in dealing with employees. Treat others as you would have them treat you.

Supporting Missile Defense

I spent the vast majority of my 36 years in management at Teledyne Brown Engineering in company operations, day to day leadership over the administrative elements of the company. The Human Resources Department recruited, then managed the compensation and benefits resources to help retain world class systems engineers and analysts. Our facilities department maintained the modern buildings in Huntsville and at facilities in Colorado, Florida, Virginia, and Tennessee. We constructed eight major buildings totaling more than one million square feet in those three decades.

No doubt of greater value to the company was my role in business development, government relations, and strategic planning. Over those years I worked closely with high-level government customers to help make the case to Congress for their programs. In the Sixties we had built the company primarily as one of the space program's key contractors, along with limited involvement in the U.S. missile programs. From the early Seventies we had been the key technical supporter for the Army's role in the missile defense program. We had targeted and recruited a key staff of senior engineers from Bell Telephone Laboratories after its corporate board decided to focus on commercial telecommunications and depart from the government contractor field. TBE won a stiff competition to become Bell's successor as the Systems Engineering and Technical Assistance Contractor (SETAC). We recompeted and won that contract every five years or so a half-dozen times. In that role we served basically as a technical extension of the government in all aspects of missile defense.

Throughout the late Seventies and early Eighties, we worked closely with the Alabama Congressional Delegation on behalf of the Army Ballistic Missile Defense Organization to avoid efforts to starve missile defense's budgets. William A. Davis, chief civilian in that agency, usually accompanied me to Washington for these meetings.

President Ronald W. Reagan desired a strategic alternative to the national security policy of nuclear deterrence and mutual assured destruction that left America defenseless against Soviet missile attacks. Our land-based ICBMs were growing more vulnerable to a Soviet first strike, and under President Carter our military was unable to satisfactorily field an upgraded missile. President Reagan launched a major new program in 1983, which he called the Strategic Defense Initiative (SDI), to determine whether or not missile defenses were technically feasible. The day after Reagan announced his plan in a national speech, the Senate's leading liberal, Senator Edward M. Kennedy of Massachusetts, labeled the speech as "reckless Star Wars schemes." SDI became widely identified thereafter as "Star Wars.". Initiated at the height of the cold war tensions, SDI played a significant role in the events that led to the end of the cold war nuclear confrontation. The Star Wars program confronted the Soviet Union with the prospect of a strategic competition in a new area, one that would require enormous Soviet expenditures to counter the threat of the technologies in which the United States was thought to be well ahead. In December 1991, the Soviet Union was dissolved.

With Best Wishes
to Charles Grainger

President Jimmy Carter greets author at White
House event honoring delegates, 1979.

Saving Money in the Costs of Health Care

I was still interested in serving the public in whatever capacity I could when I left the Legislature. While waiting for an appointment with my doctor who was also a golfing buddy, I began checking my watch. "Gosh, it's taking a long time!" I thought. I finally began converting my waiting wait into the time it was taking away from me. It takes time to save money in the health care business, I concluded.

"Time---lots of it---may be a key factor in getting on the boards that make a difference. They are right where you live. To combat rising health costs required involvement. Not only did I become involved, I served in capacities that led me to become knowledgeable in the field. This was in the early 1970s. By the middle of the decade, I had served in succession as Chairman of the following boards, all with active volunteers willing to drive the miles and spend the time necessary to make a difference: the North Alabama Experimental Health Services Delivery System, the North Alabama Appalachian Health Delivery Health Development Agency, and, most important the 12-county North Alabama Health Systems Agency.

The Alabama Hospital Association invited me and three other health care consumers to go to Great Britain to contrast their systems with ours. After ten days of looking into their system I heard the Queen delivering Margaret Thatcher's acceptance of the position of British Prime Minister on the radio in the taxi on the way in. We found, in a word, the government to be the last agency capable of running such a program. *Tuscaloosa News*, May 31, 1979.

The extended stay in London enabled me to consolidate my thoughts into a bound volume 62-page document, complete with photos by Randy Quarles of the *Huntsville Times*, that was distributed to health care providers at all levels. The study was entitled, *"The British Health System: A Management Prospective."* It was submitted in partial fulfillment of the requirements for the degree in Master of Science in Management for the Southeastern Institute of Technology. The paper helped me compile the highest grade received by a graduating student that year.

As for my doctor and golfing buddy, he told me how to get in the back door to avoid the customary wait. The rest of the poor souls would just have to await their turn. In Great Britain you would have wait in "queue" up to two years to have hernia surgery.

CHAPTER **6**

The Golden Eighties

Some have identified the 1980s as the Golden Age, when Conservatives and President Ronald Reagan revived America's economy, reoriented its politics and restored Americans' faith in their country and themselves.

The Cold War, which dominated American thinking for more than a decade became past tense as more than one billion people found themselves free of domination. From the Berlin Wall in 1987, the Western cowboy challenged the Soviet leader with these words, "Mr. Gorbachev, tear down this wall." Central to the negotiations was his "Star Wars" plan which scared the hell out of the Russians. He led the nation to the most massive military buildup in history.

On its way to space station American saw a renewed interest in space. Then the program was interrupted by the accidental loss of six lives with the explosion that occurred to the Challenger in 1986. It would not fly again until the beginning of the next decade.

The U.S. Senate Election Following the Death of Jim Allen

The background to the election of 1980 involved a series of unexpected events. First was the sudden death in 1978 of U. S.

Senator James B. Allen, a conservative Democrat from Gadsden. Jim Allen served two terms as lieutenant governor and for ten years in the U.S. Senate. In both Montgomery and Washington, he was known as a master parliamentarian. He was reserved, a man of great integrity, all business, sincere, and, even though he was one of its most conservative members, highly regarded by both sides of the aisle. He used the filibuster often and effectively.

As was the case with his colleague and my longtime friend, Senator Howell Heflin, Jim Allen became knowledgeable and highly supportive of missile defense and other military programs. His keen strategic knowledge helped us over several hurdles. One year, the cantankerous old chairman of the Appropriations Defense subcommittee, Senator Milton Young of North Dakota, caught everyone off guard by unilaterally reducing the missile defense budget by $75 million, which represented a cut of almost one-third. It took our breath away in Huntsville, where missile defense originated and was headquartered. We had the pleasure to sit in the Senate gallery later that Summer to observe the genius at work as he calmly reasoned with the veteran chairman. Then they took opposing microphones and engaged in colloquy, a back and forth discussion designed to demonstrate Congressional intent. There was some mumbling that few could understand. Senator Allen looked up and smiled. That was when we knew it meant the funds would be restored. The words that appeared in that day's *Congressional Record* confirmed that Young would address the matter in Joint Conference.

I was among the overflow crowd of mourners from Congress across the state following Jim Allen's death from a heart attack. Some of Governor George Wallace's friends encouraged him to resign and have the lieutenant governor appoint him to succeed Senator Allen, but Allen's widow, Maryon, requested the appointment and Wallace complied.

After taking her Senate seat, Senator Maryon Allen decided to run for the remaining two years of her late husband's term. Wallace had eyed the seat but chose to defer to the widow of his friend. However, Mrs. Allen suffered serious damage to her public image after the *Washington Post* published a detailed interview with reporter Sally Quinn. Allen appeared in the article to be an aloof Washington insider, critical of George and Lurleen Wallace. Even though Senator Jim Allen had been one of my heroes I had never come to know Mrs. Allen. She was opposed in the Democratic primary by State Senator Donald W. Stewart, whom she called "a flaming liberal." Stewart won fairly easily.

Donald Stewart kept in touch during the campaign and called immediately after winning the general election in November, 1978. Would I meet him in Birmingham and fly up with him and give him the benefit of my experience on Capitol Hill to help him hit the ground running, he asked. His office gave me the number of the flight the next day. I reserved an adjoining seat and drove to Birmingham for the flight. In the terminal I heard my name being paged. Stewart's secretary was calling to say something had come up and for me to go ahead and he would meet me at Senator Allen's former office the next day.

When I met him at his office, he asked me to wait while he met with a delegation from Selma. Mayor Joe Smitherman led the delegation in for a meeting Stewart had arranged with the group and a high-level bureaucrat concerning a Selma problem. As I sat in the outer office Steward berated and shouted at the bureaucrat while I wondered how this brash young man would fare in such a challenging environment. The day wore on and Donald Steward never got around to inviting me in for the advice he had so eagerly sought. I wondered why he had made such a point of inviting me to hold his hand when Mr. Stewart went to Washington, but by this point it was becoming apparent that in his mind he needed no advice. So, I quietly departed. I maintained casual contact with him during his two-year term while he served with limited distinction and was defeated in the Democratic Primary by Jim Folsom, Jr. The Republican candidate was war hero Jeramiah Denton.

Even with the emotional support Denton's story engendered, Folsom still led by a comfortable margin five days before the election of 1982. At that point the Chairman of the Alabama Democratic Party stuck his foot in his mouth at a statewide conference in Huntsville. He faulted Denton for being shot down and captured. That story was on the front pages of Alabama newspapers throughout the weekend preceding the election. Denton upset Folsom by 50.2% to 47.1%. Denton then lost his reelection bid in 1986.

The Upward Path of Jim Folsom Jr.

While I had known his dad as a young newspaper reporter, I later came to be close friends for three decades with James E. Folsom Jr.

First, the background of our relationship. We first met in 1980 when he was 32, serving his first term as a member of the Alabama Public Service Commission, and running for the U.S. Senate against my former state House colleague, freshman U.S. Senator Donald Stewart of Anniston. "Little Jim" called when he came to Huntsville and we met for coffee. He had inherited the bashful, shy smile of his beautiful mother, was well over six feet tall, laid back, with a deep South accent even more pronounced than "Big Jim's." I wound up hosting two fundraisers for him. He defeated Stewart in the Primary but lost the general election to war hero Republican candidate, Jerimiah Denton.

Folsom's next race was for Lt. Governor, which he easily won. When Guy Hunt was forced to resign, Folsom became governor. Within six days after taking office Governor Folsom ordered the removal of the Confederate flag from the state capitol. In 1994, he ran for a full four-year term in his own right, but was narrowly defeated by former Democratic Governor Fob James, who was running as a Republican. Although some regarded Folsom as a popular Governor, he won only 54% of the vote in the Democratic primary, not enough to defeat James in the general election.

Underdog Shelby Challenges Senate Incumbent

Jeramiah Denton became the first Republican since Reconstruction to represent Alabama in the U.S. Senate, and the first Catholic to be elected to statewide office in Alabama. In the U.S. Senate, he compiled a solidly conservative voting record. His strong opposition to the Supreme Court ruling that permitted abortions led to billboards across the state with a couple looking surprised at a character peering at them over their blankets with the admonition, "Keep the Senator Out of Our Bedrooms."

In 1986, I dropped by the House office of my former legislative colleague, Congressman Richard Shelby of Tuscaloosa. He told me he had decided to run against Senator Denton. He went through his plan for the campaign in excruciating detail. Shelby concluded with, "I'm going to ambush him, you wait and see."

What an ambush it would turn out to be. Shelby was a popular conservative Democrat in his fourth term in the House but few thought anyone could beat Denton, the Viet Nam hero. The film for the Shelby commercial was with a home movie camera. A Shelby campaign aide photographed Denton at a town hall meeting responding to a question about why he rarely came back to Alabama. "What do you want me to do, spend my time patting babies on the butt?" was Denton's response. The "baby butt" segment became the centerpiece of a Shelby commercial about "Alabama's absentee senator." As the date for the general election neared Shelby was running out of campaign funds.

He and his wife, Annette, decided they had come too far to fall short now. They reached into their family savings and paid for the final days of television advertising. Denton was still favored on voting day. But late that night, after calling the election for Denton, Dan Rather of CBS ended election coverage at midnight

Chuck Grainger, left, makes point to Congressman
Ronnie Flippo, 1982 as author listens

with the words, "There may be a change developing in Alabama." I called Shelby at his Tuscaloosa headquarters at 2 a.m. for an update. "We're gonna whup him," Shelby exclaimed. "Nearly all of the votes that are still out are in my congressional district." When all the boxes had been counted, Shelby won by less than 7,000 votes (50.28%) of 1,211,897 votes.

Note to Joe Willie Namath

Dear Joe Willie,

The green and black reflections off the walls of the Birmingham Civic Center, like those that mirroring the cover of your autobiography, settled on your angular face with the Roman nose. Like you were eager to see us when you beckoned to us to stop and talk with you in a friendly manner. You looked down at her and said, "You have beautiful eyes." Whereupon, you tagged my blond-headed wife with a classic Namath kiss on the forehead. It was in 1981, when we were there for your induction into the Alabama Sports Hall of Fame.

I was there when it all started, me and another 60,000-plus fans at Legion Field in Birmingham. It was back in 1962. I was sitting up in the section that had been newly renovated due to a collapse from weather damage. I was a considerable fan of Alabama's Crimson Tide and eager to see you in your first season at the helm when the guys in the crimson jerseys would compete for a national title. The Tide was playing undefeated North Carolina State. The quarterback was Number 12, from tiny Beaver Falls, PA. You described how the monumental moment occurred in your life in your autobiography, *"All the Way,"* written by you in 2019: "North Carolina State was good, and we were both undefeated at that point. We shut them out 21-0, but I didn't have a lot to do with it. Steve Sloan, our junior quarterback, led the team to victory."

I was sitting up there proud as a new dad looking down at this redshirt freshman quarterback displaying his wears. "He looks like a young buck when he goes out on the option," I said, for the benefit of those around me.

"It was third-and-2", you wrote, in describing this major event in you young life. "We needed two yards to get a first down. I had called a run-pass option around the right end. I got the snap, started sprinting to my right, and when I planted my right foot to cut upfield to run for the first down, my right knee caved in. Boom. I just went down. And it hurt. I walked off the field with some help and stayed on the sidelines. My knee swelled and the trainers took my pants off and put the ice packs on. We went to the hospital right after the game...When we looked at my shoes afterward, the cleats on the edges were bent out in all directions, so I must have hit a hole or uneven spot...So I wound up hurting it three more times in practice, we just drained it and taped it for stability and got me onto the field so I could move around gingerly, still practicing plays until the swelling took me out...

"The last time it gave out was in 1965, before the Orange Bowl in Miami against the Texas Longhorns. As we were lined up for the national anthem Coach (Paul Bear) Bryant (had an assistant coach) asked me if I could play. "I said, 'I think so.' Starting quarterback Steve Sloan hurt his knee in the second half. We had been down but came back, and on the deciding play, one yard away from the winning touchdown, I called the quarterback sneak. I carried the ball, thought I'd crossed the plane, and the linesman on the right gave the touchdown signal. But the line judge on the right came running and said I hadn't. The officials conferred and the referee ruled no touchdown, Texas ball. If it had counted, we would have won (the game and national title)," you wrote.

"I suffered numerous knee injuries, requiring a number of knee surgeries over 13 years of being a pro quarterback. What if?" Well, you were not bad in spite of those injuries. Playing on three division champions, the New York Jets and Los Angeles Rams, you passed for a total of 27,663 yards. You attributed the game when you "guaranteed" victory in the biggest game of your career. No, nothing was greater than your taking your team to that 16-7 win in Super Bowl III.

You said in a recent book that you would probably be dead if you hadn't stopped drinking in 1973. By then you were drunk many mornings. You said you had two artificial knees, a new hip, and an abnormal-looking hamstring, the latter a result of a 1973 water skiing accident.

Sincerely, from one of your fondest admirers.

Charles Grainger

Namath, Joe Willie, with Schaap Dick. *I Can't Wait Until Tomorrow.* Random House, New York. NY., 1969. Namath, Joe and Shawn Coyne. *Namath.* Boothite Publishing. New York, NY Namath, Joe. *All the Way.* Little, Brown. And Co., New York, NY. 2019.

TBE Puts Space Hardware Counterfeiters Out of Business

Those who were watching CBS's "60 Minutes" in 1986, saw a segment about counterfeit bolts on NASA's Discovery. Another contractor, Teledyne Brown Engineering, had a quality control manager who caught the supplier using counterfeit bolts, like Inspector Clouseau, and got the the company convicted for claiming the parts had been tested when they had not been. TBE's quality control manager was Charlie Blass.

Author at TBE desk, 1989.

The culprit supplying the bogus hardware was a tiny California company, the low bidder. The incident resulted in Blass being commended for catching the company in the act. Astronaut Hoot Gibson did the honors. I tagged along to observe our company being so saluted. After all, CBS did not exaggerate the story, probably because I let them know that we were filming the interview.

Brown Engineering, Now a Part of Teledyne, Inc.

Teledyne Brown Engineering's proud history involves 65 years. Based in Huntsville, it grew to slightly over 3,300, when it was acquired by Teledyne, Inc. of Century City, California. This is a history of friendly and unfriendly acquisitions.

Henry Singleton, then 69 years old who had co-founded Teledyne in 1960, retired in 1989 as CEO. He turned the company leadership over to George Roberts. The two operated in tandem in leading the fast-growing company.

In late 1994, Teledyne was subjected to a hostile takeover attempt by WHX Corporation. This was successfully challenged, but the Teledyne pension fund had a surplus of $928 million and this was of wide interest. To forestall further hostile takeovers, Allegheny Ludlum, a steel and specialty metal firm, offered to serve as a white knight friendly acquirer. In 1996, an agreement was reached to merge Teledyne with Allegheny Ludlum, forming Allegheny Teledyne, Inc., with headquarters in Pittsburgh, Pennsylvania. From 1996 to 1999 Teledyne Brown Engineering existed as part of the conglomerate headed by Robert Mehrabian, former head of Carnegie Mellon University.

Over the years, Teledyne Brown Engineering has been headed by a succession of company presidents. Following Moquin, they were Robert Rieth, Jim McGovern, Dick Holloway, Jim Link, and Jan Hess. Ms. Hess joined the company in 2000 and has been promoted to her current position as head of the Engineering segment, where she heads up TBE and three other Teledyne companies.

A Man in a Hurry: John Glenn

"I don't know what you could say about a day in which you have seen four beautiful sunsets...To look out at the Earth from this vantage point...to look out at this kind of creation and not believe in God is, to me, impossible. It just strengthens my faith." Astronaut John Glenn.

On a sparkling summer day in 1983, in a large patio rose garden packed with luncheon guests, I am standing alongside former astronaut and now U.S. Senator and Presidential candidate John Glenn, the man author Thomas Wolfe characterized as "last true national hero America has ever had." I was selected to introduce him at the fundraising luncheon at the large antebellum home of nursing home developer Bryson Hill, on a sloping hillside near downtown Huntsville. On my right is former Ambassador Marvin Warner, a Birmingham native, wealthy Cincinnati financier, Glenn's close friend and chief fund-raiser.

The audience of John Glenn's first North Alabama financial supporters reacts happily. He is the kind of candidate we from Rocket City USA can enthusiastically support---a centrist Democrat running to the right of the ultimate winner, the liberal darling of the labor unions and party establishment, Vice President Walter Mondale. And at that moment the campaign of the first man in space is bolstered nationally by Wolfe's best-selling book, *The Right Stuff*. This is his first foray into our region and it is my first effort to take the lead in coordinating a fundraising event for an out-of-state candidate. (I had never enjoyed raising money for myself when I was in the Legislature. I felt somewhat like I was begging when I asked people for money to spend on my campaign. But now I am finding it easy to solicit funds for others.).

We stop by the Hilton Hotel for a press conference afterwards. As soon as it ends, we bolt for the door with Glenn in the lead to race to the airport behind a motorcycle escort to keep pace with the tight schedule Presidential candidates face months ahead of the election. He may be an unexciting speaker, genuine but not charismatic in person, but this much is obvious about John Glenn---he is a man in a hurry. But there is a holdup. Just as he opened the rear door, Warner says, "Wait a minute. I have to go back." He runs back into the hotel while Glenn looks impatiently at his watch. Several minutes later he returns. Later a friend reported that the wealthy Warner had gone to the phone booth to retrieve a quarter he suddenly remembered he had left in the slot.

Shortly before the Super Tuesday primaries in March, 1984, we joined John and Annie Glenn on a daylong campaign swing, riding with them on their campaign RV from Huntsville for stops at Guntersville, Gadsden, and Birmingham. Even in that environment John Glenn was less than engaging, comfortably talking about computer bytes, and happily responding to my questions about his Marine Corps memories when he served as a fighter pilot in the Korean War with my baseball hero Ted Williams. He was not a bad senator but had done nothing in the Senate to attract national attention. He frankly lacked the organization, charisma, record, or ability to upend the prohibitive frontrunner Mondale. The Democratic Party was at that point becoming a party of special interests. Glenn was never a favorite of the unions, party bosses, and liberal activists. A poor showing in the Iowa Caucuses mortally wounded any serious chance he had of winning. A week later he finished third in New Hampshire, limping into Alabama and a dozen other states on Super Tuesday where he peaked with a tie for second in Alabama. He ran first in our part of the state, where the memories of his space heroism were strongest.

During his remaining 14 years in office I dropped by to see him and his longtime political advisor and Chief of Staff, Mary Jo Veno. As a member of the Armed Services Committee, even though he believed a missile deployment would be destabilizing, he helped us maintain a viable missile defense research and development program. And, of course, he was always out making the case for a viable space program. In 1998, his last year in the Senate, the first American to orbit Earth became, at age 77, the oldest person to travel in space. He had continued to pilot his own airplane and had kept in shape, persuading NASA to let him fly on the space shuttle Discovery and conduct tests on the physiological effects of nine days of weightlessness on older people. In the epilogue to his best-selling book about the original seven astronauts, Thomas Wolfe wrote that the day "when an astronaut could parade up Broadway while traffic policemen wept in the intersections," was no more. An era, he continues, "had come, and it had gone, perhaps never to be relived."

John Glenn's best friend, Marvin Warner, was a likeable sort, a flamboyant high-roller, appointed by President Carter as U.S. Ambassador to Switzerland. He made a fortune taking high risks in real estate, backed by involvement in the savings and loans business, and launched the Birmingham Stallions of the U.S. Football League in 1983.

Al Gore, the Youngest Candidate

At the age of 39, Tennessee Senator Al Gore Jr. entered the 1988 Presidential primaries as the youngest serious Presidential candidate since John F. Kennedy.

Well before the convention, it was obvious that Gore did not have enough organization, resources, or support among the interest groups to stop Dukakis. He dropped out after a poor showing in New York state. At the National Democratic Convention in Atlanta that Summer, even though his campaign now seemed like long-ago history, one delegate, Mary Grainger, still wore a Gore button to the Alabama reception. Gore dropped by, spotted the single button, shook his head to show he shared her disappointment and gave her a big hug.

Gore always opposed a "Star Wars" deployment but when we talked in person, I argued that we could deploy a treaty-compliant land-based defense, to protect, for example, our missiles at Grand Forks, S.D., from a preemptive strike. I discovered in the late 1980s why he was so inflexible on missile defense deployment. At his side, whispering arguments against missile defense in his ear, was Gore's Senate legislative assistant for national security advisor, Leon Fuerth. An important vote was coming up the next week and I figured Fuerth had been blocking out my inputs to his boss. So how to get around him? I called Clark Jones at Savannah, Tennessee, who would be driving Gore around the state during the weekend. He gave me his fax number and asked me to fax a personal note to Al. "I will make sure he reads it in the car," Clark said. The following Monday I had a call from Leon Fuerth. Gore had forwarded the personal note to him and obviously told him to solve the problem. Fuerth reluctantly agreed to meet at Gore's Senate office to hear our arguments. Wally Kirkpatrick of the Army Ballistic Missile Defense Organization had developed a presentation that made a logic-based case for treaty-limited, land-based missile defense deployment. Five minutes into Wally's presentation Fuerth stood up without comment and walked out the door. No, "I will be right back." "Or thank you for coming." Nothing. Wally and I looked at each other. "He must have an urgent call and will be right back," I said. We waited nearly ten minutes before it became clear that Mr. Fuerth had terminated our pitch in a rude, classless way.

When Gore became Vice President in January, 1993, Fuerth became his national security adviser. By Presidential order, he operated as a full member of the Principals and Deputies Committees in both the National Security Council and the National Economic Council. If Gore had prevailed in his 2000 quest for the Presidency there is little doubt Fuerth would have been named Presidential National Security Advisor---based, no doubt, not on his social graces but on Gore's appreciation of his knowledge of complex international issues.

The next time I heard from Al Gore was when he called in 1993 to complain about Senator Richard Shelby embarrassing him outside the Vice President's Senate Office on the eve of the vote to increase taxes. Gore was incensed. "Isn't there something you folks can do about Shelby?" he asked. "My boss (President Clinton) just called me from California to ask what was going on. The SOB stood outside of my office and ridiculed me."

This was on a Thursday night. "Let me call Heflin," I said. You two are scheduled to be together in Birmingham Saturday. Maybe he can come up with something." "He will get back to you." I called Heflin at home. He growled like a giant angry bear about the problem being so unnecessary, then agreed to call Gore and arrange to ride with him from the airport on Saturday morning. After that everyone cooled down.

Al Gore made numerous positive contributions to America's betterment. He was the first elected official to grasp the potential of computer communications. When the Internet was still in the early stages of its deployment, Congressman Gore provided intellectual leadership by helping create the vision of the potential benefits of highspeed computing and communication.

Coaching a Future Death Row Inmate

As a college sophomore, I coached an undefeated basketball team of 14-year-olds in the Sheffield Church League that included a player who surprisingly grew up to become a notorious killer. His name was Tommy Arthur. When a jury convicted him for the 1982 murder of his girlfriend's husband, he asked to be given the death sentence because it would give him automatic appeals and better access to law books. At age 75, the man known as the "Houdini" of Alabama's death row for escaping seven past execution dates through legal challenges, was finally executed by lethal injection on May 26, 2017.

On death row more than 34 years, Arthur was the third-longest serving inmate to await execution and the second oldest to be executed ---*Associated Press*, "Alabama Executes Tommy Arthur, Who Escaped 7 Prior Execution Dates,", *CBS News*, May 26, 2017. Lyman, Brian and Davis, Kelsey, "Asking for Death Penalty, Inmate Keeps Escaping It,", *Montgomery Advertiser*, October 31, 2016.

When I coached Arthur in church league basketball, he did not attract my attention as being weird or evil. He was just a slow, clumsy substitute who only participated when I emptied the bench with a 30-point lead. We had a great team and won every game by 30 or more points in that Winter season of 1956-57. The Baptist team featured two quick guards and three tall rebounders and a two-three zone defense that was almost impossible to penetrate. Arthur played very little, but he never complained nor, to my knowledge, brought attention to himself.

My sisters could not believe Tommy Arthur played basketball without giving me problems. Joyce said he was evil personified. Linda, in the same class with Arthur, said he gave all his teachers a hard time. "I stayed as far away from him as I could," she said. Tommy Arthur the Bad Boy stories circulated wildly for years. As a teenager, he was said to have shot monkeys in their cage with a BB gun at a bowling alley, shot the windows out of a restaurant where black people ate and shot his 14 year old cousin in the leg with a bow and arrow.

Shortly after highschool graduation, another story went, he hitched a ride to the Gulf Coast with a group of classmates. As they drove south of Moulton, he asked the driver to stop at the next service station so he could get cigarettes. When he rushed back to the car, they realized that he had robbed the store. They were riding in a conspicuous yellow Cadillac convertible. Miraculously they made it to the Florida Panhandle without being overtaken by the law.

As an adult, he would become notorious as a hired murderer whose execution was delayed eight times by his cunning "jailhouse lawyer" appeals.

Phenix City Story: Sin City

Charlie Johnson was a 17-year-old craps "stickman" in the small crime-ridden Alabama town of Phenix City which became known nationally in the early Fifties as "Sin City, USA." His job was to make sure the house won and the naive young Army soldiers from Fort Benning, GA, lost their entire paychecks. Charlie's quick hands gave the dice shooter no chance. "If he needed a point, I would switch the dice to special dice that made it impossible for him to roll his point," he recalled seventy years later. "How could you switch dice without anyone seeing you do it?" "Easy, when the dice were thrown across the throw-line everyone's eyes were glued to the blur of the dice. No one noticed my hands in my pockets."

Charlie Johnson, who spent a career as a hydraulics engineer boosting rockets into space at the NASA/Marshall Space Flight Center in Huntsville, recalled at age 87 his father was sentenced to prison for five years for cheating the customers "and the only way I avoided prison was being drafted into the Korean War." The 17-year-old was dating the 15-year-old daughter of the criminal kingpin when a thug tapped him on the shoulder. "Are you dating the boss's daughter?" he was asked. "Yes," Charlie replied. "Well you will be dead if you keep that up," the hoodlum declared. Charlie got the message. He stopped dating the underworld kingpin's daughter.

Fueled by the steady incomes of U.S. Army trainees from nearby Fort Benning, Georgia, Phenix City was notorious during the Forties and early Fifties as a haven for organized crime, prostitution, and gambling. In the 1958 Governor's Race, John Patterson ran for governor on a strong segregation and law enforcement platform. His father, Albert Patterson, was assassinated in 1954 by the Phoenix City gang when he was running for Attorney General on a platform to clean up Phoenix City.

Patterson was campaigning for the Kennedy-Johnson ticket in 1960 when we became acquainted. I covered the Governor's office as well as the Legislature through the 1964 elections. John Patterson and I got along well, even deer-hunting together once. He was a complex and likeable politician. Mullinax, Kenneth, "Governor John Patterson Interviewed by the *Montgomery Advertiser, New South Books*, April 11th, 2008. Grafton, Carl and Permaloff, Anne, "John M. Patterson (1959-1963,") *Encyclopedia of Alabama*, 2008, Grafton, Carl and Anne Permaloff. "The Big Mule Alliance's Last Good Year: Thwarting the Patterson Reforms." *Alabama Review* 47 (October 1994): 243-66. Permaloff, Anne, and Carl Grafton. *Political Power in Alabama: The More Things Change,"* University of Georgia Press, 1996. Trest, Warren. "Nobody but the People: The Life and Times of Alabama's Youngest Governor." New South Books, 2008.

The Battle of Shiloh

"On paper, Shiloh was a draw; actually, it was one of the decisive battles of the war. It was a battle the Confederacy simply had to win. It had failed, and the fact that it had come close to being a dazzling victory did not offset the failure." Bruce Catton, This Hallowed Ground.

Ernest Marsh, my maternal grandfather and close pal as I grew up, kindled my imagination with stories of the Battle of Shiloh and his grandfather's role in it. His grandfather, Hiram H. Marsh, was killed by artillery fire at his supply wagon behind the lines in a battle to force Union troops from the infamous "Hornet's Nest," where the whistling sound of bullets sounded to gray-clad soldiers like an angry swarm of hornets.

Mary and I had driven to Memphis in April 1993 with good friends JoAnne Hill and Ed McCormick to view an exhibit of historic objects from the Napoleonic era. On the return trip, we detoured from Corinth, Mississippi, 22 miles northward to Shiloh Battlefield in the southern edge of Tennessee. It was there, on tall bluffs beside the steamboat dock known as Pittsburg Landing, that the Union army had encamped in the Spring of 1862 to prepare for an invasion of Corinth, the strategic railroad center of the mid-South. The Battle of Shiloh brought 80,000 Americans---in almost equal numbers---together for a two-day battle among its thick woods, open fields, and deep ravines. It cost the lives of 3,400 men killed outright in the two days of brutal fighting.

Few of the little group of small farmers from the Summit Community of Blount County, Alabama who volunteered to serve in the Confederate Army in 1861 were slave-owners. Of a statewide population of almost one million, 45 per cent were slaves. Like most of the state's northern hill counties, in Blount County, less than seven per cent of its population of less than 7,500 were slaves. Powell, George. "A History and Description of Blount County." From the *Alabama Historical Quarterly,* Volume 27, Spring and Summer 1965, pages 95 -132:

The raggedly little band of volunteers from Blount County reported for induction in Huntsville into the newly-formed Nineteenth Alabama Infantry Regiment. Their commanding officer was Lieutenant Colonel Joseph (Fighting Joe) Wheeler. An Augusta, Georgia native and West Point graduate, the tiny-but-tough Wheeler picked up the nickname as a second lieutenant in the U.S. Army skirmishing with Indians in New Mexico.

I envision my great-great grandfather, a teamster for the Quartermaster, as he began preparing his ten-foot-long supply wagon for the march northward on April 3. Hiram Marsh would have had a six-mule team to pull the heavily loaded wagon through deep muddy ruts. Burton, Gracie, "Alabama Volunteers," *Pelican Publishing.*

The Nineteenth Alabama soldiers were likely marching to join the fight against Prentiss' forces at the Hornet's Nest when its teamster/wagonmaster, Private Hiram H. Marsh, was killed. Records show he was in the area fronting Prentiss' division in the center of the battlefield when he died from wounds to the head and neck. That would suggest he was hit by canister fire because the odds of two rifle shots hitting him simultaneously would be unfathomable. It was common in that battle for artillery gunners to aim too high to hit infantrymen. At 3:30 p.m., the time when records show Hiram Marsh died, the five-hour struggle at the center was renewed with enormous fury. The sounds of close to 100 dueling cannons could easily be heard 22 miles away in Corinth.

The Legend of Pelham Humphries

"Tell us the story about Uncle Pelham," was our usual bedtime story request when we visited our grandfather. Ernest (Pawpaw) Marsh chuckled as he repeated the exciting family legend of the cowboy who rode West to seek his fortune.

He described Pelham Humphries as a cattle rustler living in Carter County, in the mountains of Northeast Tennessee. When he "got in trouble with the law" for stealing a horse he hurriedly rode out of town, heading for Mexican Territory. Land was being granted to settlers in Nacogdoches, in southeast Texas. He was granted a large track of marshy land that was considered worthless at the time. He was killed in a barroom shootout the next year, long before the greatest amount of oil in history was discovered on a small hilltop on the 4,400 acres of land originally granted to Pelham Humphries. That story was passed down through the generations from the Langs to the Clapps to the Marshs.

As we grew to be teenagers, our grandfather related details of our family legacy: his family believed we were heirs to an oil fortune. A land grant of dubious value was magically transformed with the discovery of "black gold" in 1901 and the potential for rich heirs---including us. A thirty-foot high salt dome would come to be known as Spindletop oil field as Texas was transformed into the oil producing center of the world.

Our family's mission to become Humphries inheritors paid dividends in other ways. It brought the Marsh family and Mother's cousins closer together. Letters and calls came from relatives from several states. It led my younger sister, Linda James, to become a serious amateur genealogical researcher. She was impressed, first, by the professional research provided by Burke's Peerage. Their researchers sent copies of Uriah Humphries' will, which mentions his daughter Judy Humphries Lane. They sent census records, deeds, military service records of Henry Wade Lang's brother Joseph, who served in the Creek Indian War, and of Henry Wade Lang, who served in the Confederate Army and was at Appomattox when General Robert E. Lee surrendered in 1865. "No," Linda agreed from her own research over the years, "We are not descended from Simon Lane who married Judy Humphries. His genealogy has been proven. We are descended from Henry Wade Lang, whose father was John C. Lang, our fifth great-grandfather, not Simon."

Linda, had concluded that the lawsuits attempting to collect from the Humphries land grant was a scam, but she added this positive note in an email: "Without this scam, the family contacts would not have happened. This was the real inheritance. The Burke's Peerage genealogy report has been a great source of information in my journey as amateur genealogist. So far, I have over 16,000 in my family tree and have taken a DNA test to connect with who they are scientifically. So that's the real truth behind the "Spindletop Oil Billions."

Long Drive. Hitting it straight is required on most holes at Pebble Beach. Here author parred last hole, a total of 83, which won the Teledyne Manager's Meeting tourney.

CHAPTER **7**

The Roaring Nineties

These were the years of the tumultuous, Roaring Nineties. The Cold War ended with the dissolution of the Soviet Union. The economy boomed.

George H. W. Bush as President won the Gulf War, then Bill Clinton presided over notable advances in work for welfare and equal employment opportunities.

Alabama's National Title Celebrated

The Alabama Crimson Tide maintains the richest tradition in college football. The Paul (Bear) Bryant era, from 1958 to 1982, was acclaimed as the most magnificent, unparalleled quarter of a century in sports history. The Tide was the team of the Sixties and Seventies, winning three national titles each decade. The team of the Eighties, going into the Nineties, was the Miami Hurricanes.

I had attended most of the major Tide games at Legion Field in the decades following frequent breakfasts at the Bankhead with the *Birmingham News* sports staff and Coach Bryant in 1958, Bear's first year back at his alma mater. Our daughter, a student at Alabama, and a friend were in New Orleans with us for Alabama's near-miss in the Sugar Bowl matchup of the 1989 Bama-Miami

203

teams. The Tide was not intimidated by Miami, losing on a couple of questionable calls by officials as the Canes won their third national title of the decade.

When the Huntsville contingent of Tide fans arrived after Christmas in 1992, New Orleans Bourbon Street was a rainbow of Crimson red and white and Miami's green and orange. The cocky, trash-talking Miami players patrolled Bourbon Street looking for Alabama players to intimidate. An ugly incident occurred outside Pat O'Brien's Irish bar, as Miami players loudly threatened Tide players. Miami linebacker Rohan Marley, the son of Jamaican reggae singer Bob Marley, bragged that he would be looking to kick butts in the game, getting in the face of a 290-pound Bama tackle to call him a "fat, sloppy SOB."

"As the Miami players taunted, the Alabama guys maintained their poise. They were right up in our faces, saying that us blankety-blanks didn't deserve to be on the same field with them."—Bucholz, Andrew: "The 1993 Sugar Bowl Saw Miami's Trash Talk Go Very Wrong in an Alabama Triumph.

In the stands, we did our best to contribute to the Miami quarterback's misery. Early in the game those seated in our area were annoyed by the loud shouting of an inebriated redneck Alabama fan in the row just behind us. Supported in unison by a halfdozen of his buddies, he brayed like a jackass. Even during commercials. Finally, I turned and addressed the guy and his group. "Hey, guys, this noise is helping Alabama but we need to time it better. When I raise both hands you guys cut loose at once." Every time the Miami quarterback prepared to take the snap for the rest of the game, the conductor waved at his orchestra and the loud braying added to the noise level coming from Bama fans smelling blood. – Higgins, Ron, "Defense Lifts Alabama to 1993 National Championship." *Memphis Commercial Appeal, Fall, 2008*

At that point, a weird feeling swept across the Superdome: Hey, Alabama is going to win this game, we suddenly realized. Bourbon Street became a surging sea of red celebrants for the rest of the night. —Murphy, Austin, "The End of the Run," *Sports Illustrated, January 11, 1993*

Fans of the University of Alabama football team that had grown accustomed to winning national titles in the Bryant coaching era were starving for another one in 1992 when a Bryant disciple, Coach Gene Stallings, brought back the spirit of winning after a 13-year drought.

Stallings was one of Alabama's all time favorite coaches. Fans remembered that as a player he had been a gritty "Junction Boy" survivor of the Texas A&M team's introduction to Bryant coaching. Stallings was a hard-nosed competitor who was an inherently likeable person. As my golfing partner in a couple of charity golf tournaments, he inspired our team to relax and have fun. Always the gentleman, he insisted on Mary riding in his place on our golf cart while he walked along and constantly chatted between shots. A photo of Stallings hitting a drive with me standing close by with driver in hand appeared for several weeks in the *Huntsville Times* as part of a promotional ad for the newspaper. Stallings sent me a copy with the note that he enjoyed playing with me.

A Fundamentalist Preacher as Governor

Even though little was expected from Hunt due to his limited background, he did enough right to be reelected to a second term as governor. He pushed through major tort reform and tried to bring more industry and tourism to the state, but was ineffective dealing with the Legislature. In 1992, the Alabama Supreme Court ruled that taxpayers could sue Hunt for flying on stateowned aircraft to preaching engagements, where Hunt received monetary offerings. In 1993, when I was Chairman of the Huntsville Chamber of Commerce, Governor Hunt hosted us in Montgomery to discuss economic development. I made a carefully documented presentation demonstrating that Huntsville's Redstone Arsenal and its high technology companies were the state's greatest contributor to Alabama state revenues. Hunt listened but didn't understand. When we focused on our priorities for state support, such as the infrastructure necessary to support the economic thrust, he replied, "But Charlie, ya'll have everything. Huntsville don't need no help." Thank you, Santa Claus.

He attempted to offset his minimal knowledge of state government with clumsy party partisanship. I sat embarrassed on the platform in 1991 for the official opening of Huntsville's new interstate highway spur when I realized that the person who convinced Congress nearly 30 years earlier to add the link to the national highway system and obtained the federal funding to make it possible was not there. Afterwards, I called former Congressman Bob Jones to ask where he was. Jones, a Democrat, had not even been invited. I followed up by writing one of the few letters to the editor I have ever written to help correct the historical record.

In 1992 a grand jury indicted Hunt for theft, conspiracy, and ethics violations. Prosecutors said that he took $200,000 from a 1987 inaugural account and used it to buy marble showers and lawnmowers. Hunt was forced to resign in April, 1993. He also served a five-year probationary term. Most observers thought Hunt was guilty only of ignorance. He was a nice man whom I personally liked, who no doubt was a sincere, well-intentioned man. But country preachers were said to customarily pocket cash tithes. And since he paid no taxes on the large sum, perhaps to his way of thinking the money was a tax-free fringe benefit.

In the early Nineties, while Hunt was serving as Governor, he accompanied the Huntsville Chamber to Boston to encourage companies along the High Technology Corridor to locate operations in Huntsville. Former Lt. Governor Bill Baxley, by then practicing law in Birmingham, joined us. We had talked years before about how we both grew up as Red Sox fans. As soon as we saw each other we arranged to go to a game at historic Fenway Park, where we ate hotdogs like teen-agers and rooted the Red Sox home.

Alabama's Flawed New South Governor

Don Siegelman was elected governor in 1998, and in spite of his intense campaign style I was optimistic. Here was, at long last, a ray of sunshine in the New South. Someone not interested in chasing Lost Causes. We had finally elected someone interested in improving the state's image in race relations, education, and economic development. His inaugural address in 1999, about moving the state forward and creating a positive national image, was inspiring. I told him so when I saw him in the capitol rotunda following the event. But a young man with promise became a flawed leader.

Don Siegelman ran for reelection in 2002 but lost to Congressman Bob Riley. Siegelman sought the governorship again in 2006, but lost in the Democratic Primary to Lt. Governor Steve Windom. Riley was reelected in the general election. A few weeks after his loss in the Democratic primary, Siegelman was convicted by a federal court in 2006 on bribery, conspiracy and obstruction of justice charges after being accused of appointing former HealthSouth CEO Richard Scrushy to a health planning board in return for a $500,000 donation to the governor's campaign for a statewide lottery. Siegelman maintained that Scrushy had been on the board of the state hospital regulatory board during several preceding governorships and that his contribution towards a state lottery fund for universal education was unrelated to the appointment. The Certificates of Need Review Board reviewed expansion requests from hospitals, including those owned by Scrushy's company. The federal law establishing the certificate of need process was aimed at avoiding unnecessary health costs due to duplication of healthcare facilities. I served as a consumer representative on a similar state board in the mid-Seventies. Siegelman and Scrushy received sentences of almost six years each. --"Freed Ex-Governor of Alabama talks of Abuse of Power", *The New York Times,* March 29, 2008, p. A13. Lyman, Brian, July 26, 2012, "Scrushy Released from Custody," *Montgomery Advertiser.*

Democratic Party, Goodbye, from Yours Truly

SONG OF THE SOUTH By Bob McDill, popularized by the music group, Alabama.

Cotton on the roadside, cotton in the ditch
We all picked the cotton but we never got rich
Daddy was a veteran, a southern democrat
They ought to get a rich man to vote like that

Song, song of the south
Sweet potato pie and I shut my mouth
Gone, gone by the wind
There ain't nobody looking back again

Born on a small farm in the Tennessee Valley region of the South, we believed we were born as Democrats. Mr. Roosevelt did save us all. You were either a Democrat or you were a DamnRepublican---one word. As a youngster, my association with politics was to build a collection of the cards handed out by local candidates who came to our house. They all were the same style---across the bottom in capital letters as large as the candidate's name, "SUBJECT TO THE ACTION OF THE DEMOCRATIC PRIMARY." I grew up supporting the National Democratic Party, the party of Truman and Kennedy.

I helped organize the Colbert County Young Democrats and saw liberalism up close for the first time when I attended a National Young Democrats Convention in Washington while still in my twenties. (Steny Hoyer of Maryland was one of those persuasive liberals; in 2014 he was U.S. House minority whip). The Democratic Party in the South was a big broad party, with room for all philosophical shades. It was called the Solid South because Southerners had been voting Democratic since the Civil War. That suddenly changed in 1964 when Alabama and four other Southern states voted Republican for Barry Goldwater for President. Goldwater's appeal to most Southerners was based on his advocacy of less government and opposition to the Civil Rights Act of 1964. By the November general election so-called unpledged Democratic electors (who were in fact pledged to carry the banner for George Wallace's presidential ambitions) announced their support for the Goldwater Republican slate.

In the May primaries, Wallace's electors had overwhelmingly defeated our slate of loyalist electors pledged to support the National Democratic Party candidate for President. Five of the state's eight Congressional seats were captured by little known Republican candidates swept in on the Goldwater tide. Across the South there were stirrings of Democratic officeholders looking at changing parties. U. S. Senator Strom Thurmond (D-SC) did not have far to go. He had been a leader in the Dixiecrat movement in 1948. He switched parties in 1964, saying the Democratic Party was "leading the evolution of our nation to a socialistic dictatorship."

Two years later, at age 29, I ran on a slate of eight candidates loyal to the national party for the State Democratic Executive Committee, the statewide party governing body. My opponent was wellknown across the district as campaign chairman of Mrs. George Wallace's campaign for Governor. Preparing for a serious run for President, Wallace wanted to control his state's party apparatus, but our loyalist slate eeked out a majority. We ran in seven counties and the night they counted the votes I thought I had lost my first election. A radio station in my home county of Colbert had inadvertently shorted my vote totals by 2,000 votes. When the official returns were tabulated, I had won by a few more than 1,200 votes. I served a total of 18 years on the State Democratic Executive Committee. One of my first votes was to override the Wallace's forces by removing the "White Supremacy for the Right" label from the party emblem, replacing it with "Democrats for the Right." I was the Democratic nominee two years later to fill a vacancy for the Alabama House of Representatives, then reelected two years later for a four year term. In 1972, George McGovern, the Democratic Presidential nominee was so far to the left of my thinking that I literally held my nose when I voted the straight Democratic ticket. Like all elected Democrats in our state, I had sworn an oath to support the nominees of our party in the general election. I abided by the oath, but was becoming concerned at the extreme direction the party was taking.

In the early Eighties I had grown close to U.S. Representative Jack Edwards (R-Mobile, AL). As the Ranking Republican on the Appropriations Committee's Defense Subcommittee, Jack became an advocate for missile defense after previously voting to dismantle the U.S. deployed system in Grand Forks, ND. We thought alike on defense, we visited in the Edwards home at Point Clear, and invested the same way, buying 18-wheeler trucks from a Mobile dealer a few months after his retirement in 1984. Jack bought two and I bought one. We both lost money on the investment. As he was retiring, Edwards asked former State Senator Sonny Callahan to run for his seat as a Republican. Callahan, my colleague in the Alabama House in the early Seventies, had been elected three times to the Legislature as a Democrat and had run unsuccessfully as a Democrat for Lieutenant Governor in 1982. He switched parties and was elected to Edwards seat where he, too, would be a member of the powerful Appropriations Committee's Defense Subcommittee.

I continued working to try to keep the state party from straying further to the left in the Seventies. In 1975, at the urging of Senator Howell Heflin, I coordinated a Huntsville fundraiser for Senator Henry (Scoop) Jackson (D-WA), a fiscal conservative and original supporter of missile defense. I supported Jimmy Carter of Georgia in 1976 and 1980. I was elected as the North Alabama male delegate to the Democratic mini-convention in Memphis in 1978, where I fought antidefense issue positions proposed by what we called "peaceniks."

In 1984, I campaigned for Senator John Glenn (D-OH), who as a former astronaut had a strong identity with Huntsville and a relatively moderate record. In 1988, I was the North Alabama coordinator for our friend from Tennessee, Senator Al Gore, Mary and I were elected from our congressional district as Carter Delegates in 1980 and as Gore Delegates in 1988. It was the following year that I began my transformation---or evolution---from an activist Democratic leader to being less and less partisan. Whether I was aware or not at the time, I was evolving from a party activist to a point a few years later when I would be comfortable as an independent conservative supporting mostly Republicans. I did not seek election in 1990 on the State Democratic Executive Committee because I was feeling more and more uncomfortable in the environment of special interest groups.

By the Nineties, I hosted fundraising events for Congressmen from both parties who were strong supporters of missile defense and other national security and space issues. The member to whom I was closest was Congressman Curt Weldon (R-PA), who was the unquestioned leader for missile defense in Congress. I also hosted events for Congressman John Spratt (D-SC), who as a former DoD analyst was an effective advocate of missile defense. I continued to strongly support our Democratic Congressman, Bud Cramer of Huntsville, a leader of a fiscally conservative group of Democrats which called itself "Blue Dog Democrats." They picked that name to separate themselves from "Yellow Dog Democrats," which commonly referred to Southern Democrats said to be willing to vote for a dog rather than for a Republican. Southern Democrats who supported Republican Ronald Reagan's shift away from bigger government in the Eighties had been called "Boll Weevil Democrats." When the Democrats lost Congress in 1994, House members not blinded by party loyalty formed the "Blue Dog Coalition." They held their first meetings in the office of Louisiana Congressman Billy Tauzin (D-LA), who several years later switched to the Republican Party.

Our Congressman Bud Cramer was barely re-elected in 1994. In 1998 his opponent pressured the House Republican leadership to force Weldon to come to Huntsville to campaign with the Republican candidate, as was customary in Congressional elections. Weldon had promised me more than once he would resist those calls due to Cramer's support of missile defense and our community's consistent support for Weldon.

Gore was the last Democrat I supported for President. I quietly cast a vote for him in 2000 because of our longtime friendship with him and his loveable wife, Tipper, and because of his strong support for the space program. Gore worked daily with Senator Heflin to save Space Station when President Clinton's budget officer tried to kill it. Gore grew closer to the party's liberal left base during the 2000 campaign. In later years, he made a fortune off the green movement, and he and our friend Tipper divorced. And while maintaining my independence from being wed to a party, I have supported Republican presidential candidates since. That was not hard considering the philosophical distance between my thinking and Democratic candidates John Kerry and Barack Obama. There was no particular day I made that decision. It evolved over a period of time, beginning when it came home to me that the Democratic Party had become a party of special interests after the 1968 election and it was making its way down to the Alabama party.

Milestones in that transformation were when I ended my service on the state party governing body in 1990, relieving me from the loyalty oath of voting a straight Democratic ticket. I began hosting fundraisers for conservatives of both parties in the Nineties, voting increasingly for Republicans until the present day when I vote Republican 95% or more. In one way my biggest regret about leaving the Democratic Party was in not doing it sooner, but in another the distance it tends to create among some close friendships is regrettable. Philosophically I have always been a fiscal conservative and remain somewhat of a social moderate. But I believe government has become too big and inefficient and the Obama Administration is headed down a socialistic path that is dividing and weakening this republic.

Why I am No Longer a Democrat

Why am I no longer a Democrat? Most all politicians who have switched from Democrats to Republicans over the last few decades have said simply, "The Democratic Party left me." They say that because it is true.

Our pappies were Democrats, and their grandpappy was a Democrat, and their great-grandpappy was a Democrat, we were too. Then the party changed, along with the generations. My dad and my mother are gone now. And so is the party we all once supported. Their grandfather is gone — and so is the party which he once supported. Until the late Eighties I was labeled a "Yellow Dawg Democrat," a tag given to straight-ticket Democrat voters decades ago that meant they would vote for a yellow dog before they would vote Republican. Even then, I was an anti-union conservative.

Someone said they changed when they realized that Democrats took money from working people and gave it to people who were content not to work. All of us believed in providing a safety net for those unable to work or find jobs but were concerned that those on welfare rolls would ultimately be drawn into government dependency. As British Prime Minister Margaret Thatcher famously said, "The problem with socialism is that eventually you run out of other people's money."

My favorite syndicated columnist and political commentator, Charles Krauthammer, wrote that it was he, not the Democratic party, which changed on issues of domestic policy. "The origin of that evolution is simple: I'm open to empirical evidence. The results of the Great Society experiments started coming in and began showing that, for all its good intentions, the War on Poverty was causing irreparable damage to the very communities it was designed to help...As I became convinced of the practical and theoretical defects of the social-democratic tendencies of my youth, it was but a short distance to a philosophy of restrained, free-market governance that gave more space and place to the individual and to the civil society that stands between citizen and state. In a kind of full-circle return, I found my eventual political home in a vision of limited government that, while providing for the helpless, is committed above all to guaranteeing individual liberty and the pursuit of one's own "ends of life." Charles Krauthammer, *Things That Matter,* Random House, 2013.

After that terrible day in Dallas in 1963, media mythology turned John F. Kennedy into a liberal hero. Yet today's Democratic Party of Barack Obama and Hillary Clinton wouldn't give the time of day to a candidate like JFK because he was an ardent tax-cutter who championed reductions in personal and corporate tax rates, slashed tariffs to promote free trade, and even spoke out against the "confiscatory" property taxes being levied in most cities. He was anything but a big-spending, welfare-state liberal. "I do not believe that Washington should do for the people what they can do for themselves through local and private effort," Kennedy bluntly avowed during the 1960 campaign. By any reasonable definition JFK was a conservative — and not just by the standards of our era, but also by those of the Sixties. In today's political environment, a candidate like JFK — a conservative champion of economic growth, tax cuts, limited government, peace through strength — plainly *would* be a hero. But he could not get the Democratic nomination. Jeff Jacoby, Boston Globe, October 20, 2013. Ira Stoll, "JFK, Conservative."

So, someone asked: "So, you are now a Republican?" My answer is "not quite." I am a conservative, pure and simple. I support no other candidates than Republicans for Congress and President, but there have been one or two conservative Democrats at the local level whom I continued to support. And as the liberal Democrats' extreme policies continue to tarnish all candidates with the "D" by their names it won't be long that even they, too, will switch or retire.

Mary Grainger, Still a Sweetheart

In the mid-Sixties I was 28 and single, chairing the public relations committee for the United Way campaign when a beautiful lady sat down at the table. As company representatives took turns introducing themselves, it turned out the woman with the gorgeous eyes was representing Boeing, Huntsville's largest aerospace contractor, the builder of the giant boost vehicle that near the end of that decade would provide the initial lift for America's flight to the moon. Following the meeting, I awkwardly shook hands with attendees as they filed out of the meeting. My mind was so taken by the pretty lady that I could not shake her hand, absorb her smile, and correctly understand her last name, all without hanging on to her hand too long. It sounded like something along the lines of "Mary Shumberger" and I was too embarrassed to ask twice.

On the way back to the office I thought, "This must be the unmarried public relations person at Boeing my match-making newspaper friend has been saying he wanted me to meet." Thirty minutes later I picked up the phone and asked the information operator for help. She found a "Mary Shumberger" at Fountainbleau apartments. Mary answered but it was the wrong Mary. But fate smiled one of its biggest smiles ever down on me. "You must mean Mary Sullenberger," she said. "She lives in this apartment complex also. I have gotten other calls for her and here is her number."

Mary Grainger and author host fundraiser for U. S.
Senators Jim Sasser (left) and Don Reigle

Two minutes later the right Mary was on the line and, yes, she would meet me for a drink that night at the Sheraton. We met, we laughed, we fell in love that same night. I had never met anyone like her. The next night our newspaper friend, Dave Langford, and his wife, Royeanne, who was my secretary, met us for dinner. For the next several months Mary and I saw each almost every night. We would see each other regularly for two more years, then marry in June, 1967.

When we met, Mary Margretta Sullenberger had recently graduated the University of Tennessee in Knoxville, about 40 miles from her hometown of Dandridge, population 800, near the Great Smoky Mountains. A throw-back to the Revolutionary War, the Sullenberger house was dark brick with green shutters, a block from the Jefferson County Courthouse. Her father was the town surgical and family doctor. In the rear was a garage and a large yard that served as home for a menagerie of animals paid to the doctor when his patients could not afford to pay in cash. As a child, when she walked to the drug store two blocks away, she was frequently closely followed three steps behind by her pet, a large turkey named Tom Turkey.

Dandridge was founded in the late 1700s by settlers moving westerly across the Appalachian Mountains. The second oldest town in the state, the tiny town's future existence was threatened by the planned construction of Douglas Dam in the early 1940s. A group of citizens went to Washington, DC and lobbied for a stone and earth dike to keep the waters of the reservoir from flooding the town. They petitioned then-First Lady Eleanor Roosevelt for her help, stressing that Dandridge was the only town in the United States named for the wife of George Washington. Mrs. Roosevelt's efforts resulted in TVA building a saddle dam between downtown Dandridge and the lake.

The first time we went to visit Mary's family and hometown I learned that in a museum in the Courthouse was a copy of the Davy Crockett and Polly Finley marriage bond dated August 12, 1806. The frontiersman's formative years were spent in Jefferson County where he met and married Polly Finley of Finley Gap in Bays Mountain.

Everyone in those days knew the story of David Crockett, 19th-century American folk hero, frontiersman, soldier and congressman, commonly known as "King of the Wild Frontier." He became a national legend in the 1830s. I was a teen-ager in the mid-1950s when a Crockett craze swept the U.S. and Europe. I had my own coonskin hat like he wore. A television series and movie, and a Broadway play rekindled his frontier fame. In 1955, Tennessee Ernie Ford led the hit parade with *The Ballad of Davy Crockett* sung in his popular booming baritone voice. It began this way:

218

"Born on a mountain top in Tennessee, greenest state in the land of the free
Raised in the woods so's he knew ev'ry tree, kilt him a b'ar when he was only three
Davy, Davy Crockett, king of the wild frontier!"

Obviously, the folk hero was a skilled bear hunter at an early age, but becoming a marksman at the tender age of three was part of his mythical legend.

While Mary and I were having a soda at Tinsley-Bible Rexall Drugs, across from the Courthouse, I mentioned that the Grainger family claimed a Davy Crockett kinship. He was either my Grandfather Thomas Grainger's third cousin, which he emphasized in the family bible that I proudly inherited, or he was our fourth great uncle, according to my younger sister, Linda James' genealogical research. In both, the link was Mary Crockett, Thomas Grainger's grandmother. Her father was Benjamin Franklin Crockett, whose father was Wilson Crockett, brother of Davy Crockett. Mary Crockett married Steven T. Grainger in 1851, who during the Civil War was a private in Company B of the Eighth Confederate Calvary. Steven Grainger was born in 1822 died in 1905 and is buried in Carroll County, GA. During the War Between the States, he was a private in Company B of the 8th Confederate Calvary Regiment.

Mary's heritage included Revolutionary War soldiers and Civil War brothers fighting on opposite sides. She was a direct descendent of Governor John Sevier, who played a leading role, both militarily and politically, in Tennessee's pre-statehood period and was elected the state's first governor in 1796.

Confronting Joint Issues

Some people believe the nine lives myth is related to cats' ability to always land on their feet. Over time, people have witnessed cats survive in situations that surely would have severly injured or killed other animals.

In the mid-Eighties I did something really stupid. Across the street from our home on Dunsmore Street in Jones Valley the city had constructed a wide, flat-bottom, six-foot deep, concrete ditch, sloped at 45 degrees, to hasten the flow of water running off the slopes on each side of the valley. Between the ditch and street was a median sloping slightly toward the ditch that was filled with knee-high Johnson grass that the city had failed to cut. Annoyed by the city's lack of maintenance, one holiday afternoon when I finished mowing our large lot, I took it on myself to do the city's job. I drove my big John Deere riding lawn mower across the street to cut the Johnson grass on the sloping median. When I finished and drove the few feet uphill to the curb the lawnmower blade assembly stuck on the ground. I backed up to gain enough speed to force my way across. Suddenly, when I applied the brakes, instead of stopping the big mower moved backward toward the concrete ditch. The big tractor went backward toward certain trouble.

"Hey, this is maybe just a bruise," I thought. "Maybe I can crawl out of here." As my mind cleared, I had crawled to a wrought-iron ladder ten or fifteen yards away, when neighbors who had heard the loud noise of the crash began arriving. "I am okay. Don't call an ambulance," I mumbled. When they helped me to our house my substitute for emergency medical care was to pour a heavy shot of Jack Daniels. The pain was heavy, numbing. But I was convinced it was only a deep bruise

The next day I was at my orthopedic doctor's office as soon as it opened. First came the obligatory x-ray. When he came into the room to announce the results, Dr. Kendall Black spoke in the unforgettably deep baritone intoned every year when he presented honorees at the Cotillion Ball: "Mr. Grainger, you have broken your damn back!" Over time it healed, but I further complicated matters by rupturing L-5, the lower back vertebrae, by getting in the wrong position working out with weights at a gym. By the early 2000s, when I had transitioned into my new consulting career, I also had developed frequent pain from spinal stenosis, the narrowing of the spinal canal, in that area of the lower back.

Upon advice of medical friends, I scheduled surgery at the University of Alabama in Birmingham hospital. The surgeon was the highly-regarded head of Neurosurgery. UAB was recognized for its surgical expertise, beginning in the early Sixties with the pioneering open-heart surgery of Milburn Stone, a famous actor on the television series, "*Gunsmoke*." My lower back operation relieved the stenosis problems but I was still left with arthritic problems and scar tissue. The first casualty was golf. I found I could not continue to play the sport that I had enjoyed on the average of twice a week for 25 years at home and at some of America's top courses. It particularly hurt to bend over to putt. I tried a chest-high putter, but still it was necessary to bend over to see the ball to line up putts. After giving up after a few holes the next couple of times to try a return to golf, I gave it up totally.

My new right hip, consisting of exotic high strength metal, healed in five weeks. The doctors then informed me there was very little cartridge remaining to support the left hip joint, so it should be replaced soon. I was scheduled to have that hip replaced thirteen years later, on December 5, 2013. But as I exercised in the hospital "joint camp" in preparation for the surgery the hamstrings strengthened. That took most of the load off the worn-out hip. The pain subsided. So, I postponed surgery. Indefinitely. As long as I stretch the hamstrings regularly---rolling forward and backward on a big rubber ball to reduce the weight on the worn hip joint---there is no necessity to replace the other hip joint.

"Indefinitely" lasted nearly two years, until August 17, 2015. In spite of glucosamine lubricants and daily stretching of the hamstrings rolling forward and backward on a large rubber ball, the pain was returning. I needed to go forward with that hip replacement. But who would ever imagine how it would happen the way it did?

We were getting ready to celebrate Grainger Reeves 17th birthday and I was videoing his two younger brothers playing a game of wet football in their swimming pool. One would jump off the diving board, catching the small football thrown by his brother before breaking the surface of the water. A few minutes later Coleman swam on the other end of the pool. I shot a still photo as he treaded water, smiling broadly. The view was enhanced by beautiful plants in large pots at the end of the pool. Totally focused on the colorful scene, I took a step backward to include more of the large flowers. I was so focused on the photo that I forget that just that morning Carla had mentioned the danger of the single-step ledge at that end of the pool. She said they planned to have it redesigned because more than one person had stumbled on that step. But as I concentrated on the composition of the photograph, I took another step backward.

Suddenly I was walking in space, falling backward out of control. I pumped my legs madly trying to reach purchase with something to regain balance. That rearward pumping action of my legs propelled me just enough that the instinctive attempt to regain balance may well have saved my life. Or at the least a serious concussion. When my left hip landed on the concrete patio, the upper body snapped back sharply. But my head landed on the soft dirt of a flower bed rather that the hard concrete of the patio. Time ran together, unlike my previous encounter with a concrete ditch when my mind measured time in frame-by-frame milli-seconds as my riding lawnmower plunged backward into the concrete ditch. The sensation was sudden. I was walking backward, then struggling for balance. The point of impact was on my wallet on the rear of my left hip.

As I lay stunned Carla rushed out. She cradled my head, saying, "Just lie still, I'm calling an ambulance."

"Don't do that, I'm alright," I moaned, instinctively resisting the embarrassment of the arrival of an emergency vehicle. Surely, I would be better, I thought. It must be just a bruise. No, as sanity returned, I realized that it was more serious than that. The pain was agonizing. My mind flashed back to Dr. Kendall Black's announcement, "Mr. Grainger you have broken your damn hip." I was experiencing the worst agony of my life when the emergency medics arrived. The peak was when they partially lifted me in order to slide my 215 pounds onto a metal sheet to permit them to lift me onto a gurney. Injections of pain-killer and warnings before each bump helped, but barely reduced the suffering on the trip to Saint Joseph's hospital. There, after two hours of painful waiting by a staff overwhelmed by other emergencies and indigent walk-ins, I was transferred from my tiny cubicle to the x-ray department. That was the most painful part of the hospital process, as an aggressive technician pushed me around to film the hip from several angles. Back in my cubicle, the emergency room doctor finally appeared. He announced that I had a femoral neck fracture of the left hip. That was the same hip so long overdue for replacement.

A short time later the orthopedic surgeon arrived. He said they would be able to treat it by replacing the hip joint. "Doctor, this is a crazy, painful way for me to get the hip replacement I have postponed so long," was all I could say. An accident was forcing me to have done what I have been postponing all this time: replacement of the left hip, now worn at the joint to bone-on-bone in lieu of cartridge. What if I had gone ahead and had it done earlier? No doubt the solution would have been to replace it again. So maybe there had been an element of divine intervention here.

223

By the time the surgery began I was flying high on pain-killing chemicals. I do remember that at times toward the end of the hour-long surgery I was partially conscious for brief periods. I recall opening my eyes and seeing that I was enclosed in something that looked like a plastic tent, held tight by small ropes. A doctor leaned close to whisper assurances that everything was going fine. I vividly remember the ringing-like pounding of some sort of surgical hammer, driving the metal stake into the thigh bone that held the ball that would fit into the hip joint. I visualized the ringing sound of a railroad worker driving steel stakes into cross-ties holding the rails. I felt some pain with each stroke of the hammer, but it seemed like less than a four on a scale of ten. When asked before the anesthetic was injected, I rated the pain level at "ten-plus." As I came out of it the anesthesiologist was there to welcome me back to planet earth. I was heartened when I heard the word "perfect" coming from more than one direction. I could hear nurses celebrating in the background. The anesthesiologist explained that the celebration was for mine being the last surgery of the day.

After four days of hospitalization, where the food was terrible but the medicine helped, I was dismissed to transfer to an in-patient rehabilitation facility in East Cobb.

Mary's Life Story Is Fascinating

Mary's life story is fascinating. She had a famous father, then a famous third cousin. They were the only two pilots known as "Sully" to glide planes to safe landings, probably the only two relatives to do it. Her father was a World War II member of the Army Medical Corps, who saved the lives of both soldiers and civilians, was a flying physician after the war, who miraculously survived when his single engine plane froze up in the frigid weather over the Smoky Mountains while taking the opportunity for an aerial view of the colorful foliage in November, 1955. He glided into a tree, was attacked by a bear, and walked 15 miles to a ranger station three days later. The search for him commanded national attention. The other safe landing would be the miracle of aviation history--- Sam Sullenberger's first cousin's son US Airways Captain Chesley Burnett "Sully" Sullenberger III, 57, who 54 years later successfully glided his ailing aircraft to in the Hudson River and saving 155 lives.

Here's Mary's version of what her family experienced when Dr. Sullenberger's engine froze near the Smokies highest peak:

"When he failed to return that evening, a search began, involving the Civil Air Patrol, other agencies, and hundreds of volunteers from our community and the surrounding area. My mother, three sisters, my brother and I, were combing the mountains as part of the team. After three days, our hopes were diminishing when word came that he had walked into a ranger station at the foot of the mountain. We cheered and cried with relief and gratitude when we got the news over our car radio. It was a miracle! "When we arrived home about the same time Daddy did, our yard and the street in front of our house were filled with reporters and well-wishers. Daddy told us that when the engine froze and he knew he was going to crash, he was able to guide the plane and "soft-land" into the top of a tree. He was knocked out on impact, but when he regained consciousness, he was able to climb to the ground. He had his medical bag with him and some food, so he was able to treat his head wound and survive on the food he had. Then, he was attacked by a bear, whose cub wanted to share his food. But he was able to escape with only a large gash on his stomach, by throwing the food he was eating to attract her attention. He temporarily treated the gash, then followed a stream down the mountain to the ranger's house."

In January 2009, I was watching the nightly news in our den when I first heard the news bulletin that a commercial pilot by the name of Chesley Burnett Sullenberger III had saved the lives of everyone on board his commercial flight when the engines were clogged with a flock of geese. "Mary, come in here quickly." I shouted to the kitchen where Mary was cooking the evening meal. "I believe this pilot must be your cousin." She quickly came up with a family tree that showed her father's uncle and first cousin to have that same name. Chesley III's grandfather had migrated from East Tennessee to Texas. Mary's third cousin, "Sully" Sullenberger became an instant international folk hero after performing perhaps the greatest aviation feat of all time. Miraculously, all 155 people on board were rescued safely.

Sam Venable, a columnist for the Knoxville *News-Sentinel* described the similarities as a "family tradition." He recounted the story of Sam Sullenberger, known as "Sully" during World War II, gliding into a tree to survive a harrowing plane crash. On Saturday, Nov. 5, 1955, Dr. Sam Sullenberger had finally trekked to Big Creek ranger station in the Great Smoky Mountains National Park, after three nights in freezing weather and a black bear attack ended a massive search for the downed pilot from Dandridge.

Mary's younger brother recalled a boyhood encounter with the now-famous US Airways pilot: "In 1954, Dad and I flew in an air race to California," said Blake Sullenberger, 62, of Knoxville. "We spent one night in Denison, Texas, at the home of his cousin, Chesley. He was a dentist. "I was 8 at the time. They had a son who was about 3. That would have been Chesley III. "I don't remember much about him, though," Blake said with a chuckle, "except that he was running all around the house." Venable quoted Blake's sisters, Mary Sullenberger Grainger of Huntsville, Ala., and Priscilla Sullenberger Millard of Maryville, adding to the story after consulting the family tree. One of their ancestors was Samuel Jacob Sullenberger, who lived in Morristown in the late 1800s. He had four sons: Dan, Charles, John and Chesley. "John was our grandfather," said Grainger. "Chesley was Chesley III's grandfather." Sully Sullenberger responded to her email and told her he hoped to see his East Tennessee relatives soon.

In fact, he saw Mary and me a few months later when he was honored along with 24 Medal of Honor winners at a dinner in Huntsville. He was given the American Spirit Award during the Medal of Honor Gala - "In the Company of Heroes." The event was attended by 24 of the 87 living Congressional Medal of Honor recipients. When he arrived at the dinner event, attendees formed a long line at the entrance. Mary held a small hand-written sign welcoming her cousin to Huntsville. "There's Mary," Sully could be heard remarking to his wife. Following the dinner, the *Huntsville Times*, photographed the Sullenbergers with Mary.

According to media accounts, Chesley III went to high school in Denison, graduated from the U.S. Air Force Academy and served as a military fighter pilot. He has flown commercially since 1980, has his own safety consulting company in Danville, Calif., and has assisted in a number of investigations for the National Transportation Safety Board. Both Presidents Bush and Obama have praised his skillful demeanor for preventing a catastrophe when Flight 1549 became disabled shortly after takeoff from LaGuardia. "Sam Sullenberger's crash in 1955 was a solo affair," Venable wrote. "But the circumstances around it are the stuff of legend." A seasoned aviator who was known as the "flying country doctor," he went aloft Nov. 2 for an afternoon of viewing fall foliage in the Smokies. Thirty minutes into the journey, the engine of his Piper Cub abruptly lost power. To make matters worse, he caught a sudden downdraft. As Sullenberger described in a 1955 *News Sentinel* interview, he put the plane down in the safest place he could immediately find---a grove of saplings near the base of Mount Guyot, elevation 6,621 feet.

Howell T. Heflin, a Man of Principle

The phone voice was distinctive, like the Hollywood actor, James Earl Jones, whose booming voice made him the perfect choice to play "God" in a late Twentieth Century movie. Only this one had a Deep South accent, higher pitched but definitely distinctive.

"Choll-ee," the caller said. "This is How-well Heflin. I read your news articles about the tornado that hit Colbert County. Could we talk about that?"

"Yes, sir," I replied to the best-known trial attorney in Northwest Alabama.

"The part about the fellow you interviewed who said he was visiting from the Northwestern part of the United States. Checking the damages to the ante-bellum home he owned southwest of Tuscumbia. Do you recall for sure that he said he now lives in Oregon?"

"Yes, sir," I said.

"I am representing a party in a divorce case in Federal court in Birmingham and I would appreciate it if you would ride down there with me in a couple of weeks and let me ask you about what he said in court."

It turned out attorney Heflin was attempting to establish jurisdiction in Federal court, which tended to be more generous for spouses in the division of property than state court cases. Through my testimony, he hoped to show that his Alabama client was suing a resident of another state. He picked me up in a large Buick the morning of the hearing and we drove to Birmingham. He chewed on a cigar non-stop. He was a fascinating conversationalist.

That, in the mid-1950s, was the beginning of a long relationship with Howell Thomas Heflin, one of the most highly-respected members of the U.S. Senate from 1978 to 1997. That trip to Birmingham as a young college student was the beginning of a close, enduring friendship until his death in 2005. After a highly successful career as a trial lawyer, in 1970 he was elected chief justice of the state's Supreme Court. He took over a state judiciary in a state of severe disrepair and, through cajolery and masterful political maneuvering, turned it into such a model of judicial efficiency that he was elected president of the nation's chief justices. He was first elected to the Senate in 1978, and reelected in 1984 and 1990 — each time overwhelmingly.

I was a political writer for *Birmingham News*' in mid-1962 when I received a call from a friend, Ed Mauldin, a Leighton farmer and ginner. He asked if I would be interested in coming home to publish a weekly newspaper, he co-owned with Heflin. It was shortly after the exciting gubernatorial race, won by former Circuit Judge George C. Wallace. I had been in the middle of that three-way race for Governor, alternating riding a week at a time in the back seat between campaign stops with the three leading candidates. I was looking at weeks of relative boredom in which politics was on the back page, following the daily excitement of the gubernatorial race, statewide Congressional elections, and others.

Mauldin's timing was perfect. And I had great respect for him and his partner, Tuscumbia attorney Howell Heflin. They had established *The Valley* Voice a few months earlier to provide Colbert County with a true home county newspaper in competition with the *Florence Times-Tri-Cities Daily*, a powerful daily located across the river in Florence that served the entire Muscle Shoals area. The *Valley Voice* was published weekly, tabloid size until we graduated to a full-size newspaper the following year. *The Muscle Shoals Morning Sun*, where I had been Sports Editor a few months in the late Fifties, had tried unsuccessfully to compete with the *Times-Daily*. By 1962, Mauldin had become nationally recognized for his knowledge of agricultural issues and Heflin was one of the state's leading trial lawyers.

The three of us were partners in that enterprise for 15 months. I am convinced the true character of a person can best be realized through a business partnership. I learned that Howell Heflin and Ed Mauldin were gentlemen with high principles. They never suggested editorial content and cheered us on as we gained statewide notice with our editorials and news coverage that included an invitation to the White House. Both were active in their communities, Heflin in Tuscumbia and Mauldin in Leighton. Of the two, I thought Mauldin would someday run for a high office, but Mauldin was content with a highly successful career as a large cotton farmer, cotton ginner, tractor dealer, banker, respected advisor to Congress and the Legislature on agricultural issues---and the strongest supporter of his old high school pal in Heflin's successful campaigns for Supreme Court Chief Justice and U.S. Senate.

Ours was a great relationship in an unfortunate location. Merchants in deteriorating Sheffield, staid Tuscumbia, and still-slow-growing Muscle Shoals City, were not anxious to advertise sufficiently in a weekly newspaper for it to achieve significant growth. That was the case until our competitor's press union closed it down for two weeks in 1963 and we published fat newspapers filled with advertisements. When I came in hoping to restore a wayward paper to a successful business, the fiscally-conservative Heflin would sit behind the cluttered desk in his dimly-lit office, squirming, grunting, then writing his check to meet payroll. He was always honest and supportive.

Our association continued until Huntsville's Milton Cummings sent an emissary asking me to come over to Huntsville to talk with him about being his chief assistant. I had developed an appetite for the management side of the newspaper while supervising a total of eight fulltime and parttime employees. A management career at a blossoming aerospace company sounded like an exciting career opportunity. When I told Heflin and Mauldin that Cummings was offering the opportunity to pursue a management career with a large company they said, "We understand. Please just wait until we can sell the paper." No problem. The timing was right. We were still riding the revenue crest from our daily competitor's strike. We sold the *Valley Voice* in two weeks to a publisher in Northport, who had grown up in Colbert County.

Ed Mauldin and Howell Heflin had been close pals growing up in Leighton. When Mauldin returned after college and military service, he focused on operating family farms. He became one of the most knowledgeable and influential Alabama farmers regarding national agriculture issues. He was a pro-parity advocate, a champion of the family farm even though he was one of the Tennessee Valley's largest farmers. A Mauldin trademark was his frequent letters typed on his Royal typewriter in bright green ink to members of Congress to communicate complex farm issues. During my time at the *Birmingham News* he was a key member of the Alabama Legislature's Cotton Study Commission and was appointed to the National Agriculture Advisory Committee by President Kennedy. When I needed background inputs for stories on farm issues, Mauldin was the person I called.

Heflin worked in a general store during high school and played on the football team. As the nephew of one of the most colorful U.S. Senators in Alabama's history, Thomas "Cotton Tom" Heflin, Howell Heflin took an early interest in politics. While in elementary school he first heard his Uncle Tom speak. "I remember he quoted a poem," Heflin said. "He said it was by an anonymous poet. I was pretty young but I had read the poem. After his speech I ran home and looked it up. I ran over to the train station to give him the name of the poet he had quoted. I was trying to make an impression on him." Heflin went on from there to practice speaking in the garden to an audience of corn stalks before becoming a regular winner of oratorical contests in high school.

At 6 feet four, 275 pounds, Heflin stood out for his hulking frame, Southern drawl, and slow, deliberate gait. He wore his pants hiked so high above a mammoth stomach there was no danger of slippage. Heflin projected an image of a stereotypical Southern politician with folksy story-telling style delivered in hill country Southern-ese. All of which to the unknowing disguised a deeply intelligent and serious leader. His stories usually involved a mythical country lawyer known as "No Tie" Hawkins, whose name derived from the fact that he was constantly getting in trouble with judges because he refused to dress properly in court. "No Tie" had a cousin named "Sockless Sam," something of a courthouse loiterer who was occasionally available to provide perjured testimony when his cousin "No Tie" had a particularly difficult case on his hands.

When the First Lady was out of town for the weekend, President Ronald Reagan often invited Heflin, Senator Alan Simpson (R-Wyoming), and Democratic House Speaker Tip O'Neill to the White House to smoke cigars and tell tall tales. Politically, Heflin was said to favor Reagan initiatives so often the conservative Democrat voted with the President more often than some Senate Republicans. During the widely-televised committee hearings of Clarence Thomas' nomination to the Supreme Court, Heflin's "Senator Claghorn" Southern style attracted a wide range of international followers. Heflin fan clubs sprang up in such places as the United Kingdom.

In 1994, Senator Heflin was dining in Dirksen Cafeteria with two reporters when he felt a sneeze coming on. He reached into his pocket and pulled out a bit of fabric and---lo and behold!---began to wipe his nose with a pair of ladies underwear. His explanation: While dressing in the darkness of early morning before rushing out the door he mistakenly picked up a pair of his wife's white silk panties from a stack of linens next to what he thought was his normal stack of handkerchiefs. Heflin sheepishly replied that in the future he would be using colored handkerchiefs. The next day, I was Heflin's guest, seated on his immediate right at a White House ceremony celebrating the 25ᵗʰ anniversary of the lunar landing. Controversial First Lady Hillary Clinton was on Heflin's left. "Oh,", she ribbed him, "Thank you, Senator, thank you, for getting us off the front page."

While Heflin was hypnotizing juries in Colbert County in 1952, State Rep. Noah S. "Soggy" Sweat, Jr, a Mississippian from Corinth gave his famous "whiskey" speech to the Mississippi Legislature. "In my memory I can vividly recall the hulking, bear-like Heflin, his pants belted tightly around his chest, above his large stomach, leaning into the microphone as he read that humorous speech:

"My friends, I had not intended to discuss this controversial subject at this particular time. However, I want you to know that I do not shun controversy. On the contrary, I will take a stand on any issue at any time, regardless of how fraught with controversy it might be. You have asked me how I feel about whiskey. All right, this is how I feel about whiskey:

"If when you say whiskey you mean the devil's brew, the poison scourge, the bloody monster, that defiles innocence, dethrones reason, destroys the home, creates misery and poverty, yea, literally takes the bread from the mouths of little children;

"But, if when you say whiskey you mean the oil of conversation, the philosophic wine, the ale that is consumed when good fellows get together, that puts a song in their hearts and laughter on their lips, and the warm glow of contentment in their eyes

"This is my stand. I will not retreat from it. I will not compromise."

Heflin's humor helped him connect with voters so well that in his final race for the Senate his supporters laughed his Republican opponent away to a smashing defeat. His opponent was a wealthy Republican industrialist country clubber from the state's richest city, the Mountain Brook suburb of Birmingham, who Heflin perceived as having difficulty connecting with blue collar Alabamians. He labeled him my "Grey Poupon Republican opponent," capitalizing on a popular television ad that featured a rich stuffy man in a limousine pronouncing the name of a mustard product in ritzy tones. Campaign crowds roared as Heflin drawled in a mocking, "hoity-toity" voice, "My Gucci clothed, Jacuzzi-soaking, Mercedes-driving, Perrier-drinking polo-playing, debutante-dancing, high society ritzy-rich Republican who has a summer home in Kennebunkport" – Hayman, John and Clara Ruth, *A Judge in the Senate, Howell Heflin's Career of Politics and Principle," P366, New South Books, 2001.*

Heflin was an economic conservative, with strong support from the Alabama business community, and a social moderate, strongly supported by minorities and unions. Referring to his judicious approach to issues and the notoriety extending from his leadership in judicial reform, fellow senators called him "Judge" Heflin. For 13 years, he was viewed as the Senate's ethical guardian, passing judgment on his colleagues as a senior member or chairman of the Senate Select Committee on Ethics. "In all the years I've known Howell Heflin, I've never heard the slightest hint of scandal or unethical conduct associated with his name," wrote former Montgomery newsman Ray Jenkins in the Baltimore Sun. Jenkins, Ray. "Heflin Really Does Talk Like That." The Baltimore Evening Sun, September 29, 1991

The flag is offensive to millions of Americans because it was under that banner that blacks were enslaved." [Hayman,, 389, Flynt, Wayne, *Alabama in the Twentieth Centery. The University of Alabama Press, 2004. P.369]* In his most dramatic departure from his Confederate forbears, he made a dramatic speech on the Senate floor in 1993 urging his colleagues to respect the progress made in removing racism. His speech set off an emotional reaction in the Senate that resulted in the defeat of an amendment renewing a patent for the United Daughters of the

Confederacy to display a symbol of the Confederate flag. Some called it Heflin's finest hour. Alabama editors were mixed in their reactions. The *Gadsden Times* wrote that he had "turned his back on his Confederate forefathers" while the *Decatur Daily* wrote that he took the moral high ground.

From that early beginning as a newspaper reporter testifying at his request in a divorce case, to our relationship at the *Valley Voice,* to serving as a close advisor throughout his Senate career, my relationship with Howell Heflin grew even stronger over the years. After his election to the Senate in 1979, my boss Joe Moquin and I met with him at the Huntsville Airport as he prepared to fly to Washington, D.C. to begin an 18-year tenure in the Senate. We showed him our research that revealed that space and defense dollars ranked at the top, along with agriculture, as the largest contributors to the Alabama economy. Heflin never forgot that. From that time forward, I was an unofficial advisor to him on those issues. He was a constant advocate of a land-based ballistic missile defense and was the first senator to call for the building of a manned space station. He became the Senate strategist who saved the space station from several budget cutting attacks. He convinced Democratic Presidential nominee Michael Dukakis to change his position from opposing the station to supporting it in 1988 and helped create Huntsville fund-raisers for key members of Senate space committees.

The most serious threat to the survival of Space Station Freedom came in the early days of President Bill Clinton's first administration. His first budget recommended cancellation of the space station as a part of his program to downsize government. Heflin looked for ways to motivate his old friend and longtime NASA supporter, Vice President Al Gore, to directly engage the President on the

To Charlie Grainger
Best Wishes,

Bill Clinton

**President Bill Clinton with Senator Howell Heflin at White
House event honoring lunar landing anniversary, 1996**

issue. Heflin arranged to be in the Senate gym when he knew Gore
would be working out to squeeze in arguments as they occurred to
him for Gore to make to Clinton. After they had brought Clinton
around, the president looked to Heflin for strategic leadership
to combat Senate amendments to kill the program. As we were
leaving the White House celebration of the 25th anniversary of the
lunar landing, Clinton intercepted us in the corridor. He steered
us into a private spot in the adjacent corridor where Heflin gave
him a detailed update of his plans to combat destructive floor
amendments. Heflin extolled the space program's contributions to
medical and technology breakthroughs and detailed experiments
that would be undertaken on the earth-orbiting space station. He
often reminded friends that when he suffered heart illness in the
Nineties it was through the miracle of aerospace technology---first
installation of a stent, then a pacemaker---that he had survived.

Throughout Heflin's Senate tenure, I was an unofficial advisor on space and defense issues. He provided temporary space in a cubical outside his office for me to write speeches on space and defense issues. In 2001, Heflin's biography was published. He wrote on the first page of my copy, "To my advisor and friend Charles Grainger. I will always be in your debt! Howell Heflin." Republican Senate Majority Leader Robert Dole wrote in the book's introduction that Heflin was a "compassionate and understanding man of vision and integrity who never crossed over into the liberal realm, but he helped move the South and the nation to a greater acceptance of diversity. He represented the transition from the old to the new. – "The old South to the New South, Jim Crow to Equal Rights." Hayman, P.11

On the afternoon of March 30, 1995, I was at my cubicle when he waved me into his office for a chat. He confided that he had decided he would not seek reelection in 1996 due to the deterioration of his health and the desire to live out the remainder of his years among his old friends in his home town. He had not completely recovered from heart problems and was suffering from diabetes. We had scheduled dinner that night with our wives at the 701 Restaurant on Pennsylvania Avenue. When Elizabeth Ann Heflin arrived, he made his decision official by sharing it with his friend and advisor of a half-century. She was pleased that he had made the decision best for his health. His Senate career ended in October, 1996. As his staff cataloged his mementos to be archived at the University of Alabama Law School, a framed photograph on his office wall stood out. It was a picture snapped by our *Valley Voice* photographer of Heflin and Mauldin greeting President Kennedy when he came to Muscle Shoals in 1963 to celebrate the 30th anniversary of the Tennessee Valley Authority. His biographer John Hayman quoted me as saying, "I have never been around an officeholder who is more tenacious. In a body where processes are tied to the committee system, he regularly offers successful amendments and carries the day on issues such as NASA and defense, even though he is not a member of the committee of jurisdiction." – Hayman, P.428

Other senators recognized that Heflin was far more than a congenial humorist and entertaining conversationalist. He was exceptionally bright and a hard worker. When he announced his retirement, Senators took more than six hours marching to the microphone to offer tributes. The senator who perhaps characterized Heflin's service best was Senator Paul Wellstone (D-Minnesota): "He is the alternative to cynicism. He is hope. And he is honor." Wellstone, Paul. "Tribute to Howell Heflin." *Congressional Record*. March 29, 1995.

In his farewell address on the Senate floor in September 1996, Heflin noted that he came from "an ancestral background deeply rooted in the old confederacy," and he was "exceedingly proud" of his own civil rights record. "It has been publicly stated by black leaders that I was the first senator from my state who believed in and supported the civil rights movement," Mr. Heflin said in his farewell speech. "I worked to secure the extension of the Voting Rights Act; to appoint African-Americans and women to the federal bench and other federal offices; to support historically black colleges; to ensure passage of the civil rights restoration bill; to help pass the fair housing bill; and to establish a national holiday honoring the late Martin Luther King Jr." He found a growing trend toward partisanship and demonization of opposing views. "We must set a new course in Congress and across the land---a course of moderation, tolerance, responsibility, and compassion. We need to return to the tradition of being just plain neighborly." – Hayman, P. 431, Pear, Robert. "Howell Heflin, Former Alabama Senator, Dies at 83." *New York Times*, March 30, 2005.

During his retirement years, he hung out at his son's law office, worked out at a gym, and drank coffee with his buddies. I stopped by their historic hillside house several times during his retirement years for always-pleasurable visits. In 2005, Judge Heflin suffered a fatal heart attack at the age of 83. News of his passing was met with valedictory comments inside and outside his home state. Above all, he was remembered as a man of conscience and high principles.

Heflin Honors His Long-time
Friend and Unofficial Advisor

In 1996, following my receipt of Huntsville's "distinguished service award," my warm friend and former business partner entered the following tribute in the *Congressional Record* which became my most treasured accolade.

Tribute To Charles E. Grainger

Congressional Record
Volume 142, Number 50
Pages S3620-S3621
Legislative Body: Senate
Date: <u>Thu, April 18, 1996</u>
<u>Sen. Howell Thomas Heflin</u>

Mr. President, one of the major reasons that Huntsville, AL, has been nationally recognized as one of the country's top high-technology growth areas is the strength and vitality of its community leadership. One of these visionary leaders is Charles E. Grainger, vice president of administration at Teledyne Brown Engineering and 1992 chairman of the Huntsville-Madison County Chamber of Commerce. Recently, he received the chamber's Distinguished Service Award.

As chairman of the chamber 4 years ago, Charlie Grainger expanded its economic development emphasis to create a coordinated Partnership for Economic Development. Madison County led all Alabama's counties in new plant and equipment investments that year.

As vice president of administration at Teledyne Brown, a major defense contractor, Charlie is responsible for coordinating governmental relations activities with agencies and Congress. He has overall management responsibility for the departments of human resources, facilities, public relations, administrative services, security, technical communications, and computing resources and technology. He has held his current position since 1978, having served as director of administration from 1967 to 1978. He joined Brown Engineering as assistant to the director of administration in 1963.

Charlie was elected to the Alabama House of Representatives in 1968 and 1970, and was an award-winning legislator. He sponsored a water pollution control act and a school bus safety act, both of which became national models. Both pieces of legislation were named after their sponsor by joint resolution, which is somewhat rare. As a member of the Ways and Means Committee, he secured funding to begin the University of Alabama in Huntsville nursing education program, to establish physical health facilities at Alabama A&M University, and to complete the Huntsville-Madison County Mental Health Center. He served as an elected member of the Alabama Democratic Executive Committee from 1966 through 1990, serving as a delegate to the 1980 Democratic National Convention. He was a presidential campaign coordinator for Senator John Glenn in 1984 and Vice President Al Gore in 1988.

A native of Lawrence County, Alabama, Charlie grew up in Sheffield, attended Florence State College, and earned a master of science degree in management from Southeastern Institute of Technology. His work as a member of the Base Realignment and Closing Commission Community Task Force was invaluable during the base closure rounds of 1991, 1993, and 1995. He has received the Governor's Air Pollution Control Award; Madison County Good Government Award; Alabama Water Conservationist of the Year Award; and Huntsville-Madison County Mental Health Distinguished Service Award.

He was originally a journalist. He spent several years as a reporter for the Birmingham News. He served as editor and publisher of the *Valley Voice;* a weekly newspaper published in Tuscumbia.

One of the secrets to Charlie Grainger's phenomenal success is that he truly understands that in order to thrive and grow, the various groups and resources within a community must be united in supporting the bottom-line economic imperatives. In Huntsville's case these are the defense and space industries. He is an instrumental unifying force who sees the big picture and Huntsville's role in that picture. He is a leader who brings people from divergent points of view to common understandings so they can work together for the common good.

I congratulate and commend Charlie for all his accomplishments and for his superb leadership role in the development, growth, and vitality of the Huntsville area. He is a unique role model and a living testament to the tremendous results which can be realized through strong partnerships between government and industry.

CHAPTER 8

The 21ˢᵗ Century

Where will we be in this 21ˢᵗ Century?

A New Career, Successful in So Many Ways

In 1999, I continued to be happy. Then a friend from Boeing challenged me. "You can still do as much for them as you do now and still work for other companies." He was talking about Teledyne Brown Engineering and its external affairs, not the inside baseball we called operations. A few nights later, a group of us were having dinner in Philadelphia. Don Miller, a new friend, was sitting next to me. He brought up the same topic. "Charlie, you are known in the community as the person we see. That is not whether you can whisper in your boss' ear, it is what you do that helps everyone." He began to talk in dollars. It began to make sense. "Heck, with Boeing included, he is talking about more money than I am making now, plus all the other clients I could add."

So, that's how my new career began. I took those two and added five other clients the first year. The next one was the surprise. At the staff meeting of TBE executives who report to the president, he called on me last. I was seated on his immediate left and he went around the table before the last person was called on. As I began speaking, a few of the executives were already stirring, ready to adjourn as soon as I gave my report. But I shocked all, saying that after 36 years with the company I was planning to retire. The President was as surprised as anyone. I had just returned from the International Air Show in Paris. "I suppose that's where the conspiracy was hatched," he may have thought. He didn't ask that though, the only question he could ask was if I had already registered. Meaning that to lobby the person was required to register his intent with the proper agency. I told him that was a matter of telling the government what companies before actually I had made contact with DOD or whoever on their behalf. The meeting ended on that note. It didn't take long for his real reaction to make itself known. He asked me how much I would charge to represent TBE. The amount he offered was higher than Boing or Miltec was planning to pay. So, I took him up on it, after negotiating what I would take with me such as my computer and private papers, so the first company I officially represented was TBE. The others came easy. I had built up a reputation for success. I was going to be helping seven rather than one.

On September 1, 1999, C.G. Technologies, Inc. was ready to the face its challenges, with me at the helm and another employee, the treasurer of the company, wife Mary.

One of the first things was to register to represent my clients. TBE was followed with Miltec and Boeing. Over the next 18 years there were Sy Technologies, Gray Research, United Technologies, Camber, SAIC, Avion, Dynetics, General Atomics, and J2 Technologies. Since I was registered to lobby, I went about it with the strong belief that my lobbying was the best way for me to serve my clients and, indeed, my country. Lobbying and fundraising went hand in hand. I held events in Huntsville for Senators Glenn, Gore, Sasser, Riegle, Shelby, and Sessions and House members from Alabama, Representatives Griffith, Aderholt, Cramer, Rogers, and Roby, to name a few. And Cooper and Vann Hillary, from Tennessee, Weldon of Pennsylvania, and Wicker of Mississippi. In lobbying, we mostly dealt with legislation to get business through earmarks but often in making changes to laws.

Retiring from Big Company and Reloading in One Much Smaller

The first time I gave any thought to future retirement was when our daughter Carla was writing a research paper for a psychology class at the University of Alabama. She reviewed studies warning that those who retired from work completely were 40% more likely to have a heart attack or stroke, most of whom died in the first 18 months after retirement. "I can't imagine just suddenly retiring completely," I thought. "In my next career, I will try to pick the things I enjoy most and do them as long as I am having fun."

Carla wrote her paper in 1991. Eight years later, at age 62, I was not thinking of retiring from my high stress executive management job at a company of 2,000. At the time I was vice president of administration and government relations as well as acting vice president for business development. Events set me to thinking about retiring and reloading---taking early retirement and entering a new career in the consulting world. Those events were triggered when two company executives asked me, "Would you consider doing for us what you do best for your company?" They meant helping our government customers with their funding and helping bring in new business for the company. A one-person consulting business would permit me to focus on the fun side of business while leaving behind the stress of day-to-day management of a large organization. When I quietly shared my thinking with a third CEO, I was assured of retainers from three clients as soon as I opened the doors to this exciting new career. I could focus on doing what I loved---finding additional funding for Huntsville government agencies.

When I told my boss of my decision, he surprised me with an offer of his own. "If you are going to help other companies, we want your help, too," was the message from Teledyne Brown Engineering President Richard A. Holloway. This was exciting. Now, how to resolve the timing. First, I was working an issue that was too important to leave without resolution. When we won a major subcontract with the Boeing Company to support the Missile Defense Agency's Ground-Based Missile Defense program, the issue of a conflict of interest arose. We had been the Army's systems engineering and technical assistance (SETAC) contractor for over 25 years, serving in the key advisory role on missile defense technical matters. Working on the major Boeing subcontract, would cause us to be working on both sides of the road, as an evaluator/technical advisor on one hand and a system producer on the other. Some saw it as "grading your own papers." To avoid an organizational conflict of interest, we proposed to create a separate company with physical and legal "fire-walls" between the employees of the two companies. It would be a services company with a separate name, board of directors, and facility to provide the SETAC support.

This was new territory for the military bureaucracy. Our conflict of interest mitigation plan had been languishing for months in acquisition offices because no mid-level acquisition specialist was willing to make the decision. I had met once to explain the issue to the two three-star generals who commanded the two agencies. My credibility with them resulted from close relationships developed in supporting their budget requests on Capitol Hill. In dealing with the organizational conflict of interest issue I was wearing my contracts administration hat as the administrative head of the company. The lieutenant generals had offered to meet again if we did not receive a resolution within a reasonable period. I went back again. This time they jointly directed the decision to create the contractual "fire-wall." It worked well for both the government and our company for several years after I retired from the company and entered the consulting world. In fact, it became the template I later used for contracting officer approval of mitigation plans for other clients.

My early retirement decision was easier because I could qualify as a spouse under Mary's health insurance plan for teachers and avoid being caught without health insurance coverage for the three years preceding Medicare eligibility. I was 62; Medicare kicked in at 65. I officially retired from Teledyne Brown in the summer of 1999 to serve as President of newly-created CG Technologies, a consulting company supporting clients in governmental relations (assisting their government customers' funding pursuits), business development, strategic planning, and public relations. Mary became VP of Finance, paying the bills and handling invoices. I rented an office that I rarely used, preferring to work from an office upstairs at my home. That was how I met my number one retirement objective: avoiding long meetings. Our community covenants prohibited operating business offices within the residential neighborhood, so it was clear any meetings would be at clients' offices. As time wore on, meetings tended to be shorter and less frequent. I had a half-serious rule when taking visiting congressmen by client's offices that on the third acronym we were out of there. Of course, it is virtually impossible for almost all engineers to talk in non-technical terms. Even the Congressmen who were members of national security committees would pretend to understand the acronym so the briefer would go on to the next viewgraph.

As I pursued my new journey in the flexible world of retirement, I was again reminded of the study showing that people who retired completely were 40% more likely to die of a stroke or heard attach than those who were still working, at least part time. The increase was more pronounced during the first year after retirement and leveled off after that. Those pitfalls are mostly preventable, according to the Mayo Clinic, by lifestyles which include healthy eating and exercise, which also fuel the brain and can help delay cognitive deterioration, a part of aging for many. Experts saw the key to a healthy, happy retirement: Having fun. *USA Today*, Oct 21, 2013.

I envisioned the transition being heavily loaded on the front-end---working virtually full-time, then scaling back in future years by picking and choosing those projects I would most enjoy. Sixteen years later I was continuing on that path, gradually reducing my client base every year or two. That left more and more time to travel, exercise, read, write, and being present to witness the many proud moments of my grandsons' evolution through youth baseball and other sports.

I joined Facebook recently as a means of promoting my book. Already I can count on sales of 250 without the public relations push because many of the inquiries are from people sufficiently interested for me to count on. How long it will take for the rest is for people with more experience than this rookie author. I'm using IUniverse as the self-publishing house. A second book I'm planning to publish is virtually as complete as was this one. I am a driven high-speed guy. I'm still getting used to typing with one hand. Almost every sentence has at least one wrong hit of the keys and editing on the spot is essential. Otherwise, even I the author, might not know what I was trying to say. Thank goodness WORD has red letters for what it thinks are spelling errors and blue for questionable expressions.

The Second Visit to the Hospital, this Time Nearly Fatal

It began during one of Donald Trump's long speeches in Huntsville in 2017. It was then that I felt the first signs of the stroke that nearly took my life, although I didn't know what it was at the time. I had driven to my second home amidst the tree-tops in Sandy Springs, Georgia. I suffered my famous stroke about 2 p.m. I came to once that I recall. I was in my favorite chair, where I had been watching the Braves on television. I remember well my predicament. I kept reaching out with my left hand to retrieve my ringing cellphone. I could get within a few inches, but not the all-important full way. Oh, how I begged for Mary to come home. I stretched and kept stretching. But the distance was what was probably no more than six to 12 inches away on the nearby reading table. When I was conscious all I remember saying was, "Mary, please come home." I kept begging for her the entire 3 ½ hours that I lay there. Finally, at around 6 p.m., the face of Mary appeared like an angel.

I remember that at the night of the Trump rally, as we walked the four or five blocks from VBCC to the restaurant, I felt dizzy. I had two drinks and drove myself home. Gina Miller told Mary the day following the stroke that she had been concerned about my strange behavior the night of the Trump rally. The following Tuesday after I voted, I headed for Atlanta where a stroke awaited, just three days later.

Three-and-one-half hours was the time I was unconscious most of the time. The only thing I remember in that span was reaching for the phone and failing to reach it by less than a foot. "That was Mary calling." I had driven her to our daughter's house a few miles away earlier. She was recovering from rotator cup surgery and was unable to drive at the time. I told her I would come back in a couple of hours to pick her up, and we would go for a Friday night dinner. A little later, left was a mentally aware person who was normal except for inability to walk or operate normally from the right side. In other words, if you could function without the right leg or right arm when I had been a right-side dominant person, you had a perfect person.

After calling several times, Mary became concerned and came home, she called 911 and I was soon transported by ambulance to nearby Emory St. Joseph's Hospital, where they determined that too much time had passed to give the medication to dissolve the blood clot they found on the left side of the brain. I immediately went on a second ambulance ride to Grady Hospital, where neurosurgeon Dr. Diogo Haussen performed a thrombectomy, whereby they go through the groin to the brain and literally pluck the blood clot out of the brain, the process that saved my life!

This was on September 29, 2017. Thus, began the painfully slow process through rehabilitation. After ten days in intensive care at Grady, I spent the next 3 weeks at Emory Rehabilitation Center and another five weeks at Manor Care in Marietta. I went to our home in Sandy Springs in early December, at which time we hired Shay Welch as caregiver, and what a blessing she has been! From December 2017 until present, I have been in home health care, outpatient care, respite care, a couple of stays in the hospital with aspirational pneumonia, and presently am working out at a gym with a personal trainer, Derrick Sams, and Pilates instructor, Bonnie Spencer. I also have PT two days a week to strengthen my right side, and continue to make progress. Most recently I am participating in an adaptive golf class, a program sponsored by the GSGA. Who would have thought that having a stroke would bring me back to golf!

Second Career Lasted 18 Years

The second professional career lasted almost exactly 18 years. Where did it go? It was gone in a flash. I have gone nearly two years and the walking is gradually coming back, ever so slowly, after countless therapy sessions. The arm, not so good. It dangles with limited use when needed. But, hey, I'm not complaining. I promised the Good Lord if he would spare me that I would live out the remainder of my life serving Him in the best way I could. It has given me the time to finish writing this book. It already looks like two books realistically before final editing. The stroke ended my tenure as a lobbyist. I tired of getting extensions of time earlier this year and decided to concentrate on completion of the first one by time for friends to buy by Christmas. The prospects for that deadline are very real. I have laid the groundwork to the commercial publishing, since I originally began with an objective of having a small essay for the family and a few close friends. The response from others had been enormous. And gratifying.

Presidents I have known

I have known nine Presidents. I went to Washington in 1953 as a guest of Harry S. Truman. John Kennedy, Jimmy Carter, and Bill Clinton, I came to know on a personal basis. I met Richard Nixon in the summer of 1960, when I was a reporter and he was running for President. Lyndon Johnson was at the luncheon I attended at the White House in 1963, and along with Kennedy signed my placecard. George H. W. Bush I met when he was campaigning for his son's election reelection in 2003. George W. Bush I shook hands with at a fundraiser hosted by Senator Richard Shelby. I had a brief encounter with Donald Trump at a campaign rally for Luther Strange in 2017.

Harry S. Truman: (1945-1953). Began with Harry S. Truman's hosting a group of newspaper carriers to the White House Rose Garden for a Truman speech in 1951. "The Man from Independence" liked newspaper carriers and we liked him. He was from the school that to be a patriot one needed to support saving bond drives. That was the gist of that speech in the Rose Garden, as I recall it some 60 years later. He served in WWI, was elected to the Senate in 1940, to the Vice Presidency in 1944, and served as President from 1945 to 1953 He represented the U.S. in the peace negotiations and was the first President to preside over the atomic age. "Give 'em Hell, Harry" came to Decatur in 1960 on behalf of the Democratic candidates for President and Vice President. "*The Buck Stops Here.*" Harry S. Truman, 33rd President.

Richard M. Nixon (1969-74). Knew him in 1960 only as the reporter for the *Birmingham News* who was praised by his boss, Vincent Townsend, for his objective coverage of the then-Vice President, who stopped at Woodrow Wilson Park for a speech. Later, it became fashionable for politicians who always got a big laugh when addressing him with the nickname of Tricky Dick Nixon, or in Alabama Senator Lister Hill's manner at 1960 political rallies, Tricky-Dick-Meel-House Nix-on. He ran unsuccessfully for President in 1960 and lost a bid for California governor two years later. He became the 37th President, defeating Vice President Hubert H. Humphrey. He served as Vice President 1953-61. His administration ended the war with Viet Nam, brought home the POWs, introduced détente in the Anti-Ballistic Missile Treaty of 1971, and began the first diplomatic relations with China. He stepped down 1n 1974, halfway through his second term, rather than facing impeachment over his efforts to cover up illegal activities by members of his administration in the Watergate scandal. He resigned before the House could take the first step toward impeachment. His resignation was followed with a pardon by his successor, Gerald R. Ford. *"When a President does it, that means it's not illegal." Richard M. Nixon, 37th President.*

John F. Kennedy: (1962-63). Met him twice in one month. Also, Vice President Lyndon B. Johnson, when Alabama Editors were invited to the White House. We spent a delightful afternoon with Robert F. Kennedy, discussing how to manage the relationship between George Wallace and Martin Luther King. President Kennedy flew to Muscle Shoals for the celebration of the 30th anniversary of TVA. I was coordinator of a welcoming group of local dignitaries. Following behind me in the receiving line were Howell Heflin and Ed Mauldin, who shared in the ownership of the *Valley Voice*. As the 35th American President, he served during the heart of the Cold War and a majority of his time was spent in dealing with relations with the Soviet Union. His term was cut short by an assassin in November, 1963. *"We must use time as a tool, not as a* *couch." President John F. Kennedy. 35th President.* His life, including my rationale for selecting him as my all-time favorite President, is discussed in greater detail in Chapter 4 of this book.

Lyndon B. Johnson: (1963-70). At his nomination speech when he was running for an elected term as President at Atlantic City Democratic Convention in 1964. I was in the center as he made his points in the acceptance speech. Upon assuming the office when President Kennedy was killed, he unveiled a package aimed at creating the Great Society. First term achievements by his administration included the comprehensive Civil Rights Act of 1963, followed with the Voter Rights law of 1965. When he ran for a fouryear term of his own Johnson won the election by the largest margin of any candidate since 1820. Most historians rate him highly because of civil rights legislation and major laws dealing with gun control, wilderness protection, and Social Security while he has drawn substantial criticism for his escalation of the View Nam War. *"Until justice is blind to color, until education is unaware of race, until opportunity is unconcerned with the color of a man's skin, emancipation will be a proclamation but not a fact." Lyndon B. Johnson, 36th President.*

Jimmy Carter, (1975-1979: Met once when he was seeking reelection as President. I knew Ed Jenkins, his Press Secretary from Alabama, who hosted my wife Mary and me on a special tour of the White House after meeting the President in 1980. At a visit to Birmingham, he saw me out of the corner of an eye stepping forward, hand outstretched, was momentarily shocked at the sudden movement as he navigated his way through a large crowd. We saw him again at a Labor Day event that year at Spring Park in Tuscumbia. I met the First Lady, Rosalynn Carter, when she spoke to Monday night well-wishers when she stopped at the airport on the eve of the election. During Bush years, on a plane delayed by weather, weary passengers were surprised when a first-class passenger made his way down the aisle, shook every hand, kibitzed with each passenger from front to the back of the plane. I told him, on a hastily written note on a napkin, that I had been a Carter delegate during his 2nd campaign. He flashed the famous smile when he reached across to shake hands and was most sincere in his thanks. On my bucket list is a trip to Plains, Georgia, to attend his Sunday school class at the Maranantha Baptist Church, where he regularly teaches into his mid-90s. *"I've looked on many women with lust. I've committed adultery in my heart many times. God knows I will do this and forgives me."* Jimmy Carter, 39th President.

George H. W. Bush (1989-93): He came to Huntsville in 2003 for a fundraiser for his son, George, who was running for reelection as President. Was elected in the 1988 Presidential election as first incumbent Vice President to be elected in 152 years. Foreign policy drove his tenure in office. The Berlin Wall came down in 1989, the Soviet Union was dissolved two years later. His eldest son became President for the first of two terms in 2001. There was a need to distinguish between them, so the name, George H.W. Bush, became the means of separating him and the son. *"Courage is a terribly important value. It means you don't run away when things are tough. It means you don't turn away from a friend when he or she is in trouble…But courage is having the strength to do what's honorable and decent." George H. W. Bush, 41st President.*

William J. (Bill) Clinton (1991-2001): Met him in 1976 in Washington, when he came into the bar where I was sitting with my friend, Congressman Ray Blanton of Tennessee. I was impressed most of all with the most intense gaze I had ever seen on a politician, except for my favorite President of all, John F. Kennedy. He wore well the "you're the most important person in the world to me" expression. Mary and I attended the gala inaugural events for Clinton and Gore in 1993, where we saw a host of Hollywood stars. I met with him and First Lady Hillary Rodham Clinton at the White House when they hosted the gathering to celebrate the 25th Anniversary of the Lunar Landing. Present was astronaut Edwin (Buzz) Aldrin, who accompanied Neil Armstrong on the epic flight. I tagged along with Senator Howell Heflin, who that morning was exposed for pulling out of his pocket a pair of woman's underpants in front of a reporter from *Washington Post*, Sally Quinn at the main dining room in the Dirksen Building. Heflin, normally a plodding type, said he got in too big of a hurry that morning when he was off to work and his wife's panties were folded in the wrong stack where he kept his handkerchiefs. Hillary said in response at the White House celebration, "Thank you Senator for getting us off front page." Afterwards, Heflin and Joe Ritch and Steve Raby and I joined Clinton for their famous hallway conference on discussing ways to break deadlock on a critical Space Station vote. Heflin gave the President names of a couple of Senators he considered key and Clinton agreed to call both of them. Also attended the gala inaugural events for Clinton and Gore in 1992, which were covered with Hollywood stars. *There is nothing with America, that cannot be cured by what is right with America. William J. Clinton, 42nd President.*

George W. Bush (2001-2009): I shook hands with him once in the receiving line at a fundraiser hosted by Senator Richard Shelby in Tuscaloosa. That was at the time Bush was under attack from supporters of his opponent, John Kerry, for draft-dodging the Vietnam War. His first term came after a razor thin election over Al Gore of Tennessee, when Tennessee was won by Bush. The September 11 terrorist attacks occurred eight months after he took office. His response was to launch what was to become known as the "Bush Doctrine," launching a "War on Terror," an international military campaign that included the war in Afghanistan and the Iraq War. *We will not waver, we will not tire, we will not falter, and we will not fail. Peace and freedom will prevail." George W. Bush, America's 43rd President.*

Donald H. Trump: (2017-). When he came to Huntsville to speak at a Von Braun Civic Center rally for Attorney General Luther Strange in his campaign against Roy Moore, the week of my major stroke. He has stuck by his campaign commitments and accomplished a great deal. But Democrats and their allies, led by the media, are building their case to impeach Trump. They have the votes in the House to impeach on strictly a party-line vote. HE is their greatest ally. He and his propensity to tweet. There has been so much turnover, both from resignations and firings, that he is said to be the loneliest man in America. The trial will be in the Senate. Who knows whether the solid majority the GOP has now will hold firm like they are right now? It depends on TRUMP's behavior and whether those close to him remain so. The nation is deeply divided. *"The media is fake. Donald H. Trump, 43rd President.*

Other notable campaigns that I dealt with the candidates on a personal basis included:

John Glenn, U. S. Senator, unsuccessful candidate for President, 1973. The Ohio Senator and former astronaut, came to the Huntsville residence of Bryson Hill. I introduced him then and spent the day riding with him on a campaign bus across North Alabama on his second campaign visit to the state. He was defeated by Mike Dukakis, who was then defeated in the general election by Republican George H. W. Bush.

Al Gore Jr., U. S. Senator, unsuccessful candidate for the Democratic nomination in 1988. Mary and I served as Gore delegates at the Republican Convention in Atlanta in 1988, and became friends with Gore and his wife, Tipper. We spent an evening with them at the Governor's Mansion in Nashville, as guests of Ned McWhorter, where June and Johnny Cash were in attendance, and I was able to renew acquaintances with my buddy from rock and roll days. Gore became Vice President in 1993, and was defeated in the general election by George W. Bush in 2000 for President.

Mitt Romney, Republican nominee for President, 2013. I worked along with Stan McDonald, who served as chairman of the event, to a Huntsville rally stop at the home of Dr. Dennis Olive in his campaign in 1983.

Florida Panhandle: The World's Most Beautiful Beaches

Overlooked by most of the planet, I submit that the world's most beautiful beaches stretch along the 227 miles of the northwest Florida Panhandle where ultra-green Gulf of Mexico waves lap at blinding-white shores. From Pensacola east to Fort Walton, Destin, Panama City, and Apalachicola, clear emerald waters and towering dunes are interspersed with small towns where the fish bite, the folks are friendly, and local color abounds. It is a region that attracts vacationers from the South in spring and summer and Canadian and Midwestern Snowbirds in winter. That is enough as far as I am concerned. Beyond that, let's keep it secret from the masses.

As a youngster we went on vacation to Panama Beach where everyone else in our small town went. In time the Panhandle came to be known for the raucous spring break crowds of Panama City and dubbed the Redneck Riviera. The only time we have visited there in recent years was for youth baseball tournaments. The beaches are still great and the smallest grandchildren enjoyed a permanent carnival, but it was on the cheesy side

Forty years ago, our company located an office in Fort Walton Beach to support Eglin Air Force Base. Our frequent travelers stayed in a company-leased condominium on Okaloosa Island. Our family stayed there or in nearby locations on the island once or twice a year from Carla's early childhood until she became a college student, usually accompanied by at least one of her friends. For two decades we played in golf tournaments with our close friends from

Eglin Air Force Base. Afterwards we joined them in their homes for the finest food imaginable. We had begun a tradition of meeting at courses across the Southeast for three-day tournaments involving six golfers from Huntsville joined by six from Fort Walton.

Then we drifted to the east to Destin, the "world's luckiest fishing village," for our Gulf vacations. Destin is filled with crystal beaches and a vast array of golfing and restaurants with fresh Gulf seafood. Our favorites were fried or chargrilled scamp, shrimp, gumbo, and fried crab claws. Deep sea fishing competed for my fun time with golf and reading under the shade of a large beach umbrella serenaded by the sounds of Gulf of Mexico waves lapping on the sand. Deep sea fishing always reminded me of the times in the 1962 runoff for Governor of Alabama while riding in the back seat between campaign stops, an exhausted candidate, Ryan deGraffenried would look forward to election day, saying to us, "When this is over, I will be at Destin, Florida on a fishing boat."

A Huntsville friend who maintained a large, modern fishing boat with a year-round captain frequently invited me to join him and his wife fishing for large snapper and grouper. Fishing from ten miles further out in deeper water than the charter boats fished, we regularly caught bottom-feeding fish in the thirty-pound range. It was a thrill but the tugging of a large fish put heavy pressure on the strongest of lower backs. As my lower back problems increased as I grew older, I was forced to give up the thrill of reeling in large fish.

Along old Highway 98, near Crystal Beach in Destin, was where I came within a counter-offer of buying a beach home in 2006. The modern third floor unit looked down on the open beach west of snow-white sands and azure waters west of Jamaica Joe's seafood restaurant. The realtor was a city councilman. As we were leaving to return home one Sunday, I made an offer on the unit. He would take it to the client that night and communicate the response the next day. As I drove the six hours trip home, I began to feel buyer's remorse. The condo was perfect, even built to withstand hurricanes. But I wondered if the two or three weeks a year we would use it would justify owning an ocean residence versus leasing by the week. The biggest question was Destin vs. Atlanta for our second home. With increasing frequency, we were spending long weekends in Atlanta, watching the grandkids play youth sports. We normally stayed at the Crown Plaza Hotel at the first exit east of the I-75/I-285 intersection in northwest Atlanta. I had looked out the eighth-floor window to the nearby mountain to the south and said to myself, "I want a weekend place on that mountain." Now, as we returned home, I began hoping the seller would make a counter-offer that would permit me to legally bail out of my Destin offer. The next day the realtor called with a counter-offer, and I was off the hook.

When we drove to the top of the mountain that looked so appealing from the hotel, we found a neighborhood known as River Oaks that was similar to the closed community where we lived in Huntsville. The neighborhood was located on the mountaintop surrounded by a virtual forest of extra-tall hardwoods reaching high above the mountainside for sunlight. It consisted of around 30 townhouses. Almost any one of them would be perfect. However, in 2006 the real estate market was hot and there were no houses for sale in that neighborhood. Our realtor took us to similar homes in similar neighborhoods where she gave us the "hard-sell" but we saw nothing of particular interest. "Please understand," we insisted, "that we want to be in River Oaks." She went back and put letters in mail boxes pleading for neighbors to let her know if anyone was considering selling. She was admonished for violating the association's non-solicitation rules but a few weeks later, while Mary was visiting our daughter and her family, the realtor learned that a townhome was going on the market the next day. Mary called and I said, "Please go over and look at it right now. If you like it, tell them we want to make an offer tonight, before it goes on the market." We offered and counter-offered two or three times, but by the next day we had bought a home on the mountain south of the hotel that I had not even seen. When I saw it the next day it exceeded my expectations. I jokingly designated it as "our beach home in the tree-tops."

"War Stories" with Flippo and Shelby

In the middle of 2017, Ronnie Flippo and I renewed our long relationship at a political fundraising reception in Huntsville, exchanging "war stories" from our days in the Legislature and his tenure in Congress. Ronnie was our Tennessee Valley Congressman for 12 years, and a good one. He and I were colleagues in the Alabama Legislature in the early 1970s. I supported him strongly for Governor in 1990, but he was unable to establish name identification south of his district to qualify for the Democratic primary runoff.

We were enjoyed recalling a time when he was in Congress when I dropped by his office at the end of the day and he invited me to tag along for a meeting with his close friend, Ed Jenkins of Georgia, to devise strategies for reducing the capital gains tax. Like John F. Kennedy and Ronald Reagan, Flippo and Jenkins believed capital gains tax reductions would unleash the economy to the point that the net effect would be to increase revenues to the Federal government. Flippo and Jenkins were Southern Democrats, sometimes known as "boll weevils," who consistently voted for tax cuts, increases in military spending, and deregulation favored by the Reagan administration. As members of the tax-writing Ways and Means Committee, they sought support from other conservative Democrats. "Working with the Republicans, we had five Democratic votes and needed one more to have enough votes to pass the capital gains tax reduction," Flippo recalled. "Jenkins had a buddy from Indiana who was a liberal, but Ed convinced him to join us. He was the deciding vote that put us over the top."

Most of the boll weevils eventually retired from politics, or in the case of some, such as Senators Phil Gramm and Richard Shelby, switched parties and joined the Republicans. And, speak of the devil, Shelby saw us enjoying our conversation, and bolted across the room to add his recollections of our mutual experiences in the Legislature. By now, Shelby was in his 31ˢᵗ year in the U.S. Senate, after eight years in the House. He had become next in line to become Chairman of the powerful Appropriations Committee.

Shelby talked about the different climate in politics in the Seventies, when the media permitted officeholders to have private lives, compared with today's highly charged adversarial environment. And we chuckled when I reminded him of his entrepreneurial days in law school when he operated a laundry pickup and delivery service. He corrected my version of how he was chosen to serve on Appropriations. He said it was on the basis of seniority, not as a reward for giving the GOP the Senate majority. By switching parties in the early Nineties before two others, he said he was first in line for the committee of his choice. Over three decades, his state has benefitted enormously from that appointment.

Returning to C.C. Smith

Before moving to town, we lived on an 87 1/2-acre farm, about half of which was in forests dominated by hickory and oak trees. It was lowland with big foot-deep puddles on logging roads in Winter. The rest was in pasture, cotton, and corn. As was the case with our grandfather and other small farmers, we leased land from other farms. In late 1946, we were raising cotton along the asphalt road where Franklin and Lawrence Counties join. From picking lint cotton in that cold, wet field that December I paid for my first new bicycle. Those remnants of left-over cotton were what we counted on for "Christmas money." And it was Christmas Eve before we finished. From what I earned, I bought my first bike, a Schwann.

It had streamlined fenders, a chrome-plated headlight, and push-button bell---the "Cadillac" in cruiser bikes.

Now on a sunny June day in 2008 I am taking a trip back to childhood. I pull in to a weed-covered lot that was C.C. Smith School before it was closed. I had finished four grades there when we moved to Sheffield, returning the Summer of my sophomore year of college to spend the Summer with my grandparents and play second base on the C. C. Smith independent team. The cyclone fence and chicken-wire backstop were still standing. The dugouts were stained and faded and a clay-colored concrete-block concession stand was barely hanging on. Two giant water oaks that I had never noticed before now stood as sentinels behind home plate. I remembered the Summer of 1956, the game at Trapptown, near Phil Campbell. Their field was between two small mountains. We were tied 1-1 going into the bottom of the ninth when an old gap-toothed catcher named Trapp (one of my Franklin County cousins) hit one so far over the steep right field hill that our outfielders didn't even bother to move.

It was less than a half mile to the farm where we had lived when I was first able to walk to school until my dad left farming for construction. A couple of football fields further east is the sunken remains of the two-story house where I was born. It is vacant now, surrounded by a heavy thicket of bushes. Near my birthplace was a junkyard filled with things like old garden tractors, a rusted, wheel-less pickup truck, a faded yellow Caterpillar, and the like. The fellow who answered the door said my Grandfather's house had been abandoned since 1974. We had moved from this house to our own small shack on the south end of the 87 1/2 -acre farm when I was still a few months old. Grandfather Grainger, the itinerant preacher, sometimes deputy sheriff, and small farmer, had moved to Phil Campbell when I was in grade school.

I drove the mile or so to the deadend road on Mount Hope Rt. 2 where Earnest and Nancy Walker had lived when I spent the happiest days of my life fishing, hunting, and sitting on the front porch listening to rain on the green, tin roof and reading Erskine Caldwell and Mickey Spillane novels. Pawpaw and I read together. His favorite pastime was going to a country store, drinking a "coke", talking politics, and telling jokes.

At the other Town Creek bridge, now concrete and three times the length of its predecessor, I stopped this day to look at the creek. It looked the same as it did back then, completing an evolution that had included a TVA flood control project during my early adulthood. PawPaw voted for it because he believed it would help keep the flood waters off his land each spring; the shallow canal that heavy machinery dug out in place of our picturesque creek. Now, strangely, it had returned to looking like it had three generations earlier. This was the Town Creek God meant it to be.

Challenger Flew at The Wrong Time

On the morning January 28 1986, the Space Shuttle Challenger, mission 51–L, rose into the cold blue sky over the Cape.1 To exuberant spectators and breathless flight controllers, the launch appeared normal. Within 73 seconds after liftoff, however, the external tank ruptured, its liquid fuel exploded, and Challenger broke apart. Stunned spectators saw the explosion and the trails from the spiral flights of the solid rocket boosters, but the vapor cloud obscured how the orbiter shattered into large pieces. The crew cabin remained intact, trailing wires and plummeting to the Atlantic; the six astronauts and one school teacher aboard Perished. –Presidential Commission on the Space Shuttle Challenger Accident: Report to the President, Washington, DC: US GPO, 6 June 1986, Vol. I, pp. 19–21, 31, 40, hereinafter, PC

Vol., page; Dennis E. Powell, "The Challenger Deaths: What Really Happened?" *Huntsville Times*, 13 November 1986.

Television images of the flight revealed an anomalous flame from a joint between segments of the the righthand solid rocket motor. Photographs showed puffs of black smoke escaping from the joint during the first moments of ignition. Wreckage of the motor recovered from the Atlantic floor demonstrated the failure of the joint and proved that propulsion gases had melted surrounding metals and caused the explosion of the external tank. Propulsion engineers from MortonThiokol Incorporated, the Utah company responsible for the solid rocket motors, testified that for years they had been discussing problems with the joints and their O-ring seals, especially in cold weather. The night before the launch they had warned Marshall officials that the anticipated cold weather could freeze the rubber O-rings and trigger disaster, but company executives and Marshall project managers had rejected calls for a launch delay.

The Rogers Commission concluded that managers at Marshall and Thiokol had known that the case joints were hazardous. They had failed to inform senior officials in the Shuttle program or to act promptly to reduce risks. The oversimplifications emerged mainly because the commission dismissed the testimony of Marshall engineers and managers. Marshall officials immediately questioned Thiokol's ideas. Program Manager Lawrence Mulloy noted that NASA had no launch criteria for the joint's temperature. He asked during the pre-launch discussions of whether to launch, "My God, Thiokol, when do you want me to launch, next April?" The commission's final report stated that "Thiokol management reversed its position and recommended the launch of 51–L, at the urging of Marshall and contrary to the views of its engineers in order to accommodate a major customer."

Reactions to the Biggest Celestial Event of our Lifetimes

With thrilling cosmic clockwork, the moon began to pass in front of the sun, casting a 70-mile-wide shadow that swept across the United States, giving millions along the "path of totality" a chance to marvel at one of nature's grandest spectacles, a total eclipse of the sun. It was the first solar eclipse to cross the entire continent in 99 years. McMinnville, Tennessee, was in the path of totality for the total solar eclipse of August 21, 2017. Only a thin swath of the United States was able to see the moon completely cover the sun, and McMinnville is uniquely positioned for that. The last full solar eclipse in the area occurred in the 1460's and the next won't occur until 2566. Mary and I drove to Tennessee to witness the event with her nephew, Mike Millard, who lives on a farm there. "Wow!" was our collective reaction when it began growing dark at 1 pm, and roosters started to crow as it began to lighten again a few minutes later.

A Temporary Stop in My Hometown

It was almost two years after I had the stroke attack, and the day before the longest day of the year in late June. I was having a late breakfast with Richard Gregg and his son Richard III at Gibson's Barbecue. "There were two people responsible for getting me elected," said the now aged former State Representative. "You and my wife. You because you provided me with the ammo I used. And my wife, who made so many home visits on my behalf in that campaign." Then he told me how the angry incumbent legislator confronted him as the deadline expired on his placing an ad attacking Gregg's reputed alcohol problem. Instead, the Sunday *Huntsville Times* ran Gregg's ad showing the number of absences the incumbent legislator had plus the fact that he had voted against the school busing bill passed by the legislature. This was a factor

5">
="5">
="5">
="5">
="5">
="5">
5">
="5">
5">
5">
5">
5">

THE 21ST CENTURY

in Gregg becoming the upset winner in the legislative race of 1974. Gregg's ad, based on data I had provided him, presented his opponent as a member who missed numerous votes that session but was there to oppose a busing bill opposed by the Governor, who was running for President. The Gregg ad was the difference in a close election versus impact that an ad, which the *Times* refused to run due to the fact that the Republican missed the deadline while he lectured his opponent on the Democrat's faults. The payback I enjoyed was the fact that the local Republican Party Chairman had attacked me in my losing campaign for election to the state senate that year.

We had several other encounters while visiting Huntsville that were noteworthy. Mary and I had a delightful dinner that night with the Rocket City's newest author. The author of *The Doughnut Tree* and *The White Dove* Catherine Knowles and her architect husband, engaged us in the happy details of her book's sales of over 6,000. "I made the right decision in selecting a publisher of books versus a publishing house that did not have the distribution of the book as an investment", she said. She asked me a bit about my book. I told her about the summary of nine Presidents I had known or been physically closed to. Then Mary recounted the story of the old man who wound up making the difference in who sold the most savings bonds and was rewarded with an invitation to the White House by President Truman in 1953. Catherine predicted my book would be widely accepted from what we told her about it. I said I hoped she was right because I had come to really enjoy the networking that went with promoting the book. It is amazing how many old and new friends I have already made, I said.

Finally, John Logan, my closest buddy from the days with Teledyne Brown Engineering, joined me for the first one-on-one we had been engaged in in a long time. It was like old times, as though time and events had not separated us for that long period. He was as funny as ever. We chuckled about the untrustworthy Personnel

 265

Director I had elected once to release in favor of Logan. John Logan was a Personnel Director's Director. Those were the days at TBE.

There's a New Sheriff in Town

It is a she, the new sheriff. She has great influence with our Republican friends. The cartoon was a warning that Linda M. Maynor was in charge. She was in charge of politics in this community, and would brook little opposition. She has hosted every fundraiser before and since. I was fortunate to have been a partner during that period in our lives when companies were reaching out for our support when they needed political help in Washington. Fund-raisers she hosted were for Republican leaders, members from Alabama, and anyone else who needed financial help to keep their seats with television being so expensive. We were lobbyists. Pure and simple. Lobbyists.

Her first endeavor was in Charles Graddick's campaign for governor in 1988. Before campaign finance reform was enacted, she and her husband Bob, the premier eye surgeon in an era when laser surgery for cataract surgeries was like a slot machine for those performing the surgery, were major factors in Graddick's campaign in North Alabama. The Federal courts took a dim view of his techniques to convince Democrats that they should elect him over Democrat Bill Baxley. Graddick trailed going into the runoff before the courts declared the primary invalid. Republican Guy Hunt the first Republican since Reconstruction was to be elected. Soon the politicians flocked to Huntsville. The successful ones were those who Linda, a native of Texas, supported. She has hosted events for such unlikely senators as Don Riegle and Jim Sasser, and also Edward Kennedy.

She handled President George W Bush's reelection fundraising event in 2004. I hosted Shelby's first event in Huntsville. She still handles his PAC events. He has said he will not run again when his current term expires in three years. By then Linda will have helped most of the Huntsville companies which the appropriators choose to help. She was given the New Sheriff in Town tag after Shelby had switched from the Democratic Party to the Republicans in 1993. She handled the son of President George H.W. Bush, President Bush's reelection campaign fund-raising in 2004. Rather than try to list which politicians she raised funds for, it is a good bet that any who came to Alabama for money came for fundraiser coordinated by Linda Maynor or Charlie Grainger, or the two, teamed up.

The Presidential Election: 2020

It wouldn't be fair to the reader if I avoided making a prediction on the next Presidential election. So, here it goes: Donald W. Trump. Not by much. But enough.

I am patriotic. I love this country. I have explained in the preceding chapters why, after sometimes holding my nose (McGovern, Dukasis) I wound up voting a straight Democratic ticket. At least before the year 1999 when I changed parties. I honored the obligation because I was an elected Democrat; and I swore an oath. I have always kept the word I swore by. For about 20 years, I voted Democratic because I was a social liberal for the most part and always a conservative economically. My relatively brief career in journalism was in an era when most writers demonstrated great pride in their integrity and fairness. These were the times preceding Watergate journalism, when a movie was made about two *Washington Post* investigative journalists who brought down President Nixon. That was the advent of celebrity journalism in which reporters become the story. There was a greater acceptance of anonymous sources, a far more skeptical attitude of reporters toward government and a sharp rise in investigative reporting.

Pushing back? Yes, I and the other rednecks are joyously pushing back against what we in the South and more believe is wrong with those on the other side, beginning with those who still have the last word: the news media. Where the America is that they envision within another generation is inconceivable. And, as a former newsman who carried opinions that I honestly thought were always based on fair treatment, all I can say is that I tried. I think the average journalist is sincere in their views. I just can't subscribe to the notion that I have to agree with everything I read.

Regarding Trump, he will do what he says he will. On economic issues, like shredding the harmful policy changes enacted by others by the simple stroke on a pen. On social issues, like abortion. And on taxes, particularly on taxes.

But he is arguably politically the most vulnerable first-term incumbent since Jimmy Carter. None of the Democratic candidates at this stage carries as much ethical baggage as Hillard Clinton did four years ago. But they could also lose if they continue on the present course being too far left on the economy. Can he win with about 44% in the current polls? Yes, he can. But it will depend on his personal behavior whether the Left can obtain enough votes in the Senate to obtain the necessary votes and override a decision made by the voters who elected him.

Mary's Close Friend, Peggy Gattis, Dies

Mary's close friend Peggy Heflin Gattis died recently. Mary drove over to Huntsville for the funeral. They sent me a photo of the group of gals drinking one to Peggy from the Outback Restaurant following the service. She died three years after her husband Paul; he of Alzheimer's, she of lung cancer. She was one of those unique individuals who loved everybody and was such a positive influence on all she met. She is sorely missed and will be for years to come.

It was July 4, 2015. We ran into Peggy and Paul at the Outback in Huntsville and ordered barbequed ribs in honor of Independence Day. Peggy said, "You know, I have never had them here!" So, Peggy then enthusiastically ordered ribs. We have eaten them every Fourth of July since.

The establishment maintains a plaque in her memory above her favorite booth. And, we will eat ribs in memory of Peggy as each July 4 rolls around.

My Old Friend Sam Phillips Reemerges

The modern times still have miracles. Take a few days ago when I was on the Internet. I stumbled across an interview while dialoging with an old friend from Applebee's.

I went to search the tape replay and there he was: It was a review of Sam Phillips' life, beginning with him talking about the time he was a graduate of Florence's Coffee High School serving as director of the band, to how he had been able to elicit from the singers who came to record at Memphis' Sun Record Company the talent that was uniquely their own. Sam Phillips, in all of his preachments, lecturing a bunch of Coffee High students!

I was long since gone from Sam's life but Sally Wilburn was still there. She was the secretary who never left him. I didn't hear a word that sounded exaggerated or untrue. I had seen him but once since the Fabulous Fifties, in 1987 when he was accepting his induction into the Alabama Music Hall of Fame. He was so drunk many of the fans who did not know him were turned off. But it brought back yesteryear to me.

Go, Braves! Then Watch for My Next Book!

I recall that when I was "negotiating" with God to persuade my loyal spouse Mary to hurry up and come and take me to get medical care after being out for more than three hours from the stroke, I am fairly certain that I offered to be good until He decided to take me home, which I envisioned would be about ten years if measured in human terms. That would be a few months longer than my dad was able to go before God called him home. So, I am living out my arrangement.

In the meantime, the Atlanta Braves offer the quickest way to finish out a day. I fell in love with the Braves in 1966. Hank Aaron was a team member. I watched from a seat behind first as the Miracle Mets beat them on the way to a World Series victory. I saw them play in the 1991 World Series first game. The worst-to-first were barely edged out. But they won it all, as I continued to sneak away from my 40th high school reunion to see the Braves finally win the elusive baseball title. It was the last time they were to take it all.

Now they are showing real promise and I am more excited than ever. A young team still a year away but already a contender. They lead their division of the National League at the halfway point of the 2018 season by six games. Yesterday they won on a solid pitching by newly-acquired Dallas Kerchel, a homer by Josh Davidson, and a perfect throw from leftfielder Charlie Culbertson, to home that erased the tying run. I don't have to drive three hours to see them in person. It is a short ride to the less than three miles away home of the Braves. They have a canny General Manager who knows what winning entails. They're ridiculously young. They're a winning team in a 2 1/2-year-old ball park. They might not win the World Series this year---I am one of those betting against it---then again, if they can get into it, they can win---and they should keep getting that chance.

I am saving the interesting highlights of the Braves up to now in Atlanta until the publication of my next book, with a publication date of late 2020.

The Autumn of Our Lives

The oasis within an oasis is in our townhouse in the suburban city of Sandy Springs, Atlanta's northern neighbor. I am sitting in the sunroom, our reading room, with its panoramic view of the treetops. I become distracted from a riveting suspense novel by the sharp contrasts of sun light and shadow playing upon the leaves of trees down the rolling mountain.

On the outer side of my view are giant trees darkened by shade, reaching over 100 feet high for more sun light. White and red oaks, white pines, Southern shagbark hickories, red and white elms, a hardwood forest. Just outside the window, a brown oak leaf from the previous fall clings to the sill from the single thread of a spider's nest, tantalizingly twisting and spinning at the slightest breeze. How, I wonder in amazement, could such a tiny strand remain so strong for so long? A hummingbird suddenly appears on the limb of a wild dogwood but it vanishes seconds later. All is still. Halfway down the slope a barren spike of a tall limbless tree demands attention because of its goose-like shape. It has bark protruding like a wing, a dark spot for an eye, terminating with a pointed beak at the top. In my mind it is a long-neck goose, aimed straight up, rocket-like, prepared to launch into flight. In the center, at the foot of the little mountain, nature's palate overflows: a red maple with oak-shaped, curling leaves turns looking lime-colored in summer sunlight, to become crowned with brilliant reds in autumn.

I lay my book aside and tilt my head back to try to see the tops of the tall trees. My eyelids close, inviting reflection. I float like a leaf on a stream, awash in memories. Closing in on four score years---what a wonderful stage of life. Thank God, I feel great! I am stress-free, relaxed, feeling like the actor on the beer commercial who flashes a big smile and exalts, "It doesn't get any better than this." Most important, my spouse, my best friend, and I have enjoyed sharing a half-century of stunning sunsets and beautiful rainbows. Only when it is shared can a sunset's beauty be fully appreciated. As contrasting lights flood through the vision, I shout, "Mary come and see this beautiful sunset!"

The "Autumn of Our Lives" is a perfect metaphor to liken our lives to the season when the time for planting, growing, and flowering is over, when the temperatures begin to drop, and the days become shorter. The leaves on the trees drop, and the natural world edges toward dormancy. It is the time, someone reminds us, when death is much closer than birth. It is the oldest we have ever been but the youngest we will ever be. We look for ways to enjoy each day while it lasts.

I love the autumn-life metaphor because I love autumn like no other time of year. It represents a collection of bright colors of changing leaves in such beautiful settings as Vermont, New Hampshire, and the Great Smoky Mountains. There, on crisp cool mornings, I have carefully recorded moments of great beauty with camera and tripod.

It is the time for harvest celebrations. On Thanksgiving Day, we pause with family and friends to consider how blessed we are. We know winter is not far behind, but with winter comes the Merry Christmas celebration of Christ's birth. The flower will have faded and fallen to the ground but it presupposes Easter---and the beginning of seeds that bloom again. And, for us, our faith causes us to look forward with anticipation of a child welcoming spring vacation. Bellah, Mike. "The Autumn of Our Years" column. Best Years, March 2000. www.bestyears.com/autumn.html

The closer we are to the end, the more we have to be thankful for. Life in this world can be hard, none can deny. But even at its hardest, there are always things to enjoy: snow in the winter, flowers in the spring, a friend's smile, a grandmother's hug. The longer we live, the more these things tend to accumulate — and to give pleasure. Henry Gary. "Anticipating the End." Word Points. com, May 27, 2015.

I made a deal with God when I came to, two or three times before Mary finally figured out that something was very wrong with me when I had the stroke that afternoon of September 29, 2017. "Let me live another 10 years" I promised, "God, and I pledge that you can do anything with me---re-save me, even the full-time service route the rest of the way if You want that too." I was about fourth of the way to another year. That would mean at 81 and four months I had better assume my life was up to me. Mary was not part of it in my bargain. If she had, it would have been the last line of Harlan Howard's song of pleading, which captures the essence of my prayers to Him then and now.

The older we become, the more Mary and I tend to depend on each other. And when I sometimes think of that inevitable sunset of our lives, hopefully still many years away, an old country song comes to mind. It was entitled, "Let Me Be the First to Go," written by Harlan Howard. I have slightly re-written the lyrics to express my own wishes:

"Lord I've never asked for many favors
And I'm not too deserving that I know

"But when it's parting time for me and Mary
Please let me be the first to go

"I don't think I could live one day without her
So please let me be the first to go."

My Prayer on Father's Day

I awakened from sleep on Fathers Day, and the first thing I did was to mouth a prayer.

"Our heavenly father, thank you for this blissful day and all you did to make it as perfect as you have done everything else in these 82 years," I began. After sharing a few just-between-us moments with God, I got around to thanking him for the many blessings in my life. I thanked him first for Mary, my bride of 52 years, then for Carla, our delightful daughter, and for my saint-like son, Chuck, and the fact that he and son Carter had driven over from Montgomery to wish me a happy Father's Day, and next for my creative youngest son Bart. Then grandsons Grainger, Drew, and Coleman, for Chuck's wife Michelle and for her daughter Hannah, and finally the remaining grandson, Dalton. He is off in Columbia in South America on a mission trip, and is considering becoming a missionary for the rest of his life. "Please forgive us our sins, in the name of our beautiful Savior, Jesus Christ. Amen."

Wife Mary and daughter Carla dogsledding in Alaska, 2015

My children (left to right), Bart, Carla and Chuck

Grandsons Grainger, left and Coleman Reeves
on helicopter, Alaska, 2015

Author with grandsons (l-r) Drew, Coleman, & Grainger Reeves, 2016

Author at Trump Rally, the night of the pre-stroke, 2017

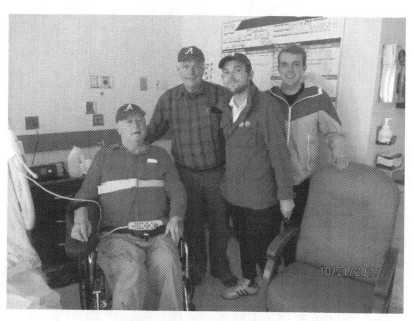

Author with son Chuck & grandsons (l-r) Carter
& Dalton Grainger, December, 2017

It's a booming drive!

First golf shots following stroke shown in sequence, July, 2019

Printed in the United States
By Bookmasters